AS Music
Study Guide

Edexcel

David Bowman
and Paul Terry

RHINEGOLD
EDUCATION

www.rhinegoldeducation.co.uk

Music Study Guides

GCSE, AS and A2 Music Study Guides (AQA, Edexcel and OCR)
GCSE, AS and A2 Music Listening Tests (AQA, Edexcel and OCR)
GCSE, AS and A2 Music Revision Guides (AQA, Edexcel and OCR)
AS/A2 Music Technology Study Guide (Edexcel)
AS/A2 Music Technology Listening Tests (Edexcel)
AS and A2 Music Technology Listening Tests (Edexcel)

Also available from Rhinegold Education

AS and A2 Music Harmony Workbooks
AS Music Composition Workbooks
AS Music Literacy Workbooks
Musicals in Focus, Baroque Music in Focus, Film Music in Focus
Dictionary of Music in Sound
Careers in Music
Understanding Popular Music

First published 2013 in Great Britain by
Rhinegold Education
14-15 Berners Street
London W1T 3LJ, UK

www.rhinegoldeducation.co.uk

© 2013 Rhinegold Education
a division of Music Sales Limited

You should always check the current requirement of the examination, since these may change. Copies of the Edexcel specification may be obtained from Edexcel: www.edexcel.com, telephone 0845 1720205, email publications.orders@edexcel.com.
Resources can be obtained from Pearson Education, Edinburgh Gate, Harlow, Essex CM20 2JE, telephone 0845 6301111, email customersolutions@pearson.com.

Edexcel AS Music Study Guide 3rd edition
Order No. RHG333
ISBN: 978-1-78305-030-7

Exclusive Distributors:
Music Sales Ltd
Distribution Centre, Newmarket Road
Bury St Edmunds, Suffolk IP33 3YB, UK

Printed in the EU

Contents

The details of the AS Music examination are believed to be correct at the time of going to press, but readers should always check the current requirements for the examination with Edexcel, since these may change. The Edexcel music specification can be downloaded from www.edexcel.com.

The authors

David Bowman and Paul Terry have co-authored many books in support of A-level music, including study guides for Rhinegold Publishing and the books *Aural Matters*, *Aural Matters in Practice* and *Listening Matters* published by Schott.

Paul Terry has taught music from primary to postgraduate level. He was a music examiner for nearly 30 years and has been engaged as a consultant by several examination boards. He also served as a member of the Secondary Examinations Council and its successor the Schools Examinations and Assessment Council. He was Chief Examiner for the Oxford and Cambridge Schools Examinations Board (now part of OCR) and he was a Chief Examiner for London Examinations (now part of Edexcel). In addition to the books listed above, Paul has written *Musicals in Focus* for Rhinegold Publishing and is co-author with William Lloyd of *Music in Sequence*, *Classics in Sequence*, *Rock in Sequence*, and *Rehearse, Direct and Play* published by Musonix Publishing.

Now retired, **David Bowman** was for many years Director of Music at Ampleforth College and Chief Examiner for the AS and A level music syllabuses of the University of London Schools Examination Board (now Edexcel). In addition to the titles listed above, his publications include the ground-breaking *London Anthology of Music* (University of London Schools Examinations Board, 1986), *Sound Matters* (co-authored with Bruce Cole, published by Schott, 1989), *Analysis Matters* (Rhinegold, 1997 and 1998) and many analytical articles for *Music Teacher*. He is a contributor to the *Collins Classical Music Encyclopedia*, edited by Stanley Sadie (Collins, 2000), and is the author of the three-volume *Rhinegold Dictionary of Music in Sound*, a unique resource for music education published in 2002.

Acknowledgements

We are grateful to the following for permission to use printed excerpts from their publications:

Webern Quartet Op. 22 No.1 © Copyright 1932 by Universal Edition A.G., Wien. Reproduced by permission. All rights reserved.

Sonata for horn, trumpet and trombone: Music by Francis Poulenc. © Copyright 1922, 2000 Chester Music Limited. All rights reserved. International copyright secured. Reprinted by permission.

The Lamb: Music by John Tavener, words by William Blake. © Copyright 1982 Chester Music Limited. All rights reserved. International copyright secured. Reprinted by permission.

'Summertime' from *Porgy and Bess*: Words and music by George Gershwin, Du Bose Heyward, Dorothy Heyward and Ira Gershwin. ©1935 (Renewed) 1962 Chappell & Co Inc. Warner/Chappell North America Ltd, London W6 8BS. Reproduced by permission of Faber Music Ltd. All rights reserved.

Honey, Don't: Words and music by Carl Lee Perkins. © Copyright 1955 Carl Perkins Music Incorporated, USA. MPL Communications Limited. Used by permission of Music Sales Limited. All rights reserved. International copyright secured.

Dialogues by Igor Stravinksy and Robert Craft © Faber and Faber Ltd 1982.

New York Counterpoint: movement II by Steve Reich © Copyright 1986 Hendon Music, Inc. Reproduced by permission of Boosey & Hawkes Music Publishers Ltd.

Introduction

About the course

Edexcel AS Music consists of three units:

Unit 1: Performing Music

This unit accounts for 30% of the marks for AS Music. You will have to give a five- to six-minute performance, consisting of one or more pieces of your choice. Any instrument (or voice) can be used, and you may perform as a soloist and/or with a small ensemble. Your performance, which can take place at any time before the end of the course, will be recorded and marked by your teacher. You are allowed to repeat and re-record the entire performance on another occasion if you are not happy with your first attempt. The final recording will be sent to an Edexcel examiner who will check the mark that you have been awarded.

Unit 2: Composing

This unit accounts for 30% of the marks for AS Music. You will have to create a three-minute piece, based on a brief that you will be able to choose from those set by Edexcel at the start of your course. You will have a total of 15 hours supervised time in which to complete the composition. The work will then be recorded, and the score and recording sent to an Edexcel examiner for marking. You will also have to write a CD sleeve note to describe the structure and other important features of your composition, and to explain how it has been influenced by music you have listened to.

Unit 3: Developing Musical Understanding

This unit accounts for 40% of the marks for AS Music. You will have to sit a two-hour exam paper in three sections, the first two of which are based on set works you will have studied:

➤ In Section A you will listen to excerpts from two set works and then have to identify specific features of the music (a skeleton score of the excerpts will be provided with the exam paper)

➤ In Section B you will have to answer questions about two other set works, this time without the aid of a recording or score

➤ In Section C you will have to identify features of the harmony in a printed score of unfamiliar music and then complete a short passage of four-part harmony. You are allowed access to an electric keyboard with headphones (but not a computer) while completing this task.

Your answers to the questions on this paper will be sent to an Edexcel examiner for marking.

Edexcel is the name of the organisation that decides what you have to do in this exam. It appoints examiners, supervises the marking, and awards grades and certificates. It is one of several similar bodies that are licensed to offer an AS qualification in music.

The set works all come from the *New Anthology of Music* (also published as *The Edexcel A Level Music Anthology*), referred to as NAM in the rest of this book.

NAM is published by Heinemann, ISBN 978-1-846-904-08-0 (with a set of four CDs, ISBN 978-1-846-904-09-7). It is available from Edexcel publications (see page 2), or from the publisher or any music retailer.

Getting started

This book will help you prepare for the exam by providing tips and advice for performing and composing, along with detailed notes on the set works that you will need to study. Explanations of technical terms printed in **bold type** can be found in the glossary at the end of the book. If you need further help with these, or with other terminology you encounter during the course, we recommend that you consult the *Rhinegold Dictionary of Music in Sound* by David Bowman. This not only gives detailed explanations of a wide range of musical concepts, but also illustrates them using a large number of specially recorded examples on CD, enabling you to hear directly how theory relates to the actual sounds of music.

The *Rhinegold Dictionary of Music in Sound* by David Bowman is published by Rhinegold Education, ISBN 978-0-946890-87-3.

Unlike GCSE, where the exam is generally taken at the end of a two-year course, AS level is usually sat after only one year's study. In practice this means that you have little more than 24 weeks in which to complete your composing and performing coursework, and to prepare for Unit 3. It is therefore essential to be well-organised from day one of the course.

Planning is the secret of success. Choosing music and beginning practice for performing need to get under way as soon as possible and initial ideas for composing are best explored during the first term. Preparation for Unit 3 needs to be done throughout the course and completed in time to allow for revision and the working of several mock papers in the weeks before the actual exam.

Take responsibility for your own progress, using this book as a starting point for your studies, and remember that by meeting deadlines you can avoid the stress of a huge workload in the final weeks of the course.

To do well in AS Music, it will help enormously if you try to spot the connections between the music you hear, the music you play and the music you compose. Understanding the context and structure of music will enhance your enjoyment when listening, inform your performing and illuminate your composing. Composing, performing, listening and understanding are all related aspects of the study of music, and this integration of activities is an important aspect of the course you are taking.

Try to broaden your musical experience by learning new pieces, taking part in group activities, improvising on your instrument to create different moods and new sounds, and listening to as wide a range of music as you can, both recorded and live. Don't just listen to comfortably familiar music – look for opportunities to broaden your understanding of new types and styles of music by listening to broadcasts and tracks available on the internet, and by going to concerts. This will help to increase your musical understanding and build your confidence as a musician. It should also make your year of studying AS Music highly enjoyable. Good luck!

Unit 1: Performing Music

What, when and where

You are required to give a performance that lasts between five and six minutes. It doesn't matter if you run a little over this limit, but if your performance lasts for less than five minutes your mark will be reduced.

It can consist of a single piece or a group of short pieces. If you choose the latter, the pieces do not need to be related, but they must all be performed in a single continuous session – you are not allowed to assemble a recording of pieces performed on different occasions.

You may perform on any instrument (including singing). You can include pieces played on different instruments if you wish, but there is no advantage in doing so. It is best avoided unless you really do play two instruments to an equally good standard.

You can perform as a soloist (with accompaniment, if appropriate) and/or as a member of a group of up to five performers. Any style of music is acceptable, but read the notes about 'difficulty level' on the next page.

Your performance can take place in class, or as part of a concert either within your school or in the wider community. Your teacher will advise what is the best type of occasion for you. It can take place at any time during the course until the date when marks have to be sent to Edexcel (usually about the middle of May). Again, your teacher will advise on a suitable date.

It is a good idea to have several practice runs at formal performance during the course, and to allow yourself enough time to give one or more later performances in case you should be unwell or not ready for the planned occasion. Remember that the performance can always be repeated if there is sufficient time – but it must be the complete performance, and not just selected parts from it.

Throughout this chapter the word 'instrument' includes the voice.

Choice of music

Choosing the right music is very important. The piece(s) should allow you to show technical and expressive control as a performer as well as an understanding of the music you present. Some types of music, such as technical studies, easy arrangements and certain styles of pop music, tend to focus on a limited range of techniques and so may not give you much chance to show what you can do as a performer. Music that offers some contrasts in mood and the opportunity to show different types of technical skill is likely to serve you best. The same considerations apply if you choose to perform your own composition(s) – the music needs to give you the scope to show a good range of your performing skills, which may be difficult if the piece is technically simple.

Difficulty level

Edexcel expects the pieces performed for this unit to be of about Grade 5 standard, although they do not have to come from the lists of pieces specified for grade examinations. Your teacher will be able to advise you on the difficulty level of specific pieces. In addition, the AS Music section of the Edexcel website includes a booklet listing the difficulty levels of many different pieces.

A small amount of additional credit is available if you give a good performance of music that is of Grade 6 standard or above. If the pieces you present are of a lower standard than Grade 5, it will not be possible to get the maximum marks available for this unit.

Whatever your technical standard it is better to choose music that you can perform with confidence than to attempt a difficult work which stretches your technique to its limit. A work that is too demanding will leave no leeway for the inevitable nervousness that *will* arise under exam conditions. The anxiety and tension it generates will be communicated to the listener, and will inevitably impair your musical interpretation.

Easy pieces played musically are more likely to be successful than difficult pieces marred by hesitations and breakdowns. Choose music that you enjoy playing, but be wary of well-worn 'party pieces' – it is easy to lose sight of musicality and communication if a performance becomes complacent. A *little* adrenalin arising from a work which is a challenge, but not an insuperable obstacle, usually enhances the work of even the greatest performers.

Note that you can omit repeats in your performance and shorten long sections that consist purely of accompaniment, but it is not acceptable to cut passages because they happen to be too difficult or to stop in the middle of a movement because it is too long. If this seems likely it is better to choose a different work.

Accompaniment

If the music is intended to have an accompaniment (as will be the case for most music apart from that for piano and other chordal instruments) then it must be played with the accompaniment.

Try to work with an accompanist who can rehearse with you regularly, or at least on several occasions before the day. Even the most skilful accompanist will be unable to let you sound your best if the first time you perform together is at the actual performance.

Unless you are performing in an ensemble, the accompaniment should be played by just one person on a contrasting instrument. This will usually be a piano but other combinations are allowed – for example, a flute solo could be accompanied on an acoustic guitar or a jazz saxophone solo could be supported by a double bass. You can use a pre-recorded backing providing it is appropriate for the style of music and your own part can be clearly distinguished. This is often a good option for electric guitarists and rock drummers.

Ensemble performing

You can, if you wish, perform as a member of an ensemble for this unit. If you choose to do so, note that there mustn't be more than five performers in the group, including yourself, and your own part must be clearly audible and not doubled by anyone else. Suitable ensembles include wind trios, string or vocal quartets, and small rock groups. You could include both a solo and an ensemble item within the six minutes allowed for the performance, but there are no additional marks available for doing this and it could prove more difficult to organise the necessary resources.

A useful book which gives many ideas for getting the best out of ensemble performing of all kinds is: *Rehearse, Direct and Play* by William Lloyd and Paul Terry, published by Musonix (www.musonix.co.uk).

Scores

You will have to submit a photocopy (not the original copy) of the music you perform for this unit. Only your own part is required, not the accompaniment nor the parts for others in the case of an ensemble.

If your performance is improvised, as often occurs in jazz and rock music, you will still need to submit something that will allow the examiner to follow the performance – if a score in conventional stave notation is not available this could be a lead sheet, chord chart, track sheet, table or diagram, along with a description of what is being attempted in improvised passages.

Preparation

Having chosen and studied your piece(s) with your teacher, and practised to a standard that you feel is acceptable, it is essential that you try out the music under performance conditions – not to your instrumental teacher, parents or anyone else who has heard you working on the music week by week, but to someone who is able to hear the performance fresh. This could be a visiting relative, your fellow students, or another teacher at your school or college.

A small slip or two in this trial performance should not concern you greatly, but if you find that you are often hesitating in difficult passages or that the music completely breaks down, it is a warning that you may have chosen something which might be too difficult. This means that you will need to decide if the work is viable or whether it would be better to make a more realistic choice.

In planning this run-up to the performance allow much more time than you think you need. Illness may curtail practice time and other commitments may prevent adequate rehearsal with accompanists or other members of an ensemble.

Try to have a run-through of the music in the venue in which you will be performing. If it is a large hall you will probably find that you need to project the sound and exaggerate the contrasts much more than when practising at home. Conversely if you are playing a loud instrument (brass or electric guitar, for example) in a small room, you will almost certainly need to limit louder dynamics.

Decide where you are going to sit or stand and check that the lighting is adequate but not dazzling. If you have an accompanist make sure that you have good eye contact without having to turn away from your listeners. If the piano is an upright one it may take some experimentation to find the best position. If you play an instrument that needs tuning before you start, plan how you are going to do this and remember that tuning is not necessarily something that all accompanists are able to help with.

Whether the piece is accompanied or not, spend some time trying out the opening in various ways. For pieces with a tricky start it can be easier to set the right speed by thinking of a more straightforward phrase from later in the piece and establishing a mental image of the right tempo from that.

If the performance is to be given to an audience of any size you should also spend a few minutes practising walking on and off stage, and deciding how you will react to applause. The audience will be disappointed if you shamble on at the start and rush off at the end. Audiences need plenty of time to show their appreciation: a hurried nod in their direction as you exit will appear clumsy, if not downright rude. If there is no printed programme, it makes a friendly start if you announce the piece(s) you are going to perform.

The performance

On the day make sure you leave time for a warm-up. Check that you have to hand any extra equipment you might need (mutes, guitar foot-stools, spare strings and so on). If you require a music stand, check that you know how it is adjusted and secured – collapsing music stands are good for comedy acts but they can seriously undermine your nerve in a performance.

Expect to be a little nervous but remember that the more experience you can get of performing to others during the course, the more natural and enjoyable it will become. Blind panic will only normally set in if the music is under-rehearsed or too difficult and this, as we have explained, can be avoided by selecting suitable music and preparing it thoroughly.

How is the performance marked?

Each piece (or movement) that you perform is marked out of 40, with eight marks available in each of five categories:

1. Quality of outcome: security and effectiveness, interpretation and communication; reaction to other parts in an ensemble; sufficient minimum length

In the case of improvisation, marks in category 2 are awarded for the use of the stimulus in the performance; marks in category 3 are awarded for the coherence of the work (structure and balance), and marks in category 5 are awarded for use of instrument or voice (including appropriate range of timbre and management of texture).

2. Accuracy of pitch and rhythm

3. Continuity: fluency and control of tempo

4. Tone and technique, including any specific matters that are appropriate, such as bowing, intonation, pedalling

5. Phrasing, **articulation** and dynamics.

The total mark for each piece is balanced against an overall mark for the total impression of the performance, and then the mark is adjusted if the piece is above the standard Grade 5 difficulty level. If you perform more than one piece or movement, the others are marked in the same way and then an average is calculated for the entire performing unit.

A good mark requires technically secure performing, although the occasional well-covered slip that can happen in even the best-regulated performances should not be a matter of great concern. However, if your performance lacks fluency and coordination, perhaps being marred by stumbles, poor intonation or inability to maintain the correct speed, it is unlikely to be awarded a satisfactory mark. You can avoid this danger by choosing simpler music in which you have mastered the technical challenges and can there-fore concentrate on communicating a really musical performance with good tone, effective and appropriate contrasts, and a sense of the style of the music.

It will help if you have a clear image of what you are trying to convey in the performance, such as rhythmic energy, a dreamy atmosphere, elegant phrasing, dramatic contrasts or subtle blends. Focus on the detail throughout the music. Rather than thinking of a passage as merely 'happy' try to decide if you mean boisterous, contented, frivolous, celebratory, cheeky or just cheerful. If it is 'sad', do you mean tragic, doom-laden, nostalgic, angry or solemn? Then try to evoke the moods you intend in your interpretation of the piece, whether it be the glittering ballroom of a minuet, the moonlit night of a nocturne or the smoky languor of a blues club. Never be content with merely 'getting the notes right'.

Unit 2: Composing

What, when and where

For this unit you have to create a three-minute composition based on one of four briefs that will be set by Edexcel in September at the start of your course:

Examples of each of these briefs are discussed in the section beginning on page 19.

➤ **Composing expressively**: a piece based on different moods and emotions for acoustic instruments and/or synthetic sounds

➤ **Composing idiomatically**: a piece for piano or for two or more acoustic instruments that exploits the characteristic sounds of the resources used and makes use of variation techniques

➤ **Words and music**: a vocal piece that explores the relationship in structure between text and music

➤ **Text, context and texture**: a piece that explores vocal textures and techniques suitable for a given context.

Unless directed otherwise in the brief, you are allowed to write in any style you wish and there is considerable flexibility about the resources you can use.

Once the work is finished you will have to submit three items:

1. A detailed score of the piece, either hand-written or computer-printed. Stave notation should be used if this is the convention for the style that you have chosen. However, other forms of notation are acceptable if they are sufficiently detailed and more usual for the type of music you have created. For example, a pop or jazz composition might be presented as a lead sheet (melody and chord symbols) or as a chord chart; an electronic piece might be shown as a detailed track diagram, or a work in an experimental style might be notated as a prose score (a detailed table of instructions) or in graphic form.

2. A recording of the piece on audio CD or MiniDisc.

3. A 'sleeve note' that describes the structure and other important features of your composition, and explains how it has been influenced by music you have listened to.

It is important to spend time practising your general composing skills before starting on the brief, and to continue doing so while working on it. The score of your composition has to be completed within a total of 15 hours of supervised time, although you can (and should) start making plans and sketches before this.

Additional time is allowed for recording the work, but if you then need to make any changes to the score, these must be completed within whatever is left of your 15 hours. It is therefore best not to leave making the recording until after your supervised time has been used up.

Research and preparation for the brief, including listening to and studying relevant music, can be done outside of this supervised time, but your teacher is required to check that any rough drafts or sketches that you use when working on your exam submission are your own work.

Your composition, recording and sleeve note will all need to be completed in time to send to the examiner by the specified date, which is likely to be in the middle of May.

Getting started

Once you have chosen a brief, you can do some valuable research and planning before starting to use up your permitted 15 hours on producing the final score. Listen carefully and analytically to plenty of relevant music and start to gather information about the resources you intend to use. You will then be in a good position to start sketching ideas and trying out some preliminary drafts.

Related listening

It is important to study as many models as you can for the brief you choose, as this will provide you with a variety of ideas on how to go about structuring and developing your own piece. You will also need to list relevant listening in your sleeve note. In many cases there will be suitable works to study in NAM (which you are allowed to consult while actually working on your own piece). Other ideas for related listening are included in the sample briefs later in this chapter, but obviously you will need to find pieces that are relevant to your own chosen brief.

When studying other music it is important to realise that you are not expected to write in the style of any specific composer. In fact attempting to do so is likely to make the job much more difficult since it would require a very thorough understanding of the style to sound at all convincing. You should instead be looking at the ways in which composers:

➢ Begin and end a piece

➢ Establish and develop ideas

➢ Create specific moods

➢ Introduce contrasts (of key, mood or texture)

➢ Use structure – not just a form, such as theme and variations, but also how the music is paced to include areas of tension and relaxation, and points of climax

➢ Unify their music, so that it sounds like a satisfying whole rather than a succession of unrelated ideas.

Getting the right balance between unity and diversity is one of the most important tasks for a composer. Too much repetition and the piece will sound boring. Too many new ideas and it will not gel. Careful listening to relevant music will show you how composers throughout the ages have evolved various techniques to solve this problem.

Resources

You will need to decide on the resources you are going to use for your piece. If other performers are to be involved it is best to write for people who will be available to work with you during the whole composing process, so other students in your group would be the obvious choice.

Start by planning how the characteristics of the instruments and/or voices might best be exploited. Try to identify the skills (and weaknesses) of each performer so that you can use their individual strengths in your composing. You could discuss what sorts of things are easy and what are difficult for each instrument or voice – although improvising, both separately and together, is often much quicker and more productive than using words.

Your research should include the ranges and characteristics of the instruments and/or voices you intend to use. There are many different matters to consider, including the fact that you may sometimes want to nudge your performers away from their comfort zones into less familiar areas of technique. Here are just some of the issues you may need to consider, depending on the resources you choose.

Woodwind instruments

Explore the ways in which different types of tonguing (slurred, legato-tongued, staccato and accented) can be used for contrasting effects. Remember that all wind players need space to breathe, so rests in suitable places are essential.

Notes at the extremes of the range can be difficult to control on some wind instruments, so if you plan to use very high or very low notes, get your players to try out such passages at different speeds and various dynamic levels.

On many woodwind instruments the contrast in tone between different **registers** offers a valuable resource for composers. For instance, the lowest notes of the flute have a beautifully expressive quality, but are easily obscured by other instruments. On the other hand, the high register (which requires leger lines above the treble stave) is clear, bright and penetrating.

The clarinet has three distinctive registers. Notes in the lowest octave are often described as dark, oily, hollow or haunting – they can even sound sinister if accented. The notes from G to B♭ in the lower half of the treble stave have a rather thin sound and there is a tricky change of fingering and breath control between B♭ and B♮ on the middle line of the stave (the point known as the break). It is therefore better to avoid hovering around these notes in solo passages. Above the break the tone up as far as top C, two leger lines above the stave, can be bright and flexible or expressive and warm, depending on the dynamic. Above top C the very highest register tends to be penetrating and shrill.

Various special effects are available on woodwind instruments. These 'extended techniques' include **pitch bend**, flutter tonguing (rolling an 'r' while blowing), multiphonics (creating more than one note at a time), air notes (blowing without producing tone) and key clicks (rhythmic sounds produced by the keys).

Look up 'extended techniques' on the internet to hear examples of some of the effects possible.

Some wind instruments, including clarinets, saxophones, horns and trumpets, are transposing instruments, which means that their notes are not written at sounding pitch (see page 46). You can write parts for transposing instruments at sounding pitch in the score if you wish, but you will need to produce a transposed part for the player if you intend to record your piece with a live performer when other non-transposing instruments are involved. Think carefully about the key(s) to use in these circumstances. For example, music in A major, which is an easy key for the violin, has to be written in B major for the clarinet – a rather tricky key for inexperienced players. The key(s) you choose may have to be a compromise if you include both transposing and non-transposing instruments in the same piece.

Transposing instruments

The points in the first two paragraphs on woodwind *above* apply equally to the brass family. Brass instruments are capable of a wide dynamic range, but less experienced players may have difficulty with quiet passages and are likely to need plenty of rests because playing a brass instrument is tiring on the lips.

Brass instruments

As with any instrument that you don't play yourself, research the available range and check with the performer what is practical. For example, if you write for the trombone you need to be aware that its normal bottom note is E below the bass stave, not C like the cello. Alternating between B♭ and B♮ on the bottom line of the bass stave is not easy for the trombonist, since it involves moving the slide over its maximum distance. If you want to use a **glissando** between notes, check what is possible with your trombone player.

Special effects on brass instruments, depending on the experience of the player, include pitch bend, growling tone and ghost notes (faint, almost pitchless sounds). In addition, various type of mutes are available:

➢ The straight mute is the most common type and produces a distant effect in quiet passages but a piercing and metallic tone in very loud passages

➢ The cup mute provides a muffled, rather dull sound

➢ The bucket mute gives a soft and mellow sound

➢ Harmon and plunger mutes can be used for 'wah-wah' effects and for sounds that can seem to imitate a blues singer.

An additional muted effect, called cuivré ('brassy'), can be obtained on the horn by inserting the hand into the bell further than normal. When played loudly, the result is an arresting sound often heard in the scores for horror movies.

All four members of the bowed-string family have a range of three octaves or more, allowing considerable contrast within a single part. Each string on an instrument has a subtly different sound. For example, on the violin the lowest (G) string tends to be rich and warm, especially when played with plenty of **vibrato**, while the top (E) string tends to sound much brighter.

Strings

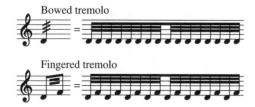

Bowed tremolo

Fingered tremolo

String players use a range of bow strokes for different types of articulation. As well as slurred bows, separate bows (for detached notes) and staccato, various types of hammered or bounced bow movements are available for particular effects. Bowed **tremolo** requires short, very fast bow movements in order to rapidly repeat a single pitch; fingered tremolo results in the rapid alternation of two different pitches, often a second or a third apart (see *left*).

Also, remember that the strings are among the few instruments that can sustain a note with the bow for as long as required.

Unless you are a string player, it is better to use standard marks of articulation (slurs, staccato and so on) in your music, and leave the precise decisions on bowing to the player(s) concerned.

In addition to playing with the bow (**arco**), string players can be directed to pluck the strings (**pizzicato**). The effect is rather quiet, unless you have a lot of players, and so easily masked by other instruments, but it is often a good way to lighten a cello or double bass part. When changing between arco and pizzicato, remember that it may take players a few moments to get their hands into the right position.

String players can use a mute, which gives a softer and more veiled sound. Again, the performer will need a few beats' rest in order to position and remove the mute.

Chords are possible on all string instruments, although they are best used sparingly and are rarely employed on the double bass. The simplest kind of chord involves **double-stopping** – playing two notes at the same time – and is relatively easy if one note can be played on an open string and the other on an adjacent string. **Harmonics** are very high, pure sounds that are easier when played on an open string. If you want to use either of these techniques, check what is possible with your player(s).

The range of more unusual and extended techniques available on string instruments includes playing with the wood of the bow ('col legno'), bowing near to, or on the wrong side of, the bridge, bowing close to the fingerboard, using 'snap pizzicato' in which the string is allowed to snap percussively against the fingerboard, and tapping with the fingers or bow on the body of the instrument.

Piano   The piano has an enormous range, so try to avoid restricting the hands to the octave or so either side of middle C. Try both hands in the treble clef or both in the bass. Think about allocating the melody to the left hand, with the accompaniment above it, or even placing the tune in the middle of the texture.

Explore ways in which chords can be patterned to give your music the character you want:

➤ Placing the bass note on a strong beat and the rest of the chord on weaker beats in march or waltz style

➤ Repeating chords in pulsating quavers or semiquavers

➤ Splitting the harmonies into patterns of broken chords

➤ Decorating the patterns with non-chord notes.

The way in which you do this can give real character to your music, establishing styles such as a march or tango, or moods of urgency or relaxation. Listen to lots of music and use your imagination!

A proficient pianist can manage a wide range of textures, from simple two-part writing (one note in each hand) to thick chords of eight or more simultaneous notes. But remember that the pianist doesn't always have to play chords – a section in which the piano presents a melody in bare octaves can sound very effective. Try other combinations, such as playing the same melody in both hands, but *two* octaves apart.

The piano can respond to a wide variety of touch, from a very smooth legato to the driest staccato. Such contrasts, like those resulting from using different textures and different parts of the piano's range, are an excellent way to achieve variety, expecially if you are writing for piano alone.

Tone can also be varied by the use of the pedals. The sustain pedal, often (but incorrectly) called the loud pedal, enriches the overall sound and can also help the pianist produce legato tone. You can mark a passage *con ped.* – 'with the (sustain) pedal'– leaving the player to decide how to use it, or you can show precisely where it is to be used like this: Ped. ⎯⎯⎯⎯⎯⎯⌐. The left-hand pedal is called the *una corda* (or soft) pedal and on a good piano produces a thinner as well as quieter tone because fewer strings per note are struck by the hammers.

Extended techniques available on the piano include tone clusters (dissonant groups of adjacent notes played with the side of the hand, the forearm or even with a stout piece of card), singing into the case of the instrument while holding down notes and/or the sustain pedal, and altering the sound by 'preparing' the piano (for an example, see NAM 10).

Singing

When writing for singers it is particularly important to work closely with the intended performer. Vocalists who are happy at presenting art or folk songs without amplification may not feel comfortable singing soul or heavy rock into a microphone. Some singers are good at sustaining a long melodic line in ballads while others may prefer a more dramatic style, or a light and lively song, or a piece which needs getting lots of words across in a rhythmically chanted rap. In other words, your choice of singer and musical style are likely to be closely linked.

You need to consider the vocal range of the singers and, perhaps more importantly, their preferred **tessitura** (the part of the range in which they prefer singing). For instance, many female singers in stage shows prefer to use a low chest voice which, although quiet, can be effectively amplified with the aid of a microphone.

What about high notes? Can your singer deliver a triumphant top note for a climax, or does the voice sound strained – and if it does, can you nevertheless make effective use of that tone in your piece? Think carefully about the syllable you set on any high, climactic note – most singers find that an open vowel sound (as in 'far') is much easier than a closed vowel (as in 'feet') because the tongue is lower and doesn't impede the airway. What about breathing? Can your singer sustain long phrases, or would it be better to use short melodic ideas separated by rests?

A wide range of extended vocal techniques are available to singers. Some, such as the 'vocal percussion' sounds of beatboxing, yodelling, whistling, ululation (a whooping sound like a battle cry), and modifying the amplified voice with various electronic effects, are relatively easy. Others, such as singing chords or harmonics, require a great deal of skill and practice. The half-speech, half-song style of **Sprechgesang** is illustrated in NAM 40, while an extensive range of unusual vocal sounds can be heard in NAM 11.

Electric guitar

Lead guitarists tend to specialise in playing melody lines while rhythm guitarists concentrate on chords, but some players are happy to take either role. Chordal parts are usually notated in the form of chord symbols above the stave, such as C or Gm^7, leaving the player to decide on the precise layout of the notes. However, it is possible to show exactly which strings and fingering you want if you add guitar 'tab' (tablature), as shown by the grid above the stave *left*. However you write the part, it is important to give a clear indication of the rhythm and style at the start, as shown in this example, and at any points where these features change. You may also want to indicate if the chords are to be strummed or picked (played in a broken-chord fashion).

= repeat previous bar

Slow rock feel

A lead guitarist can pluck the strings with the fingers (finger picking) or opt for the more incisive sound of using a pick or plectrum (flat picking). Other techniques particularly associated with lead guitar solos include:

➤ Pitch bend (moving a string sideways across the fingerboard while it is sounding, to alter the pitch of a note)

➤ Vibrato (repeated slight fluctuations in pitch, generally used to give warmth to the sound of long notes)

➤ Sliding between notes

➤ Hammer on (sounding a note by sharply bringing a finger down on the fingerboard rather than plucking it)

➤ Pull off (allowing a new pitch to sound by releasing a finger while the string is still vibrating)

➤ Tapping (playing fast passages by tapping on the fingerboard rather than plucking the strings)

➤ Palm muting (gently placing the palm of the hand on the string while playing to produce a muffled, chunky sound)

➤ Harmonics (high, pure sounds produced by lightly touching a string with the left hand while plucking with the right).

Some electric guitars have a 'whammy bar', which alters the string tension and can be used for slides and pitch bend, or to add **vibrato** to the sound. Various more specialised techniques are available. For example, in bottleneck playing, a tube around the player's finger (originally the neck of a bottle) is used to slide across the fingers oard, resulting in a continuous gliding between notes, sometimes used in blues styles.

The most common effects heard in electric-guitar playing are, of course, electronic and include:

➤ Delay, which adds simple repetitions of the sound that can sound like an echo

➤ Reverb, which adds complex repetitions of the sound to give the impression of playing in rooms and halls of different sizes

➤ Distortion, which adds the gritty sound of over-amplification and is often used in hard-rock and heavy-metal styles

➤ Chorus, which thickens the sound by adding variable amounts of small delay and/or pitch change to the original signal

➤ Compression, which evens up the sound to provide a more uniform dynamic level.

There are many other types of effect: see what your guitarist has available, and ask for a demonstration of anything unfamiliar.

The four briefs

In this section we will look at the four types of brief from which you will be able to choose, and consider some of the issues involved in each of them.

Topics 1 and 2 are based on instrumental music. Only acoustic instruments can be used for Topic 2, so if you prefer computer-based electronic music this is not the brief for you.

Topics 3 and 4 are based on vocal music. The briefs may specify whether or not it is to be accompanied. Unless instructed otherwise, any accompaniment can be for instruments or synthesised.

Whichever brief you choose, the recording can be mocked up using sequenced and synthesised sounds if any live musicians required are not available. However, it is not easy to create a convincing electronic impression of singing, so if you choose one of the vocal briefs it may be easier to make the recording with live singers, perhaps using a multi-track recorder to build up the piece in layers if you don't have enough competent singers available.

Topic 1: Composing expressively

Instrumental music

The focus of this brief will be a composition centred upon the creation and contrast of different moods. Your work can, unless specified otherwise, be in any style and designed for any instrument or group of instruments, acoustic and/or synthesised. Here is an example of the type of brief that could be set:

Compose a piece based on contrasting aspects of water. The music should use instrumental timbres and textures to create atmosphere alongside other musical elements such as harmony, melody and rhythm.

Although the brief focuses on contrasts, one of the areas in which marks are awarded is coherence – in other words, how well the piece hangs together. A patchwork of different ideas that seem unrelated is unlikely to do well. There needs to be a strong sense that the different moods you create belong to the same piece. You could do this by developing the same melodic material in different ways, or by using similar chord progressions to underpin well contrasted themes.

Think about the range of moods that could be derived from the brief. Water can be dark and mysterious in a forest pool, sparkling and brilliant in a mountain stream, drenching in a tropical storm playful in a fountain or cascade, awesome and powerful in a storm at sea, bleak and desolate when frozen to ice. How many moods would you include? Consider the way you move from one mood to another: will you do so abruptly or gradually? Will you give a hint of what is to come in the next section before the current section has ended? Will some sections return to give your music structure? Will there be a musical climax? How will you end?

Before starting to draw up ideas, ask your teacher to suggest some appropriate listening for the brief concerned. In the case of our example your imagination might be triggered by pieces such as Mendelssohn's *Hebrides* Overture, Debussy's *La Mer*, Britten's 'Sea Interludes' from *Peter Grimes*, Vaughan Williams' *A Sea Symphony* and *Sinfonia Antartica*, Saint-Saëns' 'Aquarium' from *Carnival of the Animals*, Ravel's *Jeux d'eau*, the flooding of the castle at the end of Dukas' *The Sorcerer's Apprentice*, Respighi's Fountains of Rome and the opening of the fourth concerto, 'Winter', from Vivaldi's *The Four Seasons*. Smetana's *Vltava* would be particularly worth studying, since it traces in music the growth of a mighty river from its beginnings as a mountain stream, creating contrasting moods from basically similar melodic material.

Topic 2: Composing idiomatically for instruments

Composing idiomatically means designing your music to bring out the particular qualities of the instruments concerned, rather than writing a piece that would sound much the same whichever instruments are used.

The focus of this brief will be a composition that exploits the characteristics of the instrument(s) that you choose and that uses some type of variation structure. Your work for this topic can, unless specified otherwise, be in any style and must be for either solo piano or for 2–4 acoustic instruments. Because you have to write idiomatically for the instrument(s) concerned, synthesised sounds are *not* appropriate for this topic. Here is an example of the type of brief that could be set:

Compose a theme and use this as the basis for a set of variations. Each variation could have its own character – for example, playful, sombre, dance-like and brilliant, or you could use a different dance style for each, such as waltz, salsa, foxtrot and jig. Aim to exploit the characteristics and ranges of the instrument(s) you have used.

The notes on 'Resources' (page 14) should provide some starting points for considering how to write idiomatically for instruments. The secret of writing variations is to start with a strong theme harmonised by a simple chord progression. This will give you a secure foundation on which to build your set of variations.

The brief suggests some ways in which each variation could be given its own character. You don't have to follow these suggestions, but try to avoid anything too repetitive, such as a **ground bass** structure. Ways of varying musical material include:

- Changing the metre, rhythm and tempo

- Decorating the melody with additional notes

- Using different harmonies and perhaps writing a variation in the tonic minor key to contrast with a major-key theme

- Varying the texture, perhaps by placing the melody in the bass, adding a countermelody or using fewer instruments

- Varying the accompaniment (sustained harmonies, pulsating chords, repeated rhythmic figures, arpeggios and so on)

- Changing the instrumentation, perhaps using fewer instruments or splitting the melody between different instruments

- Fragmenting the melody (for example, writing a variation based entirely on the first few notes of the theme).

Whatever techniques you use, try to include some melodic interest for all the instruments or, if writing for solo piano, create variety by using some of the methods discussed on pages 16–17.

A good starting point to prepare for this brief is to listen to Mozart's 12 Variations on *Ah! vous dirai-je Maman* for piano. The composer's treatment of the theme is easy to follow because you will already know it – it is the tune sung to *Twinkle, Twinkle, Little Star* in English. Other sets of variations to explore include the fourth movement of Schubert's *Trout* Quintet, Brahms' *Variations on a Theme by Joseph Haydn*, Rachmaninov's *Rhapsody on a Theme of Paganini* and (using the same theme) Andrew Lloyd Webber's *Variations* for cello and rock group (also arranged for cello and orchestra).

Works in variation form that feature a solo instrument, such as Lloyd Webber's *Variations*, are also valuable as models of idiomatic instrumental writing. Others include the last movement of Mozart's Clarinet Quintet, Paganini's Introduction and Variations on 'Non più mesta' from Rossini's *La Cenerentola* for violin and orchestra, Arban's *Carnival of Venice* for cornet, and Britten's *The Young Person's Guide to the Orchestra*, which includes variations for a wide range of orchestral instruments.

Variation technique is also at the heart of much jazz. For example, NAM 48 consists of improvisations over the well-known 12-bar blues chord pattern.

As you listen to any of these works, make notes on the techniques used, and how the variations are ordered to create sections of light and shade, intensity and relaxation. Is there a musical climax – if so, is it the most technically brilliant variation or is it perhaps a broad and heroic version of the theme? Are the variations self-contained sections or does the music flow directly from one to the next? How does the piece conclude – does a simpler version of the theme return at the end? These are all important points that you need to consider when planning your own work.

Two works that use variation form very freely (making the theme sometimes hard to detect) but that focus on giving each variation a distinctive character are Elgar's *Enigma* Variations and Britten's *Variations on a Theme of Frank Bridge*. Both are much longer and more complex than anything expected at AS, but they could suggest ideas for you to explore.

Some 20th-century composers were attracted to 'hidden variation' form, in which the variations appear first and the theme is not revealed until the end. If you plan anything this subtle, be sure to explain it in your sleeve notes!

Vocal music

Topic 3: Words and music – structure in vocal music

This brief focuses on structure in vocal music. Your work can, unless specified otherwise, be in any style and written for one or more singers, with or without accompaniment. If you decide to include an accompaniment, it can be for acoustic or amplified instruments, or for synthetic sounds. Here is an example of the type of brief that could be set:

Choose a text and compose a song in verse-and-chorus form with an accompaniment for any instrument(s) of your choice. It must have an ending suitable for live performance rather than finishing with a fade-out.

> Other types of structure that could be set in this brief include **strophic** form (the same music for each verse, either exactly as in NAM 37, or varied as in NAM 41) and ternary form (ABA).

Your text could be a poem or the lyrics of an existing song – or you could write your own words. To form the chorus you will need a poem that has a refrain, or some lines that could be repeated after each verse to act like a refrain. Don't spend too long working on the words, as marks are not awarded for the quality of the text, only for the way in which you set it to music.

Verse-and-chorus form is potentially very repetitive. Although the verses have different words, the music is the same for each one (save for any slight adaptations to fit the text) and each verse is followed by a chorus in which both the words and the music are usually virtually identical each time it returns. You should therefore be wary of techniques that add to the repetition, such as too much use of unchanging **riffs** or using the same chord progression for both the verses and the choruses.

> At one time a common way to create a climactic ending for a popular song was to modulate up a semitone for the final chorus. The resulting lurch, nicknamed 'the truck driver's gear change', has long been a cliché (although it can still often be heard in the Eurovision Song Contest) and is best avoided in examination work.

There are a number of ways in which you can prevent a song in this form sounding too predictable. You could vary the texture and/or instrumentation in each verse, and perhaps use different singers for alternate verses if that suits the lyrics. You could make the chorus more interesting each time it appears by gradually building up the texture, perhaps adding backing vocals or countermelodies to the basic structure. The final chorus could be repeated (with an extended ending) to form the climax of the song.

Another way to prevent verse-and-chorus form sounding too predictable is to include some additional sections:

> An introduction to set the mood (and help the singer find the starting note)

> An instrumental instead of a sung verse (generally using the same music as the verse, or at least the same chord pattern, and often featuring an elaborate improvisation on the melody)

> A short **coda** to end the song.

Short instrumental links or 'fills' can be used to bridge the gap between sections and give the singer a chance to breathe. One common type is the **turnaround** – a few bars ending with chord V^7 to lead the song back to a repeat (as in bars 33–34 of NAM 53). Another possible addition to the basic structure is a **pre-chorus**: a section at the end of each verse, often with the same words every time it occurs, designed to propel the music into the start of the chorus, as in bars 13–24 of NAM 57.

> NAM 57 is an example of a song in expanded verse-and-chorus form: see the notes on page 121.

The chorus is usually the catchiest part of the song and in popular styles may be based on a **hook** (a short and memorable musical figure, sometimes using the title words of the song).

Plan the phrase structure of both the verse and the chorus with care. There is usually quite a lot of internal repetition in popular songs, so four phrases in a pattern such as ABAB, ABCA or ABAC are common.

One of the most traditional structures for a chorus, particularly in songs from stage shows, is known as **32-bar song form**. It consists of four eight-bar phrases in the pattern AABA. Each phrase has different lyrics, but the A phrases all have the same chord pattern and melody (possibly based on a hook), while the B phrase has a contrasting tune with different harmonies, and lyrics that generally offer a different slant on the idea expressed in the A phrases.

> The B phrase in 32-bar song form is known as the 'middle eight' or 'bridge' (although note that the term 'bridge' is sometimes used for any contrasting middle section in pop music and jazz).

However, remember the warning about over-repetition in verse-and-chorus structures and consider how you might vary phrases when they return. For instance, the first two phrases in an AABA structure could have different endings, and the final A phrase could be extended by a few bars in order to create a more climactic ending to the chorus or to incorporate a turnaround.

Try to use the verse-and-chorus structure creatively. The singing doesn't *have* to start with a verse – it could begin with the chorus. And there is no need to keep to a rigid division between verses sung by a soloist and choruses sung by a larger group. The soloist could improvise over the other vocal parts in some of the choruses, or the larger group could add a brief comment at the end of the soloist's phrases in the verses. Use your imagination!

Before starting to draw up ideas, listen analytically to a variety of songs – even better, sing them. For a brief such as this, material could range from such well-known songs as *Rule, Britannia!* and *Waltzing Matilda*, through popular numbers from opera (such as the 'Toreador's Song' from Bizet's *Carmen*) and musicals (such as 'The Surrey With the Fringe on Top' from *Oklahoma!* to pop songs of the last 50 years or more. *Penny Lane*, *All You Need is Love* and *She Loves You* by the Beatles are all in verse-and-chorus form, as is Nirvana's *About a Girl*, Madonna's *I Deserve It* and *Don't Look Back in Anger* by Oasis.

Topic 4: Text, context and texture

The brief for this topic focuses on how text and musical texture work in the context of vocal music. A few examples should clarify this requirement:

➤ Church music uses religious words, is often written for a choir and, if intended to be performed in a resonant cathedral, might be relatively slow-moving and make best use of the acoustic by employing dramatic pauses and perhaps echo effects between contrasting and separated groups of singers positioned around the building

➤ A vocal ensemble for a stage show (such as a trio of accompa-nied voices) will have a text relevant to the plot and, thanks to the dry acoustic of theatres, is likely to have much faster word-delivery than is found in church music, probably including some lively interaction between the three singers:

➤ In a musical, the textures may be fairly simple (often with just one voice at a time), the setting may be largely **syllabic** (to get the words across to the audience), and the vocal parts may be in a fairly low register (since they are likely to be amplified)

➤ In an opera, the vocal parts are likely to have a wider range and be more technically demanding, and the textures are more likely to include **counterpoint**, with the vocalists singing independent melodic lines at the same time.

➤ A piece of experimental vocal music might be presented in a studio or performance space with a range of equipment that allows live and electronic sounds to be combined; it could be semi-staged, with some acting required of the singers, and it might use text in unusual ways, like the re-ordering of words, syllables and letters of the poem in NAM 11.

Here is an example of the type of brief that could be set:

Choose a suitable text and compose a piece for unaccompanied voices suitable for performance at a contemporary arts festival. Include changes of texture and a range of vocal techniques, which might include speech, wordless singing or the electronic processing of vocal sounds.

As in Topic 3, avoid spending too long choosing or writing a text, as it is the musical setting of the words rather than the words themselves that earn marks. The text for this brief could be quite short – a sentence or two containing a thought-provoking idea or some interesting word sounds could work just as well. It doesn't need to be a poem, although you might get some ideas from the work of poets such as e. e. cummings and Bob Cobbing.

Different types of texture are discussed on page 45. You could contrast homophonic and contrapuntal writing, and/or sections in a thin texture, perhaps for just a solo voice, with passages for all the singers. If you write for soprano, alto, tenor and bass voices, you have the opportunity to contrast different vocal groupings, such as a phrase for upper voices answered by a phrase for lower voices, or groupings such as SAT contrasting with ATB.

We looked at writing for voices on pages 17–18: the section ends with a discussion of some extended vocal techniques that could be used for this brief. If you decide to use ideas of this sort, be careful that your piece is more than just a collage of sound effects – it needs to have structure and a convincing musical purpose. You don't have to use unusual vocal techniques – some sections of humming or vocalising to 'ah', would be enough to fulfil the requirements of the brief. Notice that it allows you to include electronic processing of vocal sounds if you wish. This could include simple amplification of voices, or more adventurous methods, such as employing tape loops, digital delay and echo effects.

Because it might be difficult to find and rehearse enough competent singers to record your work for this topic, you are allowed to use melody instruments or synthesised sounds for the recording. If you do this, make sure that your score nevertheless includes all the detailed performing directions that singers would need, so that the examiner can see exactly what you intend.

Before starting to draw up ideas, ask your teacher to suggest some appropriate listening for the brief concerned. In the case of our example this might include studying the varied vocal textures in Tavener's *The Lamb* (NAM 32), the writing for six amplified singers in Stockhausen's *Stimmung*, the use of wordless singing in vocal arrangements of Bach's instrumental music heard in recordings by the Swingle Singers, the vocal writing in Penderecki's *St Luke Passion* (a work that also contains orchestral writing), choral music by Arvo Pärt and Henryk Górecki, and the solo vocal writing in Berio's *Sequenza III* (NAM 11).

Working the brief

All work on the final score, apart from the recording, must be done under controlled conditions in the 15 hours allowed, although you can (and should) practise your general composing skills, listen to relevant music and sketch your plans for the brief outside this time. Concentrating on the following three aspects of composing should help you achieve a good mark.

Development of ideas

Many of us stumble across good musical ideas when doodling at the keyboard or singing to ourselves in an idle moment. The difficulty is usually deciding what to do next, after that initial bar or first phrase. Many promising openings are spoilt by excessive repetition in the bars that follow, leading to little variety and no sense of alternating tension and repose. Just as common are openings that are followed by too much diversity – so many new ideas in rapid succession that the piece fails to hang together.

Some minimalist and riff-based music is highly repetitive. If you choose one of these styles it may be wise, as mentioned earlier, to consider writing a relatively long piece in order to show that you can achieve some variety and a sense of development in your work.

The best way out of this dilemma is to discover what happens in music that you know. Start from:

➤ The music you play or sing

➤ The works you are studying from NAM

➤ The pieces you have listened to in preparation for the brief.

Try to identify the ways in which composers unify their music by varying and developing ideas, and by repeating sections in different keys, or with different textures, rather than constantly introducing entirely new material.

Apply the principles you discover to your own music. Instead of searching for new ideas, take time to explore your opening material in more depth. Break it up into smaller motifs and try to give these a life of their own before introducing new material. Above all, aim for a balance of unity and diversity in your work.

Control of texture

Most composition examiners would agree that this is the area in which candidates have the most difficulty and yet varied textures are vital to most types of music. If you assign your melody to the same part throughout and condemn the others to dull accompanying lines, you risk the wrath of your performers, the boredom of your audiences and a low mark in the exam.

Try to distribute thematic material among *all* the resources you employ, remembering that each instrument and voice can be used in different parts of its range. Make use of well-contrasted dynamics and articulation to help achieve variety. Break longer melodies into short motifs that dart from one instrument or voice to another. Accompanying parts will be far more interesting if lugubrious semibreves are replaced with some rhythmic movement or interesting figuration. The use of a countermelody or other simple contrapuntal device can transform an ordinary piece into a work of real interest. Pay particular attention to phrase endings. If phrases often end on a long note try to add some decoration or a linking motif in another part to propel the music forwards, or see if the end of the phrase can be overlapped with the start of the next.

Points of tension and relaxation are vital in most music and such moments need careful planning throughout the piece. Changes in texture play a vital role in defining points of climax, where a thickening of chords, an increase of **harmonic rhythm**, an ascent to a high note, the addition of extra parts and an increase in rhythmic activity can combine to maximise the impact you intend.

Above all, remember that *rests* are the key to achieving good variety of texture. They are essential if singers and wind players are not to expire before the final cadence, but they are also essential to give relief to the ear. Assign solos to different instruments and don't feel obliged to occupy all the players in every bar. Experiment with different combinations, such as a melody in the bass or inner part, and remember that occasional moments of totally unaccompanied melody can be ravishingly beautiful.

Refinement of ideas

You would be talented indeed to compose a piece of music and not then need to refine and polish it. At the very least you are likely to have to make adjustments as a result of trialling the work in performance. In addition to matters such as unplayable passages or miscalculated balance, you should be prepared to use a critical ear to identify places where the music loses its impetus. Perhaps a long note at a cadence needs to be sparked into life by adding an embellishment in another part, or perhaps a tendency for the piece to sound too sectionalised and predictable needs to be corrected by overlapping the phrases or adjusting the lengths of sub-phrases.

Gnawing away at the details in order to refine the work is part of the compositional process, but there will also be a time when you should let go – a point at which further change is likely to be counterproductive and could result in inconsistencies of style that detract from your original concept of the piece.

Composing involves a certain amount of risk, and your efforts are more likely to be successful if you attempt a piece that displays a real sense of character and ambition. The criteria for a high mark require confident and creative handling of a number of aspects of the work. Examiners will rarely be impressed by Adagio movements in an unvarying C major that attempt to reach a length of three minutes by means of excessive repetition, since these are unlikely to meet many of the criteria for a successful mark.

How is the composition marked?

Compositions can be in any style, providing it is appropriate to the topic you choose, but you will want to show the best you can do, so use a format that will allow adequate variety. If you adopt a style that is exceptionally repetitive or very slow-moving you may have to write a piece longer than the three-minute minimum in order to show that you can achieve contrast and a sense of development in your work.

The examiner will give a mark for overall impression created by the composition, and will balance this against marks for five of the six categories *below* – the first three, plus whichever two of the last three are most appropriate for the composition concerned:

1. Quality of ideas and outcome. To do well in this category, your composition needs to sound convincing and should contain some exciting musical ideas.

2. Coherence. This category concerns the structure of your piece. To do well you need to balance unity and diversity, so that the work is neither over-repetitive and boring, nor so full of un-related ideas that it fails to hang together.

3. Forces and textures. Marks in this category are awarded for how effectively you have written for the instrument(s) and/or voice(s) you have chosen, and how you have combined them to create an interesting range of textures.

4. Harmony. Marks here are awarded for your choice of chords, use of harmonic progressions, treatment of dissonance and, if appropriate to the style, handling of modulation.

5. Melody. The examiner will look for good melodic shape and interesting use of motifs within phrases, not just in the main melodic line but also in accompanying parts.

6. Rhythm. To do well in this category, aim for distinctive and varied rhythms with appropriate use of patterns such as dotted and tied notes, triplets, syncopation, or cross-rhythms.

Notice that there are marks for two out of the three categories, harmony, melody and rhythm. This suggests that the full mark range would not be available for a piece written for only untuned percussion, such as a drum kit. If you are planning such a piece, try to include melody and/or harmony parts, either for tuned percussion or for another instrument.

Composing takes time and most people find that initial ideas have to be worked over repeatedly before a satisfactory shape starts to emerge. Sometimes it is even necessary to start afresh if you find a piece is not progressing well.

Some people find that developing compositions at a MIDI workstation can be a good way of working, even if the piece is destined for eventual performance by live musicians. Sequencer systems can also be useful to produce an approximation of a performance for recording purposes if live instrumentalists are unavailable.

This method needs a few words of caution, though. Firstly, MIDI software is not very good at warning you that what you write may be unplayable by live musicians – you can easily find that the string chords which sound so good on a synthesizer are simply impossible on a violin, or that 80 bars of flute music without a breathing point will cause your flautist to faint, or that your untransposed trumpet part descending into the depths of the bass clef leaves your trumpeter totally bewildered. If you are using a sequencer to develop a piece for live players it will therefore be wise to try out ideas with the performers at every opportunity. Secondly, you will need to clarify whether your work is conceived as an electronic studio piece or as a composition for live musicians. There is a great deal of difference between the two, and your intentions will seem confused if you submit a score that seems to fit neither type of resource very effectively.

The score

Your score may be fully notated or, if appropriate to the style of the music, it could take the form of a lead sheet, chord chart, track diagram or annotated graphic. Whatever format you use, it must be sufficiently clear, detailed and unambiguous for the examiner to make an assessment of your composition.

A well-chosen title can help to make your intentions clear but features such as computer-typeset title pages, colourful artwork and elaborate bindings will gain you no extra marks. Aim for a clear, simple layout with numbered pages clipped together in the right order. Bar numbers, either at the start of each system or every ten bars, are a helpful addition to any score.

If you use a fully notated score and the piece includes a number of different instruments, make sure the staves are labelled with an instrument or voice name at the start of every system, although abbreviations can be used for this after the start of the piece. When writing more than one system on a page it will help the layout if you leave a blank stave or two between systems. Remember that you can use conventional repeat signs in the score to avoid copying out identical sections of music.

Whatever type of score you submit, remember to include full and clear performing directions, showing how you want the music to be performed. However, there is nothing to be gained by using lots of Italian terms (English is perfectly acceptable) or by peppering the music with a random selection of dynamics and phrase marks. All markings should relate clearly to the music.

Computer-generated scores

Computer-generated notation is allowed and can produce very neat results, but there can be many pitfalls, especially if you generate a score from sequencing software such as Cubase. Sequencers record the exact length of sounds that are played, without rounding them to the nearest note value. If the recording is displayed as a musical score, the result can be a performer's nightmare. For example, a simple crotchet might appear as triple-dotted quaver followed by a hemidemisemiquaver rest or as a long succession of very short notes tied together. It is not that the software is wrong – it is simply displaying note-lengths in far too much detail for a performer to interpret easily.

Most sequencer software has facilities, such as score quantization, to help achieve more acceptable results, but you will still need to check the output carefully for eccentric note-lengths, and unnecessary rests and ties.

Software usually handles pitch better than rhythm, but again you must be on your guard for incorrect accidentals (e.g. A♯ in F major, when the note should be a B♭). Check carefully for mistakes such as printing low clarinet notes in the bass clef. Excessive leger lines should be avoided, either by using a different clef if appropriate, or by using an *8ᵛᵃ* sign. In particular, be sure to check that the software is correctly handling parts for instruments whose music should be written an octave higher or lower than it sounds.

Remember that you will probably need to edit in the phrasing and articulation you require, and to make sure that the staves are labelled with the instruments you intend, and not just track numbers. Most software should be able to produce correct stem directions and accurate beaming (grouping of notes), but again you should check that you have the right settings for the music concerned.

You will also need to know how your software handles repeats. It may well print the music out again in full, when what is really required is a repeat sign or a *da capo* direction, perhaps with first- and second-time bars in order to differentiate different endings.

Most of these problems can be overcome by careful study of the software manual, but remember that it is most unlikely that you will be able merely to press the 'Print' button in order to achieve an acceptably accurate score. If you are lucky enough to have access to high-quality software optimised for music notation, such as Sibelius, the task will be easier, but will still need careful checking. Again, remember to make it clear whether computer-printed staves are intended for live musicians or sequenced synthesizer sounds.

If you intend to rehearse and record your piece with live musicians, notation software can make the task of producing parts from the score very much quicker, but remember that your performers will need page turns in suitable places and players of transposing instruments will require their parts to be in the correct key. Also, try to use a decent quality of paper for printing the parts since flimsy computer-printout paper will not stay upright on a music stand.

In the end you may not be surprised to learn that some people find it quicker, and more satisfying, to use traditional pen and ink!

The sleeve note

One third of the marks for the composing unit are allocated to the sleeve note, so it is something to plan with care. The quality of your written English will be taken into account in the assessement.

The sleeve note has to be written in one hour, under supervised conditions. This hour is in addition to the 15 hours allowed for the actual composing. You are allowed to make notes in advance and to consult them while writing. It is particularly important to keep a list of not only which pieces you have listened to in preparation for the brief but also precisely what in those pieces has influenced your own composition, and how (because you will be asked to give full details of the processes involved).

You have to complete the sleeve note by answering the following three questions:

1. *Explain and comment on form and structure, indicating in particular how repetition and contrast are balanced.* (4 marks)

    It is not enough just to offer a label such as 'verse-and-chorus' form. You need to give specific examples of repetition and contrast in your composition, using bar numbers or CD timings. Draw attention to things of which you are especially proud, such as how apparently contrasting passages are subtly linked, and matters such as the use of abbreviated or extended repeats.

2. *Mention **four** other features of interest. You can refer to any two or more of the following: rhythm, melodic development, texture, handling of instrument(s) and/or voice(s), harmony.* (4 marks)

    This is a good opportunity to explain how you have designed your music to suit particular instruments or voices. By highlighting areas that you feel are particularly strong, such as the development of motifs or the use of cross-rhythms, you can hint to the examiner which two of the three optional criteria (melody, harmony and rhythm) should be assessed.

3. *Refer to pieces from the* New Anthology of Music *and/or elsewhere, to explain how other pieces of music have influenced you in your composition.* (12 marks)

    Most of the hour should be spent on this last part because you will need to make a lot of valid observations to gain high marks. This is where your notes will be essential since the examiner will want to see precise details of pieces that have influenced you, and how (including locations in the music where appropriate). Vague statements such as 'I listened to songs by the Beatles' will get little if any credit. Instead, each of your points needs to offer really well-focused information, such as this:

    'My use of a double bridge structure was influenced by studying this form in the songs *We Can Work It Out* and *You're Going To Lose That Girl* by the Beatles. The prominent use of appoggiaturas at the start of bars 1, 3 and 5 of *Yesterday* by the same group inspired the use of this device in the chorus of my own song.'

The recording

You must submit a recording of your composition, which can either be performed as intended, arranged for whatever resources are available, or synthesised. Although the recording is not marked, it plays a valuable role in showing the examiner what you intend, especially if your score doesn't use detailed stave notation.

The recording is made outside the 15 supervised hours allowed for composing but if, after recording the piece, you decide to make changes, you won't get extra time, so don't leave recording until after all your supervised time has been used up.

Submission checklist

Use the following list to ensure that you haven't overlooked any important points when it comes to submitting your work.

❏ Have you given the composition a meaningful title?

❏ Is there an indication of the tempo?

❏ Have you remembered the time signature?

❏ Are all the staves or tracks unambiguously labelled with the relevant instrument or voice names?

❏ Have you included a key for any parts, such as drum-kit, that use non-standard notation and for any graphic notation that you may have used?

❏ Have you included dynamics and other performing directions that are important to the realisation of the piece?

❏ If any sections are expected to be improvised by the performers have you provided them with adequate instructions?

❏ Are all the pages numbered and in their correct order?

❏ Have you included the recording?

❏ Have you completed and signed the statement provided by Edexcel to confirm that the composition is your own work?

If you are submitting a score in conventional notation, also check:

❏ Do all the staves have the correct key signature?

❏ Have marks of articulation and phrasing been included? Phrase marks should always begin and end on specific notes, not on barlines or between notes.

❏ Are all the notes for each instrument playable?

❏ Does every bar have the correct number of beats? Checking is tedious but essential if you are to avoid this common fault.

❏ Have you numbered the bars for easy reference?

❏ Are there any blank bars? If a part is not playing it should either be omitted from the system or be given whole-bar rests, since blank bars can be ambiguous.

Further reading

AS Music Composition Workbook by Alan Charlton (Rhinegold Education, 2008) ISBN 978-1-906178-31-4

The Composer's Handbook by Bruce Cole (Schott and Co Ltd, 1996) ISBN 978-0-946535-80-4

The Pop Composer's Handbook by Bruce Cole (Schott and Co Ltd, 2006) ISBN 978-1-902455-60-0

Orchestral Technique by Gordon Jacob (Oxford University Press, 1931/1982) ISBN 978-0-193182-04-2

Rock, Jazz and Pop Arranging by Daryl Runswick (Faber, 1992) ISBN 978-0-571511-08-2

Unit 3: Developing Musical Understanding

Practice questions for Sections A and C are provided in *Edexcel AS Music Listening Tests* by Hugh Benham and Alistair Wightman (Rhinegold Education). Section B practice questions can be found in *Edexcel AS Revision Guide* by Alistair Wightman (Rhinegold Education).

For this unit you will be studying four instrumental set works, five or six vocal set works and the basic principles of tonal harmony.

At the end of the course you will sit a two-hour exam paper, marked out of 80 and consisting of the three sections described *below*. Section A, which must be completed first, takes about 30 minutes (including five minutes' reading time at the start). You can answer the other two sections in whichever order you wish, allowing about 45 minutes for each.

Section A: Listening (32 marks)

You will hear two extracts of music, each about one minute in length. The first will be taken from one of your instrumental set works and the second from one of your vocal set works. Each will be played five times, with pauses between playings. You will be given a skeleton score of each extract and will have to complete a set of short-answer questions on both extracts.

Most of the questions will involve identifying musical features in the extracts, but you are also likely to be asked to indicate from where in the set work the extract is taken (note that you will *not* have a copy of NAM to consult during the exam).

Section B: Investigating musical styles (28 marks)

You will have to answer one question, divided into two parts, for this section. The first part (worth 18 marks) will be about the musical style of one of the set works. The second (worth 18 marks) will ask you to compare and contrast two musical features (such as harmony and form) of two set works. The works concerned will not be the same as those in Section A.

Remember, you won't have access to recordings or to NAM in this section, but you will be able to choose between answering questions on either the instrumental set works or the vocal ones. The questions will require longer answers than those in Section A, but you can write in note form or continuous prose, as you prefer.

Section C: Understanding chords and lines (20 marks)

There will be two questions. In the first (worth 8 marks) you will be asked questions relating to the harmony of a printed passage of unfamiliar music. In the second (worth 12 marks), you will have to complete a short passage of four-part harmony by adding alto, tenor and bass parts to a given soprano part. You are likely to have to add five chords, ending with a cadence.

You are allowed to use a keyboard with headphones to complete this section, but you are not allowed to use computer software.

Understanding chords and lines

Although Section C is the last part of the paper for Unit 3, we will deal with it first, because the skills involved will also be needed in your study of the set works.

Identification

In the first of the two questions in this section you will have to identify keys, chords, cadences and non-chord notes in a printed score of unfamiliar music.

The first task is to identify the key at the start of the passage. It could be any major or minor key with up to four sharps or flats, as shown *right*.

You may find it helpful to remember that:

➤ The name of a major key with sharps is the note above the last sharp in its key signature

➤ The name of a major key with flats is the same as the next-to-last flat in its key signature (you will just have to memorise C major and F major!).

Each major key has a **relative minor** key which has the same key signature. The two keys are related because they have many notes in common. The relative minor is always two scale steps below its **relative major**. For example, the relative minor of F major is D minor (F → E → D).

Because a major key and its relative minor have the same key signature, we need a way to tell them apart. The simplest method is to see if the fifth degree of the major scale has been given an accidental to raise it by a semitone. If so, the note concerned is likely to be the seventh degree of the relative minor, shown as a black note in the minor-key examples *right*.

The seventh degree of the scale is often followed by the key note, either immediately or soon after, which can be useful confirmation that you have named the key correctly:

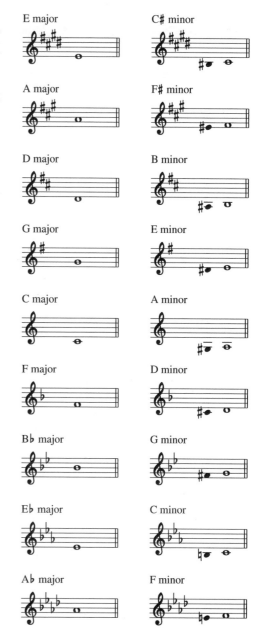

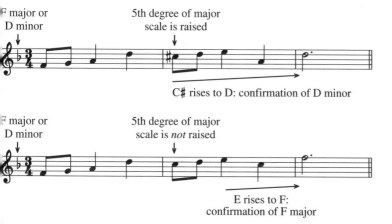

The seventh degree of all major and minor scales is called the **leading note**, because it leads the music towards the key note, or **tonic**. All seven degrees of the scale have names, which are the same whether the key is major or minor:

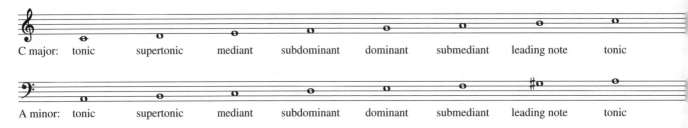

C major: tonic   supertonic   mediant   subdominant   dominant   submediant   leading note   tonic

A minor: tonic   supertonic   mediant   subdominant   dominant   submediant   leading note   tonic

Exercise 1

1. Name the key of each of the following melodies.

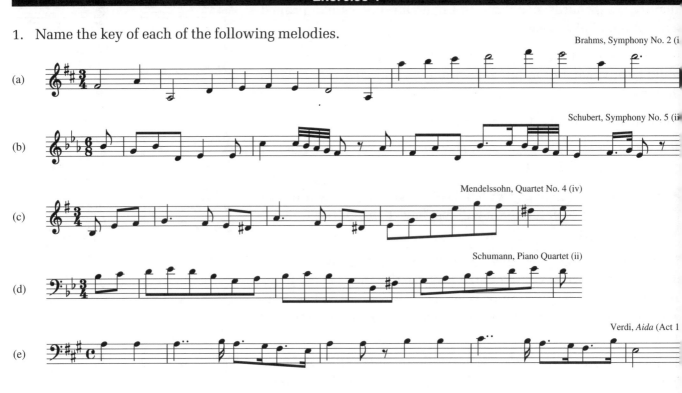

Brahms, Symphony No. 2 (i)

(a)

Schubert, Symphony No. 5 (ii)

(b)

Mendelssohn, Quartet No. 4 (iv)

(c)

Schumann, Piano Quartet (ii)

(d)

Verdi, *Aida* (Act 1)

(e)

2. Name the key of the following scale and add the missing degree names:

tonic   mediant   dominant   submediant   tonic

Chords   To be really certain of a key, we need to consider the harmony as well as the tune, and this means identifying the chords used.

Three-note chords called **triads** can be built on any note of a scale. They are formed from alternate scale steps and are identified by the scale degree of their lowest note, using Roman numerals.

D major: I   II   III   IV   V   VI   VII   I

If we add another alternate scale step to a triad, we get a **7th chord**, so called because the interval between its outer notes is a 7th. In the exam you may be asked to identify chords II^7 and V^7 (shown left). Remember to write a superscript 7 after the Roman numeral if the chord includes a 7th.

D major: II^7 V^7

The note after which a chord is named is called its **root** and the other notes in the chord are named according to their interval above it, as shown *right*. Any of these notes could be used as the lowest note and we need to include this in the chord description by adding a lower-case letter to the chord's Roman numeral:

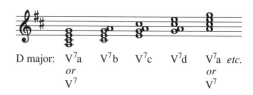

D major: V^7

7th (d)
5th (c)
3rd (b)
root (a)

➤ If the root is the lowest note, we say the chord is in **root position** – strictly we should add the letter 'a' after the Roman numeral, but it is always assumed that a chord is in root position if there is no letter.

➤ If the third is the lowest note, the chord is in **first inversion** and we add the letter 'b'.

➤ If the fifth is the lowest note, the chord is in **second inversion** and we add the letter 'c'.

➤ If the chord has a seventh and if this is the lowest note, the chord is in **third inversion** and we add the letter 'd'.

D major: V^7a V^7b V^7c V^7d V^7a *etc.*
          or   or
          V^7 V^7

The notes of a chord may appear in any order and will usually be spread over more than one stave. Some notes may be **doubled** (that is, they may appear more than once in the same chord), the fifth may be omitted, and sometimes each of the notes may be sounded separately to form a **broken chord**:

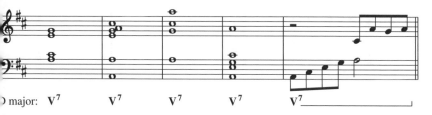

D major: V^7 V^7 V^7 V^7 V^7

Despite their different layouts, these are all versions of chord V^7 of D major in root position (A^7), because each contains the notes A, C♯, E and G, with the root of the chord (A) as the lowest note.

Here is a step-by-step method for identifying chords, using the example printed *right*:

1. Work out the key of the passage and make a chord chart for that key, like this:

7th	(d)		(D)			(G)		
5th	(c)	A	B	C♯	D	E	F♯	G
3rd	(b)	F♯	G	A	B	C♯	D	E
root	(a)	D	E	F♯	G	A	B	C♯
D major:		**I**	**II**$^{(7)}$	**III**	**IV**	**V**$^{(7)}$	**VI**	**VII**

2. Write down the names of the notes in the chord you want to identify, ignoring any duplicates and writing the lowest note of the chord at the bottom.

3. Match the notes you have listed with a chord in your chart and write down its Roman numeral.

4. Check the chord's lowest note against the inversion letters in your chart and then add the correct letter after the Roman numeral, as shown *right*.

Step 2:

A		D	C♯	
A		B	G	F♯
D		E	E	A
F♯		G	A	D

Step 3:   I   II^7 V^7 I

Step 4:

D major: **Ib**   **II^{7}b**   **V^7(a)**   **I(a)**

Diminished 7th  Minor 3rds

There is one other chord that you could be asked to identify – the **diminished 7th**. It is named after the interval between its outer notes and is a very symmetrical chord – the interval between every pair of notes is a minor 3rd (see *left*).

Chord VII⁷ in a minor key is a diminished 7th, but if the chord occurs in a major key at least one of its notes will be **chromatic** (not part of the key) – it is the only chromatic chord you may be asked to identify. It can just be labelled 'dim⁷' – it doesn't need a Roman numeral or an inversion letter.

Exam tips

Note that the only second inversion chords you will be asked to identify in the exam (and in this chapter) are **Ic**, **Vc** and **V⁷c**, and remember that you are allowed to use an electric keyboard (with headphones) if you want to try out the sounds of the chords you are being asked to identify.

Exercise 2

Name the key and complete the labelling of the chords in each of the following passages.

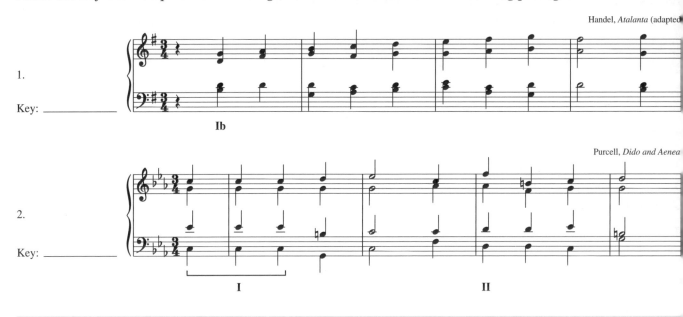

1.

Key: _____   Ib

Handel, *Atalanta* (adapted)

2.

Key: _____

I   II

Purcell, *Dido and Aeneas*

Non-chord notes

If music consisted of nothing but chords it would be very dull. Although harmony forms the foundation of many types of music, it is usually decorated with notes that do not belong to the chord that supports them. These **non-chord notes**, which can occur in any part, not just the tune, help give rhythm and melodic shape to the music, and can also create excitement and tension if they clash with the underlying harmony. You will need to be able to recognise the following types of non-chord note.

Passing notes move by step between two different chord notes. Because they occur between beats, or on weak beats, their effect is largely decorative. **Accented passing notes** also move by step but, as their name suggests, they occur on stronger beats than the harmony notes that follow them, creating a more obvious clash with the supporting chord:

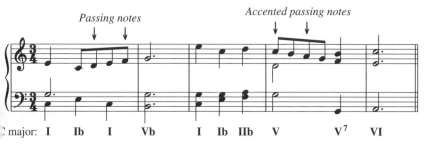

C major: **I   Ib   I   Vb   I   Ib   IIb   V   V⁷   VI**

Auxiliary notes are similar to passing notes, except that they occur between two harmony notes of the same pitch. An upper auxiliary is one step above the harmony note while a lower auxiliary is one step below.

An **échappé** (escape note) starts like a passing note, moving by step away from a harmony note, but it then leaps in the opposite direction to a new harmony note.

An **anticipation** occurs when the next harmony note (usually the tonic) comes in fractionally early on a weak beat.

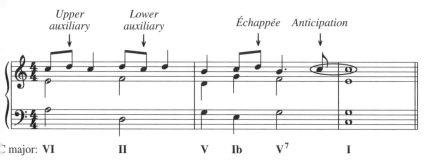

C major: **VI   II   V   Ib   V⁷   I**

An **appoggiatura** is an on-beat dissonance that clashes with the harmony and then moves by step to a chord note. Unlike an accented passing note, it can be approached by a leap, which often results in a particularly expressive effect.

A **suspension** also produces a clash with the harmony, but instead of being approached by a step or a leap, the dissonant note is 'prepared' by being sounded as a chord note on the previous beat. This note is then either repeated or extended (sometimes by means of a tie) while the chord beneath it changes. Finally, the dissonance is 'resolved' when it moves by step to a note of the new chord.

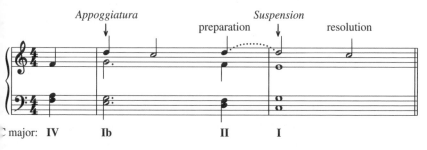

C major: **IV   Ib   II   I**

Non-chord notes may be chromatic (outside the current key). For instance, the C♯ in the example *right* is a chromatic lower auxiliary note.

Finally, the following signs for ornaments are shorthand ways of showing the use of non-chord notes. Each is followed by an example of how it might be played (although the precise interpretation of an ornament tends to depend on its musical context).

| Trill | Turn | Lower mordent | Upper mordent | Appoggiatura | Acciaccatura |

Exercise 3

Name the key of the following passage, label the last five chords (indicated by a bracket beneath the stave) and identify each of the non-chord notes marked *.

Handel, *Jephtha*

Modulation So far we have looked only at music that stays in one key, but in the exam you will also need to recognise **modulation** (change of key) to one or more of the following related keys:

➤ The relative minor or major

➤ The dominant and its relative minor or major

➤ The subdominant and its relative minor or major.

The following diagram shows all of these modulations in relation to the keys of C major and A minor:

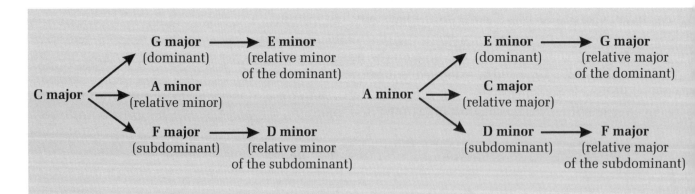

Some notes of the original key have to be changed in order to create a modulation. This usually means that accidentals are needed, although this is not always the case. For example, it is possible to modulate from A minor (a key that requires G♯) to C major (a key that requires G♮) simply by ceasing to sharpen the note G.

When looking for modulations, don't rely on accidentals alone. Accidentals are used for notes in the current key if it is minor, and they are also used for chromatic decoration rather than modulation. If the music changes key, you need to seek confirmation by looking for a cadence (preferably V⁷–I) in the new key.

We can see the different roles played by accidentals in the following short example. C♯ in bar 1 is part of the opening key of D minor, B♮ in bar 2 also occurs in that key, but it is immediately followed by C, not C♯, and then B♭ – an indication that the music is leaving the key of D minor. The progression V⁷d–Ib in F major strongly suggests that the modulation will be to the relative major. Now for the important bit – the key of F major is confirmed by the V⁷–I cadence at the end of the phrase.

Schumann, *Nordisches Lied* (adapted)

D minor: **IVb**   **V**   **Ib**   **Vc**   **I**   F major: **V⁷d**   **Ib**   F major: **II**   **V⁷**   **I**

But what about the F♯ at the end of bar 3? It is simply a chromatic note that adds colour by pointing towards the *chord* of G minor on the next beat. There is no modulation to the *key* of G minor, because there is no cadence in G minor at the end of the phrase.

Exercise 4

Study the passage printed *below* and then answer the following questions.

1. (a)   Name the key at the start of this extract.

   (b)   Name the key in bars 7–8.

2. Label each of the chords marked **1** and **2** in bar 1, and **3**, **4** and **5** in bar 3.

3. Name each of the following non-chord notes:

   A (bar 2, melody)

   B (bar 4, bass)

   C (bar 6, melody).

Beethoven, Piano Sonata Op. 28 (ii)

Chords

In the second question on 'Understanding chords and lines', you will have to complete a short passage of four-part harmony by adding five chords to a given melody. You can use an electric keyboard with headphones while working the test.

The passage will be in a major or minor key of up to three sharps or flats. The given melody may contain non-chord notes and it will end with a cadence.

It will be laid out for soprano, alto, tenor and bass on two staves, known as a 'short score'. The soprano and alto parts are written on the upper stave, with stems pointing in opposite directions, and the tenor and bass parts are written on the lower stave, again with stems pointing in opposite directions. If two parts on the same stave are to sing the same note, write a single notehead and stems in both directions (as on the bass stave of the second chord *below*):

J. F. Lampe, *Kent*

We'll work through this example in stages.

Step 1   Identify the key. The key signature suggests D major or B minor. The latter would need A♯ as its raised seventh degree, but the first note is A(♮), so D major seems more likely, especially since the soprano parts ends on D.

Step 2   Make a chord chart for D major (like the one on page 35) and label the given chords in pencil.

Step 3   Choose two suitable chords for the cadence. It could be any of the four types of cadence that you probably learned for GCSE:

➤ Perfect: V$^{(7)}$ – I

➤ Imperfect: any suitable chord followed by V

➤ Plagal: IV – I

➤ Interrupted: V$^{(7)}$ – VI

Since perfect and imperfect cadences are much more common than the other two types, you should always consider these first. An imperfect cadence wouldn't work here because it ends with chord V (A–C♯–E in the key of D major), but a perfect cadence would. Chord V can harmonise the E in the melody and chord I can harmonise the final D. Lightly sketch in the bass notes of the cadence and label the chords, as shown *opposite*.

Step 4   Add a cadence approach chord (a chord that leads into your cadence). The melody at this point has two quavers. That does *not* mean you need two chords – it is an indication that one of them is a non-chord note. You are unlikely to be expected to use complex melodic decoration in this test, so first consider if the second of

---

The six steps outlined on these pages follow the method recommended in the *AS Music Harmony Workbook* by Hugh Benham (Rhinegold Education, 2008, ISBN 978-1-906178-34-5). This offers a detailed guide to the study of harmony from first principles, with numerous examples and tips, as well as many practice exercises designed to prepare students for AS Music examinations.

this pair could be a passing note. F♯ is approached and quitted by step, so treating it as a passing note seems the obvious choice.

That means that G must be the chord note, so we need to choose a chord that contains G and that sounds good before chord V. We've chosen II, although IV could work equally well. Sketch in its bass note and label the chord.

Step 5

Choose chords for the remaining unharmonised notes. You may prefer to continue working backwards from the end, but whether you do or you don't you will have to make sure that the transition from the last given chord (chord II) to your first added chord sounds convincing.

The chords you choose don't have to be complicated. You are only expected to be able to use I, II, IV and V in root position and first inversion, plus VI in root position only. Of course, you can use other chords if you prefer and you can add occasional non-chord notes in the lower parts – but not too many, and don't add or make any changes to the given melody. If you use a 7th chord, make sure that the seventh is prepared and resolved, like a suspension, since it is regarded as a dissonant note in this style of music.

There will usually be several possibilities for each chord. Although you may have to change some of your initial choices later, the following tips should help your decisions:

➤ Chords whose roots fall in 5ths make strong progressions (for example, VI–II–V–I)

➤ Chords whose roots fall in 3rds or rise in major 2nds also work well (for example, I–VI–IV–V)

➤ Using chord I shortly before a perfect cadence will weaken the impact of the cadence – Ib would be a better choice

➤ Good bass parts move in **contrary motion** to the tune as much as possible – first-inversion chords can be very useful in helping to achieve this

➤ Avoid second-inversion chords completely unless you really understand where they can be used.

Following these principles, we have sketched in the following working for the exercise *opposite*:

D major: Ib   IV   II   V   VI   II   V   I

Step 6

We are now ready to add the inner parts. While leaps in the bass part are to be expected, because it is often moving between the roots of chords a 4th or 5th apart, the inner parts should move as smoothly as possible, either staying on the same note from one chord to the next or moving by step and small leaps.

Because we are using mainly triads but writing in four parts, at least one note in most chords will have to be doubled. That should normally be the root or the 5th. Try to avoid doubling the 3rd in root-position major chords and don't double the leading note in any chord. If you need to omit a note to get a smooth line in your inner parts, it should be the 5th of the chord. Aim for no more than an octave between any of the three upper parts; the gap between the bass and tenor can be wider than an octave if necessary.

Following these principles, we now have the following draft ready for checking:

D major: Ib   IV   II   V   VI   II   V   I

One of the most common faults in completing harmony exercises of this sort is including parallel 5ths, octaves or unisons between parts, as shown *left*. These should be avoided, since they weaken the musical effect of the part writing.

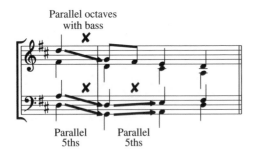

Parallel octaves with bass

Parallel 5ths   Parallel 5ths

If your bass moves mainly in contrary motion to the melody and your inner parts move as smoothly as possible, there is far less risk of these parallel intervals appearing. Nevertheless, check all six pairs of parts (SA, AT, TB, ST, AB and SB). If you do find any there are various possible solutions: try doubling a different note, omitting the 5th, changing from a root position to a first inversion (or vice versa) or choosing a different chord.

Finally, look to see if any improvements could be made. Our working is simple and could benefit from a little decoration – a passing note in the tenor between A and F♯ would work well, since these two harmony notes are a 3rd apart. Avoid cluttering your work with too much decoration, though. Perhaps more of a concern is the fact that our II–V progression in the last bar is rather similar to the II–V progression between chords 3 and 4. There are various ways to tackle this, but we spotted that the last chord II could include a 7th (the note D) since the alto already has a D on the previous beat, providing a preparation for the 7th, and it has a C♯ (the resolution of the 7th) as the penultimate note of the exercise. So this was the solution we adopted for the final working:

Once you are satisfied with your own draft of an exercise, carefully copy it out in ink on the staves provided on the answer paper, making sure that all noteheads are clearly on a line or space, and that all note stems and beams are added. You don't need to include chord labels.

Exercise 5

Complete each of the extracts *below* for SATB voices in short score choosing suitable chords. Remember that in the exam a couple of extra marks may be awarded for the appropriate use of non-chord notes, including correctly prepared and resolved 7ths, but there is no need to include more than two or three such notes.

Studying set works

Information about all of the set works for each year until 2018 is given in the chapters that follow. The questions during the course of these chapters will help you check your understanding of the context, style and technical features of the music – some, but not all, are similar to the type of question set in the exam. If you have difficulty with these, you will generally find the right answers by rereading the preceding pages. On pages 73–75 we have included Section A and B sample questions for the 2014 set works, and at the end of subsequent chapters there are Section B questions for the set works in later years.

Before starting on the set works it will be useful to look at some of the musical concepts that are likely to arise. Although you may be familiar with many of these from your work on GCSE music or from your general musical knowledge, study the following points carefully because some of these concepts – particularly texture and tonality – are often misunderstood.

Terms in **bold** can be looked up in the glossary, but if you find this section a bit daunting right now, come back to it later.

Melody

When discussing melody you may need to state which voice(s) or instrument(s) it is scored for. Amplify this by indicating if the melody is doubled by other parts and, if so, whether it is doubled in octaves, in **unison** or, more rarely, in 3rds or 6ths.

You may wish to discuss the range of the melody (is it wide or narrow?) and perhaps its **tessitura**. You may also want to comment on the nature of the melody – is it **conjunct** or **disjunct**, continuous or fragmentary, **diatonic** or **chromatic**?

The structure of the melody is also usually important. Does it consist of regular phrase lengths (if so, how many bars in each) or irregular phrase lengths? Is it formed from short motifs that are repeated or varied? If the latter, how are they varied? Does the melody have a clear overall profile – rising, falling, or arch-shaped? Is there an obvious point of climax in the melody?

Rhythm

Questions involving rhythm may require identification of some important pattern, such as dotted notes, even-length notes, triplets or **swing quavers**, or perhaps some particular rhythmic device such as **syncopation**, **hemiola** or the use of **anacrusis**.

You might also encounter the term **metre**, which refers to the organisation of strong and weak beats into patterns of bars. Metre is not quite the same as time signature – for example, a piece in duple metre could be written in $\frac{2}{2}$ (or $\mathauthornotkown$) time, or in $\frac{2}{4}$, $\frac{6}{8}$ or $\frac{6}{4}$, all of which have bars of two beats, the first strong and the second weak. Similarly, triple metre can refer to $\frac{3}{4}$, $\frac{3}{8}$ or $\frac{3}{2}$ time and quadruple metre can refer to $\frac{4}{4}$ (or $\mathbf{C}$), $\frac{4}{8}$ or $\frac{4}{2}$ time. Not all music has a regular metre. The rhythm in NAM 32, for example, is dictated by the words rather than by a firm, regular pulse.

Harmony

Questions on harmony refer to the use of chords in a piece. You may need to identify particular chords (your work in the first half of this chaper will be useful here) or discuss the use of chord progressions, such as the **circle of 5ths**, the 12-bar blues or the pattern of chords at important cadences. It may be relevant to discuss whether the harmony is **diatonic** or **chromatic**, the way in which dissonance is treated, and the use of any devices such as a **pedal** that impact on the harmony.

If chords, particularly I and $V^{(7)}$, and cadences are used to define a clear structure of keys in a piece, we say that the harmony is **functional**. We use the term **harmonic rhythm** to describe how quickly the chords change: do they stay the same for several bars at a time, or change on almost every beat? Does the rate of change increase as the music moves towards a cadence?

Structure

Structure refers to the form of a piece – the way in which repetition, variation and contrast are used. Often this will concern the piece as a whole, involving descriptions such as ternary form or verse-and-chorus, or it may involve discussing the structure of just a section or a phrase in the music.

Texture

Texture describes the way in which the simultaneous lines of a piece (melody, bass and harmony) relate to each other. Although texture is sometimes described with vague adjectives such as thick or thin, at AS you are expected to be more precise than this. The main terms used to identify textures are:

➢ **Monophonic** (an unaccompanied melody). If the melody is performed by more than once person, is it played or sung in unison or in octaves?

➢ **Homophonic** (one main melody with accompaniment). If the accompaniment follows the rhythm of the melody the texture is said to be chordal or **homorhythmic**, but if it has some degree of independence the texture should be described as **melody-dominated homophony** or **melody and accompaniment**.

➢ **Polyphonic** or **contrapuntal** (several melodic parts heard at the same time). If the parts copy each other a few beats apart, the texture is described as **imitative counterpoint**, but if totally in-dependent melodies are combined, the texture is described as **free counterpoint**. When describing contrapuntal music, try to identify the number of simultaneous melodic parts involved – for example, 'two-part counterpoint' or 'four-part counterpoint'.

➢ **Antiphonal** (the alternation of different forces, such as a soloist and a brass section or two separate choirs).

➢ **Heterophonic** (different versions of the same melody heard simultaneously, such as a simple version of the melody in crotchets and a decorated version in semiquavers).

Textures often change during a piece and are sometimes combined. For instance, even in a basically homophonic passage, a main melody might be accompanied by a **countermelody** to add contrapuntal interest, or might be underpinned by a **pedal**. Or two parts might exchange ideas in **dialogue** above a chordal accompaniment. However, exam questions are likely to be about clearly identifiable textures rather than anything complex.

Tonality

Tonality refers to the use of major and minor keys in music and the ways in which these keys are related. It is nothing to do with the tone colour of musical sounds. In tonal music, keys are usually established by cadences, particularly perfect-cadence patterns such as V^7–I. When writing about tonality you are likely to need to identify specific keys and modulations, and perhaps to show how sections in related keys help to clarify the structure of the music. You may need to point out features that help to affirm the tonality of the music, such as themes which outline notes of the tonic chord, pedal points and cadences at the end of sections.

Not all music is tonal – some is modal (based on a **mode**) and some (like NAM 59) makes use of non-western scales. Western pieces that use neither keys nor modes, such as NAM 8, are described as **atonal** (without tonality).

Forces

Questions about the forces used in a musical work are likely to require more than just a list of instruments or voices. You may need to discuss *how* they are used. Who has the melody? Is it doubled and if so, how? Is the melody distributed among different instruments or voices? If there is a countermelody, who plays it? What roles do the accompanying instruments play – do some sustain notes while others decorate them? Which instruments supply the bass part and how are they used?

It may be relevant to refer to specific instrumental effects – the use of mutes or pizzicato, and to the **timbre** (the specific tone quality) of certain instruments. Are some instruments used in a particularly idiomatic way, such as brilliant scales for flutes, wide-ranging arpeggios for clarinets or a plaintive sustained melody for oboe?

Transposing instruments

When reading the scores in NAM you need to be aware that some instruments do not sound at the pitch at which they are written. Two common examples are the double bass and the bass guitar, both of which sound an octave lower than their notated parts suggest.

For some wind instruments, such as the trumpet in B♭ and the clarinet in B♭, the relationship between printed note and sounding note is more complicated. 'In B♭' means that B♭ sounds when C is played. It follows from this that every note sounds a tone lower than written – something to bear in mind when studying the scores in NAM.

Since a clarinet in B♭ sounds a tone lower than written, if you compose a part to be played on the clarinet, it has to be notated a tone higher than you want it to sound. Fortunately, good score-writing software can manage this task for you.

Other transposing instruments work in a similar way. For example, the horn in F sounds F when C is played – all of its notes sound a perfect 5th lower than written. The alto saxophone is 'in E♭', so E♭ sounds when C is played – all of its notes sound a major 6th lower than written. The tenor saxophone is 'in B♭' so B♭ sounds when C is played, but in this case it is an octave plus a tone (a major 9th) below the written notes.

For most common transposing instruments:

➤ The description of the instrument tells you the note that sounds when C is played, from which you can work out the interval of transposition

➤ The sounding notes are lower than the written notes.

Some of the scores in NAM include parts written in the C clef which straddles the stave line for middle C (see *right*). Remember to take this into account when working out chords or how precisely different instruments double one another.

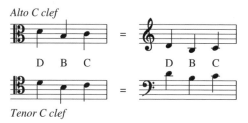

Alto C clef

D   B   C   D   B   C

Tenor C clef

All of these points concern your study of NAM and your general music knowledge – in the exam paper, scores will be printed at the correct sounding pitch, using only treble or bass clefs.

Style

If you are a follower of fashion, you will know that style is about a combination of factors – the things you wear, how you wear them, the places you go, the things you say. Style is not easy to define, but you know it when you see it!

Much the same is true of style in music. There is no single feature that allows us to be sure that a piece is Baroque, Latin American, Soul or Britpop. Style is a combination of factors working together that we get to recognise through experience. To put it another way, the more music you study, the easier it becomes to recognise the style of a piece when you hear it for the first time.

For those reasons, we have left detailed discussion of style until we look at each set work, but there are some general concepts that we can consider now.

Many people describe any sort of art music as 'classical', but musicians usually reserve this term for one of several stylistic periods in the history of music:

1550	1600	1650	1700	1750	1800	1850	1900	1950	2000
Renaissance		Baroque			Classical	Romantic		Modern	

1825

Although dates spaced at 75- and 150-year intervals are easy to remember, they are only approximations. Clearly people didn't decide to burn their harpsichords in January 1750 and go out to buy pianos and sheet music in the new style of the Classical period. New approaches appeared gradually and experimentally at first, with some composers responding quickly to the challenge of new ideas, new instruments and new types of audience while others continued to write in older styles for some years to come.

When writing about dates, be careful not to confuse years with centuries. We live in the 21st century, but the years begin with 20, not 21. Similarly, 1750 is in the 18th century, not the 17th century.

Before the Romantic period, concert audiences expected to hear mainly new music and therefore the latest styles. However, as the 19th century progressed, increasing historical awareness led to the rediscovery of older styles. At the same time, greater ease of travel and international exhibitions resulted in some composers hearing, and being influenced by, the sounds of less-familiar music, from folk traditions and from other cultures around the world.

The speed of change accelerated enormously in the 20th century as recording and broadcasting enabled new styles of music to be distributed much more rapidly. There is no single style that has dominated the years since 1900. Some composers continued to develop the styles of the previous century, while Modernist composers explored new worlds of extreme dissonance and exciting rhythms. Others were influenced by folk music from different parts of the world, or by new ideas from popular music and jazz.

Increasing leisure time in the late 19th century led to a commercial demand for popular music, initially to play and sing at home. The appearance of new styles, influenced by ragtime, jazz and the blues, soon led to popular music acquiring its own distinctive voice. Popular songs were first introduced in variety shows on stage (and later in musicals) but by the 1920s the new media of recording and radio were attracting huge audiences for popular music and bringing early jazz to international attention.

During the swing era of the 1930s, popular music and jazz were often close in style, but they went their separate ways after World War Two. Jazz became influenced by Latin-American music and later by developments in contemporary art music, while popular music was given new impetus when rhythmic blues styles developed into rock and roll.

The succession of distinctive styles in pop and rock over the last 60 years arose from a myriad of influences, often with technology playing an important role. However, style knows no boundaries, and it is remarkable that in the closing years of the 20th century a reaction set in against some of the more brutal experiments of earlier decades. In the concert hall, Postmodernist composers returned to simplicity with Minimalism. In the charts, Britpop groups sought to recreate the mood of 1960s pop. In the theatre, revivals of old musicals (and new musicals based on old chart hits) far outnumber the production of new works.

This stylistic change is not limited to music. For example, architects in recent years have sought to replace the harsh modernism of pre-1975 concrete-slab buildings with designs based on new interpretations of classical features. Perhaps we should add another 75-year division to our chart on the previous page, recognising the move from Modernism to Postmodernism in the years after 1975: what do you think?

There is one final point to mention at this stage. If you are asked to comment on the style of a piece, you must give precise details in your answer. Simply saying that a piece is Baroque 'because it sounds like Baroque music' will not earn a mark. You have to say exactly which features in the music identify it as Baroque.

Section A questions

In Section A of the paper you will have to answer a group of questions on an extract from one of the instrumental works you have studied, plus a further group of questions on an extract from one of the vocal works. The compositions from which the extracts are taken will be named and each extract will be played five times (with pauses between) on CD. You will also have a skeleton score of the extract for reference.

The skeleton score will give an outline of the music, printed on one or two staves, with enough information for you to follow as you listen, but with much detail omitted. The bar numbers in the skeleton score will start from 1, so will not match the bar numbers in NAM unless the extract comes from the start of the work.

Most of the questions will ask you to identify musical features in the extracts and will require only short answers. Some may be multiple-choice questions, others can be answered with a correct technical term, and a few will require you to give two or three phrases of brief description. You may be asked to:

> Name an instrument, type of voice, key, texture or device such as a sequence or a pedal heard in the music

> Explain a term or sign printed in the score

> Describe a feature, such as a melodic line, bass part, cadence or other chord progression

> Show how one section relates to another, perhaps because it is a varied repeat of earlier material

> Identify the structure of the excerpt (but not the form of the complete movement from which it is taken)

> State from where in the complete work the excerpt has been taken (for example, the second section or the last chorus).

Answers need to be precise. For example, if you are asked to name an instrument, you need to state its exact name, not just a general description such as wind, bass or drum.

The number of marks allocated to each quesion provide a good clue to the amount of detail you should give. For example, if two marks are available for naming a feature, you should make two accurate points in your answer – for example, dominant (1) pedal (1), or rising (1) scale (1), or chromatic (1) appoggiatura (1).

Similarly, if three marks are available for describing a passage, you should make at least three distinct points in your answer. For example, if you are asked to describe a bass part, you might say that it is syncopated (1), conjunct (1) and diatonic (1).

Notice that the questions concern the *sound* of the music – you do not have to learn information such as composers' dates or lists of their other works, but you do need to understand technical terms correctly. For example, if a motif is simply repeated by the same voice or an instrument, you will not get a mark for saying that it has been imitated.

The types of question that might be set for Section A, using the set works for 2014 as examples, are shown on pages 73–75.

Section B questions

In Section B you can answer questions on *either* the instrumental works you have studied *or* the vocal works. Whichever you choose, the format will be similar:

➢ The first question will ask you to describe the features in one named work that indicate the style of the music

➢ The second question will ask you to compare two specific elements (resources, form, texture, tonality, harmony, melody and rhythm) in two of the other works you have studied.

There are examples of Section B questions for you to practise at the end of each of the chapters on set works.

The works involved will be different from those used in Section A, and in this part of the exam you will not have access to scores or recordings of the music. You should spend about 45 minutes on this part of the paper, of which about 30 minutes should be allowed for the second question, since it is worth 18 marks, compared to 10 marks for the first question.

Your answers to both questions will need to be much longer than those in Section A, but you are not expected to write a structured essay. You could answer in continuous prose, but a list of points may be preferable if it helps you to check that you have included enough information.

One mark is awarded for each accurate and relevant point that you make, so you need to concentrate on getting plenty of information across as quickly as possible. There is no need for an opening paragraph to set the scene, and you should avoid personal opinion of a general nature, such as stating how much you like the music. You won't get marks for repeating the same point in different words or for digressing into unrelated matters. However, some additional marks are available if you can illustrate a point with a specific example – for instance, you might get one mark for mentioning syncopation and another for saying that it occurs in the bass part of the middle section of the work.

When answering the first question, don't overlook features of the music that could also be found in other styles. For instance, things such as homophonic textures and diatonic melodies are found in many different styles, but if they are important in the piece concerned, you are likely to receive a mark for mentioning them.

When dealing with contrasts in the second question, don't just state what is different but say *how* it is different. For example, 'X is in the key of B♭ major throughout, although there are few cadences to define the key clearly, while the main key of Y is G major, with contrasting episodes in the related keys of E minor and C major, each defined by a perfect cadence at the end of every section'.

Finally, remember that you also have to answer the two questions in Section C, described on pages 33–43. You can tackle these before Section B if you wish, but don't spend more than 45 minutes on either section; otherwise you will not have sufficient time to do yourself justice in all parts of the paper.

Further practice questions for sections A and C of the paper are provided in *Edexcel AS Music Listening Tests* and for section B in *Edexcel AS Music Revision Guide* (Rhinegold Education).

Set works for 2014

Instrumental music

Pavane 'The image of melancholy' and Galliard 'Ecce quam bonum' (Anthony Holborne)

These two movements were first published in London in 1599, during the reign of Queen Elizabeth I, as part of a large collection of similar pieces by this composer. Little is known about Anthony Holborne, who died in 1602, but he was highly regarded as a writer of instrumental music by his contemporaries.

They are written for five soloists and were probably intended for performance in the home, either for the enjoyment of the players or for a small, educated audience. **Chamber music** of this type was known as consort music in Elizabethan England and was usually played on whatever instruments were available (as indicated in the note printed above the score). Music printing was still relatively new (and expensive) in the late Renaissance and so publishers frequently indicated that pieces could be played on a variety of instruments in order to maximise sales. The parts are not typical of any one particular instrument and are fairly limited in range.

On CD2 Holborne's pieces are played by a consort of viols of different sizes. These were bowed and fretted string instruments, held uproght on the lap or between the knees. A consort of five viols was the most popular medium for the performance of chamber music at this time, but wind instruments (such as a consort of recorders) were also used.

The pavane was a moderately slow courtly dance in duple time, performed by couples in a stately, processional style. In contrast, the galliard was much more energetic and in triple time. The two dances were often paired in Renaissance music. However, while the pavane and galliard in NAM 13 were printed next to each other in the original publication, it is unlikely that they were intended as a matching pair – their keys, instrumental ranges, themes and descriptive titles are all different.

Although Holborne used dance forms for both movements, the dense **counterpoint**, which provides independent melodic interest for all five players, indicates that this is music for the ear rather than the feet.

Holborne added descriptive titles to a number of his dances, often of a seemingly private nature that is now sometimes unclear. Many of these, such as 'The image of melancholy', express sorrow and may reflect the grief of his patron, the Countess of Pembroke, who had lost three close family members in a single year. 'Ecce quam bonum' ('Behold how good a thing it is') is the Latin title of one of the Biblical psalms that she had famously adapted into English rhyming verse and presented to Queen Elizabeth in 1599.

Context and forces

NAM 13 (page 191)	CD2 Tracks 1–2
Rose Consort of Viols	

One of the best ways to get to know NAM 13 is to play or sing it with a group of friends. It will suit various different combinations of performers, as the original publication indicates.

'Ecce quam bonum' is also a quotation used by the Italian poet Dante, to whose works Holborne refers in several other of his descriptive titles.

Structure

Like much dance music of the period, both movements consist of three independent sections (at the time known as 'strains') each of which is repeated. We could summarise this as AA BB CC form. The symmetry of the galliard, in which each strain is eight bars long, with cadences every four bars in sections A and B, reflects the dance style of the movement. But the sections in the pavane are 16 + 17 + 26 bars, such irregularity being another indication that this is not music for dancing to.

Tonality

The pavane is in D major, with perfect cadences in the tonic at the end of the first and third strains, and in the dominant (A major) at the end of the middle strain. The tonal system of related major and minor keys was only just beginning to emerge in the late Renaissance, but here it is reinforced by a tonic **pedal** in bars 34–39 and a dominant pedal in bars 54–57. However, traces of older modality are evident in **false relations**, such as the G(♮) followed by G♯ in the outer parts of bar 13.

Today D minor is written with a key signature of one flat, but at this time it was usual to flatten the 6th degree of the minor scale (B♭ in this key) with accidentals where needed, rather than using a key signature.

The galliard is in the key of D minor (see *left*). The first and last strains end with perfect cadences in D minor (both including a **tierce de Picardie**), while the second strain ends with a **phrygian cadence** (IVb–V) in the same key.

Melody and rhythm

The pavane starts with a dotted figure in the top part that descends by step from tonic to dominant. Holborne's contemporaries would easily have recognised this as a gesture frequently associated with grief in Elizabethan music – compare it with the start of the vocal melody in 'Flow my tears' (NAM 33).

The melodic writing is much like that found in vocal music of the period – mainly **conjunct**, with occasional small leaps. Wider leaps are generally followed by balancing stepwise movement in the opposite direction, as in the top part of the pavane, bars 34–37. The lowest part has more leaps than the others, because it is often providing the bass of chords whose roots are a 4th or a 5th apart.

Holborne captures the elegant style of a pavane through the use of simple minim- and crotchet-based rhythms, enlivened with a little discreet **syncopation** (as in the top part of bar 19).

The lively style of a galliard is conveyed in its first section through the use of dotted rhythms and two different types of syncopation. The first is caused by the off-beat entry of the dotted figure in the fourth voice down and occurs every time this rising figure enters (the second crotchet of bars 2, 5 and 6). The second is caused by temporarily switching from triple to duple metre, although without changing the time signature. There are clearly three minim beats ($\frac{3}{2}$ time) in each of the first two bars, but in bars 3 and 7 the metre changes to two dotted-minim beats, as found in $\frac{6}{4}$ time, emphasised by the change of chord halfway through these bars.

The rhythms in the second and third strains of the galliard are less busy, but are enlivened by the use of **hemiola** in bars 10–11 and 14–15, where the triple pulse becomes, without change of time signature, a count of 1–2, 1–2, 1–2, in each pair of bars. Hemiola is yet another type of syncopation and is characteristic of many triple-time dances written in the Renaissance and Baroque periods.

Texture

The pavane is written in five-part imitative counterpoint. A lack of rests means that the imitation is not always obvious. For example, the opening notes of the top part are imitated one minim later by the fourth part down. At the start of the second section this figure is adapted to make a longer motif, imitated by the second part down in bars 18–19. The third section begins with a scalic figure in the middle part that is an **inversion** of the initial 'melancholy' motif and that is imitated by all parts except the bass.

Despite an even greater scarcity of rests, the texture of the galliard is more varied, with imitation in the first and last sections and a largely **homophonic** central section.

Harmony

The majority of chords are root-position or first-inversion triads. Cadences at the end of strains are perfect, except in section B of the galliard, which is imperfect (or, more precisely, phrygian). The only on-the-beat discords are **suspensions**, often decorated as they resolve and sometimes overlapped with suspensions in other parts. In the example *right* you can see how the dissonant 7th between the outer parts at the start of bar 4 is prepared (P), suspended (S), decorated (D) and resolved (R). As it resolves to C♯ the second part down starts a similar process with a note that is to form a 4th above the bass (regarded as a dissonant interval in Holborne's day) in bar 5.

Be aware that not all tied notes are suspensions: for example, those in bars 1 and 2 of the pavane do not form discords. There are only three suspensions in the galliard: can you find them?

The score

Notice that the third part down has an alto C clef, in which the middle line of the stave represents middle C. The first note of the pavane in this part is therefore A. Also be aware that the parts frequently cross each other so, for example, the highest notes in bar 41 of the pavane are played by the middle part.

Upper three parts (bars 9–10)

In common with most music of the period, there are no performance directions, not even tempo or dynamic markings. However the performers on CD 2 introduce variety by adding ornamentation when each of the sections is repeated, some of which is shown *right*. Decoration of this sort was an important performing convention at the time this music was written. Can you identify other places where the music is ornamented in the repeats?

Second part (bars 13–15)

Exercise 1

1. What is a false relation? Identify the location of a false relation in bars 17–33 of the pavane.

2. Name the harmonic device used in bars 54–57 of the pavane.

3. In bar 1 of the galliard, how does the music played by the fourth part down relate to the music played by the top part?

4. How does the top part in bar 22 of the galliard relate to the same part in the previous bar?

5. What are the main similarities and differences between the pavane and the galliard?

6. Which features of NAM 13 suggest that this was not music intended for actual dancing?

7. Which features of NAM 13 indicate that it dates from the late Renaissance?

Symphony No. 26, movement 1 (Haydn)

Context and forces

The type of music that most people associate with the orchestra is the three- or four-movement symphony. It first became popular in the Classical period and central to its development were the 104 (or more) symphonies of Joseph Haydn.

NAM 2 (page 31)   CD1 Track 2
Academy of Ancient Music
Directed by Christopher Hogwood

For much of his life Haydn was director of music to the Hungarian Prince Esterházy at a magnificent palace 50 kilometres south-east of Vienna. Here he had a small orchestra and every facility to perfect his craft. He said to his friend and biographer, Georg Griesinger,

> I could experiment, observe what created an impression and what weakened it, thus improving, adding, cutting away, and running risks. I was cut off from the world … and so I had to become original.

The title of Haydn's *Lamentatione* Symphony comes from an inscription on a manuscript of ancient plainsong melodies which reads *Passio et Lamentatio* (Passion and Lamentation). This is a reference to the passion of Christ, the story of which is told in the plainsong. Here is its opening:

Pas – si – o   Do – mi – ni   nos – tri   Je – su   Chris – ti   se – cun – dum   Mar – – cum

Translation: The passion of our Lord Jesus Christ according to Saint Mark

This chant was well known in Austria at the time when Haydn composed the *Lamentatione* Symphony since it was sung, with congregational participation, on the Tuesday of Holy Week (the week before Easter). It is therefore almost certain that the Esterházy household would instantly have recognised it when they heard it played on oboe and second violins in bars 17–38. The pitches shown *above* exactly correspond with those in bars 17–21. The various words above the score refer to the plainsong passion. The *Evangelist* is the narrator of the story while the passages labelled *Christ* (bar 26) and *Jews* (bar 35) are direct speech in the original plainsong. When the Jews call for Jesus to be crucified, the semiquaver run (bar 37) and the following wild leaps (bars 40–41) suggest the excited cries of the crowd.

Haydn used a wide range of material in his many symphonies; the idea of basing a movement on plainsong, as happens here, is highly unusual.

It is likely that the first performance took place on the Tuesday of Holy Week 1768, in the lavish concert hall of Prince Esterházy's new palace, where regular concerts were given on Tuesdays and Saturdays. These were primarily for the pleasure of the prince and his court, and to demonstrate his wealth and culture to his guests, but rather unusually they were also free for others to attend.

Haydn's orchestra at this time consisted of only about 13 players (although it was soon to grow in size). Usually there were two first violins, two second violins, and one player to each of the other parts. Although not shown in the score, a double bass would have joined the cello on the lowest part, sounding an octave lower than written. The Italian word 'cembalo' in bar 1 indicates that this part would also have been used by a harpsichordist as the basis for improvising chords to bolster the rather thin textures. This had been an almost universal practice in Baroque music, but it was to become unnecessary as orchestras grew larger during the Classical period.

The viola part is written with a C clef, but it is easy to follow since it doubles the cello part in unison or an octave higher for much of the movement. The horn parts are marked 'in D' – they sound a minor 7th lower than printed. These parts would have been played on natural horns, which have no valves and so can play only a limited selection of pitches.

Haydn includes detailed articulation (slurs and staccato markings) and dynamics, unlike Holborne in NAM 13. The direction 'a 2' in the wind parts tells the two players to play the same notes.

The score

As you listen to the music see if you can follow its structure:

Structure and tonality

> An opening idea (called the first subject) in D minor followed by a contrasting second subject in F major (the plainsong theme starting in bar 17). These 44 bars are then repeated

> A middle section (bars 45–79) in a variety of keys

> A return of the opening section at bar 80. The first subject is extended by four bars and is again in D minor, but the second subject (bar 100) is now in the **tonic major** (D major).

This is known as **sonata form** and it was one of the main musical structures of the Classical period. The first section is called the exposition and introduces the idea of two contrasting keys. Most (but not all) sonata-form movements also use, as Haydn does here, contrasting melodies for the first and second subjects.

Can you hear how the music of the middle section sounds different and yet seems to fit into the whole? This is because it develops ideas from the exposition and is thus called the development. For instance bars 45–52 are based on a variant of the syncopated idea from the first subject, transposed to F major and treated in sequence. The more extended sequences of bars 57–64 are based on a **circle of 5ths** (B♭–E–A–D–G–C♯–F♮–B♮ in the bass part on the first beat of each bar) that carry the music to the key of A minor. Above a dominant **pedal** in this key (bars 65–68) the oboes play a variant of Christ's plainsong (first heard at bar 26). Of which bars in the exposition are bars 74–79 a development?

The final section recaps (with changes) the exposition and is therefore called the recapitulation. Compare bars 92–99 with bars 13–16 to see how Haydn modifies and extends the end of the first subject to allow the second subject to return in the tonic major (D major). The movement ends with a **coda** (bars 126–133) which is an expansion of bars 43–44 from the end of the exposition.

We can summarise this structure in the following diagram:

Bar numbers: 1	17	45	80	100	126
Exposition :‖		Development	Recapitulation		
1st subject 2nd subject			1st subject	2nd subject	Coda
Main keys: D minor F major		Various	D minor	D major	

Understanding how structure and tonality are closely linked in Classical music can help you to identify the location of an excerpt used in the exam. For instance, if you spot the start of Haydn's second subject in an excerpt, the key will tell you if it is from the exposition (F major) or the recapitulation (D major).

Other points Haydn uses mainly root-position and first-inversion chords and, as in almost all music from the Classical period, chords I and V$^{(7}$ play an important role in defining the main keys of the movement. However, listen for the dramatic use of **diminished-7th chords**, for example in bar 13 and (marked f) in bar 69.

While most of the chords are fairly simple, Haydn creates tension with the **syncopation** and **suspensions** that dominate the first subject. **Appoggiaturas** also play an important role in the melodic writing. Some are long and diatonic, such as the E in the melody of bar 16 against D in the bass, while others are short and chromatic, such as the F♯ in bars 40 and 42.

While the score may look complex, your ears should tell you that the textures are often thin (there are effectively only two parts in the first eight bars, for instance). This is because:

➢ The violas mostly double the bass part

➢ The two violin parts are sometimes in unison

➢ The two oboes and bassoon mainly double the string parts

➢ The horns are used sparingly until bar 99 because of the limited pitches available on natural horns – when the music moves into D major at bar 100 a greater number of notes can be used.

Haydn uses one of his favourite techniques at the start of the second subject (bar 26) – the theme in the oboes and second violins is simultaneously decorated by the first violins, creating a **heterophonic** texture between the two parts. In general, though, the texture is mainly one of **melody-dominated homophony**.

The dramatic style of this music, and of other Haydn symphonies of the same period, later became known as *Sturm und Drang* (Storm and Stress), a term borrowed from German literature of the time. It is characterised by many of the features present in this movement – minor keys, syncopation, sudden contrasts, wide leaps and bold diminished-7th chords.

Exercise 2

1. What is the pitch of the first note sounded by the horns? (Remember that they are transposing instruments.)

2. Describe the rhythm of the bass part in the first seven bars.

3. Name the cadence heard in bar 12.

4. Identify the chord in bar 71.

5. Name the key and the type of cadence in bars 73^3–74^1.

6. Compare bars 100–104 with bars 17–21.

7. Why was Haydn able to make a significant contribution to the development of the symphony?

Piano Quintet in F minor, movement 3 (Brahms)

A piano quintet is a work for five solo instruments – often, as here, two violins, viola, cello and piano. It is therefore a type of chamber music, like NAM 13, but there the similarity ends. This is just one of four movements in a substantial work with a total length of around 45 minutes, not a short pair of dances.

Brahms clearly intended this work for highly skilled performers. The movement in NAM is fast and technically demanding, and all of the instrumentalists are required to use a wide range, which is particularly evident in bars 146–157. Compare the string writing throughout with that in NAM 13.

Brahms was a Romantic composer with a great respect for earlier music. He studied Baroque counterpoint, helped to edit the music of Handel, and wrote variations on themes by Handel and Haydn. He was also strongly influenced by Beethoven's music, especially its intensive use of short motifs and its use of tonality to define the structure of large movements. These influences led some of his contemporaries unfairly to dismiss Brahms' music as conservative, but in other respects, such as lyrical melody and rich harmonies, he was as Romantic as most late 19th-century composers.

Brahms often revised his music many times before he was satisfied; this work was first composed as a string quintet in 1862 then rewritten for piano duet in 1864. NAM 18 is from the third version, composed in 1865 for piano quintet. It was first performed, probably privately, the following year, but its scale and difficulty suggest that Brahms intended the work for professional performance in small concert halls, for audiences who enjoy chamber music.

NAM 18 consists of a scherzo followed by a trio, after which the scherzo is repeated. This gives the overall movement a **ternary** (ABA) structure. A scherzo (meaning a joke) was a fast triple-time movement in the Classical period, but Brahms uses both $\frac{6}{8}$ and $\frac{2}{4}$ metres, and his style is much more serious than that found in the light and witty of scherzos of earlier times.

First listen for the three themes of the scherzo:

The first is a rising melody in C minor and compound time. It is characterised by frequent syncopations and is *pianissimo*. Brahms' interest in counterpoint is evident at bar 9 where the theme played in octaves by violin and viola is imitated by the piano.

The second is a jerky melody (staccato notes separated by tiny rests) also in C minor but in simple time. It revolves obsessively around the dominant and is also played *pianissimo*.

The third is a very loud march-like theme in C major with strong second-beat accents (marked *forzando*). It is immediately repeated at bar 30, where Brahms adds variety by using the piano to imitate the strings two beats later (starting at the $\textit{ff}$ in bar 31).

There are then varied repeats of A (bars 38–56) and B (bars 57–67), modulating rapidly in the process. This leads to the distant key of E♭ minor and the central section of the scherzo, in which counterpoint becomes the most important element.

Context and forces

NAM 18 (page 231)   CD2 Track 7
Guarneri Quartet with
Peter Serkin (piano)

Structure

The trio is a section which contrasts with the outer parts of the movement. Its name derives from the fact that such sections were once written for just a trio of instruments.

A (bars 1–12)

B (bars 13–21)

C (bars 22–37)

Notice how the motif in bars 22–24 is an **augmentation** of the semiquaver figure in bar 14, now in the major.

Fugato (bars 67–100)

Brahms uses a **fugal** texture in which the viola treats the first four bars of theme B as a fugue subject (bar 67). This is answered by the piano (right hand, bar 71). There are further entries of the subject starting in bars 76 (violin) and 84 (viola). These are combined with no fewer than three countersubjects, introduced as follows:

1. Piano left hand, bar 67 (next heard in viola, bar 71)
2. Piano left hand, bar 71 (next heard in viola, bar 76)
3. Viola, bar 80 (next heard modified by violin 2, bar 84).

In bars 88–100 all of these melodies are fragmented into tiny cells in a complex five-part contrapuntal texture. The example *below* shows how, in the first-violin part, ten notes of the subject are detached (*a*), then just five notes (*b*), then three notes (*c*). Notice how the pitches rise sequentially until the climax at bar 100.

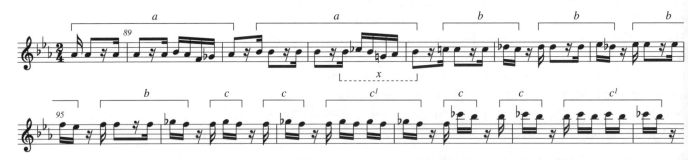

Can you spot similar processes at work in the cello and piano parts in the same passage? These fragments (and those of the viola from bar 92) are heard in a type of close imitation known as **stretto**.

The fragment marked *x above* is a motif that will recur in various transformations, imparting a sense of unity to the structure.

After this central section Brahms repeats the themes of the first part in the following order:

B (bars 100–109): E♭ minor
C (bars 109–124): E♭ major (the relative major of C minor)
A (bars 125–157): E♭ minor modulating to C minor
B (bars 158–193): C minor (greatly extended to form a coda and with a **tierce de Picardie** in the C major chord at the end).

Shown *left* are just two of Brahms' transformations of motif *x*. The first is an **augmentation** of *x* (every note is four times longer than before). The second is in E♭ major instead of E♭ minor and its fifth beat has been decorated (at *y*).

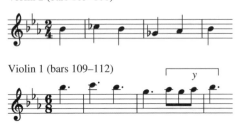

The entire work is unified by devices of this sort. The falling semitone that constantly appears in the final bars of the example printed on the previous page is heard prominently throughout the scherzo. Even the contrasting trio is linked with the scherzo by several common motifs, the most obvious being motif *y* (*left*) which becomes an integral part of its main melody (bars 197 and 199).

Trio (bars 193²–261)

The trio is in ternary form:

A Bars 193–225: This section begins with a broad 16-bar melody in C major that modulates to B major in the last five bars. It is introduced by piano and then repeated by strings, and strongly contrasts with the episodic nature and contrapuntal textures of the scherzo.

B   Bars 225–241: Legato melody with staccato bass; these parts are then reversed in bars 233– 241 – melody in the bass with staccato accompaniment above. The harmony is chromatic but anchored to C major by a dominant pedal (on G) whose triplets form **cross-rhythms** against the quavers in the other parts.

A   Bars 242–261: The first 11 bars of the melody from the first section return, in a dark texture in which all instruments are in a low **tessitura**. This leads to a plagal cadence in C (bars 253–254) and a tonic pedal (bars 254–261).

The performers are then instructed to repeat the scherzo – *Scherzo da Capo sin al Fine*, meaning repeat the scherzo as far as the word *Fine* (the end).

Other points

Apart from the bold, rising theme at the start, Brahms' melodic material is based mainly on motifs of a narrow range which are manipulated in many different ways, as we have seen. His textures are equally varied, ranging from the **monophonic** opening to the **fugal** texture starting in bar 67. Question 4 in the exercise *below* invites you to identify some other textures for yourself.

One of the hallmarks of the Romantic style is the use of chromatic harmony. Even in the first phrase Brahms gradually builds up the notes of an **augmented-6th** chord (A♭–C–E♭–F♯) that resolves to chord V in the second half of bar 6 over a continuing tonic pedal in the cello part. Pedal points also play an important role in the trio, which begins and ends over a tonic pedal on C (bars 194–201 and 249²–261). The chromatic writing of its entire central section (bars 226–241) is underpinned by a dominant pedal on G, which starts in the piano and then transfers to the cello in bar 233.

But occasionally, Brahms' interest in early music seems to surface. For example, the root-position triads in bars 18–21 are given a modal colour by the minor version of chord V (bar 19²), and the cadence in bar 21 contains chord V without a 3rd, a feature often found in Renaissance music.

Brahms' preference for the dark sound of E♭ minor as a secondary key, rather than the simple relative major of C minor (E♭ major) introduces a more complex type of tonal relationship than we saw in the Lamentatione symphony, although Brahms slips from the tonic minor to tonic major (C major in bars 22–29), just as Haydn did at bar 100 in NAM 2.

Brahms establishes each key in the movement with clear cadences, and the pedal points also help to reinforce the tonal structure. However, notice that most sections end with an imperfect cadence to project the music forward, rather than with a decisive perfect cadence to punctuate the onward flow.

Exercise 3

1.   What in the music suggests that this movement was written to be played by professional performers in the concert hall rather than by amateurs at home?

2.   Describe some of the ways in which the main themes of the scherzo (up to bar 193) are contrasted.

3. In bars 18^2–20^1 the first violinist is required to use **double-stopping**. What does this mean?

4. Look at the texture in bars 15–17, 57–59 and 88–90. Use an appropriate word or phrase to describe each of these textures.

5. Name the harmonic device used in the bass part of bars 53–56.

6. How is the trio contrasted with the scherzo?

Pour le piano: Sarabande (Debussy)

Context

The 19th-century interest in older music, that we noted in passing when studying NAM 18, is much more explicit in this work. The sarabande is a Renaissance dance that remained popular as an instrumental movement throughout the Baroque period, long after people had ceased dancing to it (see NAM 21).

NAM 24 (page 260)   CD2 Track 16
Zoltán Kocsis (piano)

The performance direction at the head of the score ('with slow and solemn elegance') captures the stately, triple-time mood of the Baroque sarabande, with its characteristic accent on the second beat of the bar (bar 2, 4, 8 and so on). Also similar to Baroque dance movements (including those in NAM 21) is the binary structure in which a short A section (bars 1–22) is followed by a longer B section (bars 23–72).

This movement was originally composed in 1894, shortly after Debussy's compatriot Erik Satie had published three sarabandes that similarly applied sensuous harmonies to an ancient dance style. Debussy himself had used historic dance forms such as the minuet and passepied in his *Suite bergamasque* of 1890.

Like Brahms, Debussy frequently revised his works, and the music printed as NAM 24 comes from a later version of the Sarabande, published in 1901 as the second of three movements in a suite entitled *Pour le piano* (For the piano). The outer movements of the suite also draw on 18th-century forms (a prelude and a toccata), and the composer used the preface of this edition to make his purpose clear: the pieces are 'not for brilliantly lit salons … but rather conversations between the piano and oneself'.

Tonality

When we listen to the sarabande it is obvious that Debussy is not seeking to copy the style of 18th-century music, but merely using some of its features as a springboard for his own ideas.

Debussy's handling of key is nothing like the mainly clear-cut tonality that we have seen in the three previous works from NAM. The key is C♯ minor, but there is no sign of conventional cadences with sharpened leading notes (B♯) to define this key. Much of the music is in fact modal. Debussy uses the aeolian **mode** (which you can find by playing an octave of white notes on the piano starting from A as the home note) transposed to start on C♯. The difference between this mode and C♯ harmonic minor is shown *left*.

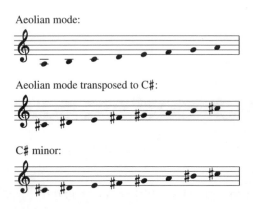

Aeolian mode:

Aeolian mode transposed to C♯:

C♯ minor:

The first eight bars are entirely modal, with cadences on the fifth note of the mode (G♯) in bars 2 and 4 and the seventh note (B) in bar 8. The melody throughout the first 22 bars is modal, although the harmony becomes richer and more chromatic after bar 8.

Debussy's use of modality harks back to music of a much earlier era, and this ancient quality is underlined by the chant-like parallel 4ths and 5ths of the opening bar (a technique of early medieval church music). However these notes are just part of the series of lush parallel-7th chords which enrich Debussy's harmony and form a much more modern feature of the work.

Harmony

There are many other colourful chords that help to give the work its rich sonority. In bars 11–13[1], for instance, the accompanying harmonies are a series of parallel dominant 7ths that never resolve. In fact they are built on a series of notes each a whole tone apart (D–E–F#–G#–A#); such **whole-tone scales** were used by Debussy in a number of later works. In bars 23–28 he builds his gently dissonant harmony on chords constructed from superimposed 4ths (known as **quartal harmony**). This technique returns in the last six bars where the bass moves up through a C# minor triad to the final modal cadence (B natural rising to C# in the outer parts).

Debussy reflects the characteristic second-beat emphasis of the sarabande style by stopping the flow on a minim in a number of bars (2, 4, 8 etc.), or by using a dotted crotchet, tied note or tenuto mark (as in bar 21) on the second beat of the bar. He also reflects the dance style by often writing in two- and four-bar units. The opening, for example, falls into two two-bar phrases, followed by a four-bar phrase. The next phrase is six bars long, but an eight-bar unit returns with the varied repeat of the opening material in bars 15–22.

Rhythm

However, just as Debussy's harmonies cloud the tonality, so his phrasing starts to obscure the dance rhythm as the piece progresses. This is most obvious in bars 38–41, where the phrasing across the barlines cuts across the triple-time pulse. In bars 67–68 Debussy introduces a **hemiola**, in which two bars of triple time sound like three bars of duple time – look at the position of the tenuto marks and the two-beat left-hand figure, and listen to the effect on the recording. Hemiola is another acknowledgement of the past – it was often used in Baroque and late Renaissance music (see page 63) – but never with such dissonant chords as these.

The music is homophonic, with a passage of bare octaves in bars 20–22 but with mainly thick chords elsewhere (notice the massive ten-part chord in bar 53). The successions of parallel chords, such as those in bars 35–41, form a distinctive element in the texture. Debussy uses a wide range of the instrument (notice the sonorous low melody in bars 20–22 and the final bass notes), and there are passages with both hands in the bass clef (bars 23–26) and both in the treble clef (bars 38–40).

Texture

Like almost all late 19th-century composers, Debussy includes detailed performing directions throughout the work. These include instructions for tempo fluctuations of a sort that would never occur in actual dance music – *retenu* (holding back), *Au mouvement* (return to the original tempo) and *Animez un peu* (a little more animated). The letters *m.d.* in bar 72 stand for *main droite* (right hand), indicating that the tied chord must be held with the sustaining pedal so that both hands are free for these bass notes.

The score

Exercise 4

1. What are the main features of a sarabande?

2. Which aspects of Debussy's sarabande are new and forward-looking and which are drawn from older types of music?

3. Compare bars 42–49 with bars 1–8.

4. Where is the melody that starts in bar 56 first heard?

5. List three ways in which Debussy deliberately obscures the C♯ minor tonality of this piece.

Vocal music

Sing We at Pleasure (Weelkes)

Context and forces

NAM 34 (page 349) CD3 Track 12
Purcell Consort of Voices
Directed by Grayston Burgess

An English madrigal is a musical setting of a poem for several solo voices, usually unaccompanied but sometimes supported by a plucked string instrument such as a lute. This type of work originated in 16th-century Italy (see page 87) but soon spread to other countries, notably England where Italian culture was fashionable in the late 16th century. For example, *Romeo and Juliet*, published in 1597 (the year before NAM 34), is just one of a number of Shakespeare's plays set in Italy.

Madrigal singing in the home became an important social accomplishment for educated Elizabethans, as the following quotation, which also dates from 1597, indicates:

> But supper being ended, and Musicke bookes, according to the custome being brought to the table: the mistresse of the house presented mee with a part, earnestly requesting mee to sing. But when after manie excuses, I protested unfainedly that I could not: everie one began to wonder. Yea, some whispered to others, demaunding how I was brought up …

This quotation comes from *A Plaine and Easie Introduction to Practicall Musicke* by the Elizabethan composer Thomas Morley, in which he explains how a gentleman risks appearing socially inadequate if lacking skill in sight-singing from music notation.

The popularity of such amateur music-making was helped by the invention of music printing earlier in the century. Collections of madrigals were usually published as a set of part books, each containing the music for just one voice part. Others were were printed with the parts at right-angles to each other so that the book could be put on a table with all the singers sitting or standing around (see *left*).

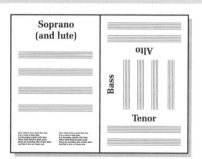

The first collections were mainly translations of Italian madrigals, such as the appropriately named *Musica transalpina* ('Music from across the Alps') published in London in 1588 and *Italian Madrigalls Englished* (1590). However English composers soon started to produce great quantities of their own music for the domestic vocal-music market, resulting in a brief but glorious age of English madrigals in the late 16th and early 17th centuries.

Thomas Weelkes was one of the greatest of the English madrigalists. His settings range from intensely serious works full of poignant dissonances to the carefree jollity of *Sing We at Pleasure*, first published in 1598.

This type of madrigal is known as a ballett and is characterised by a light, dance-like style and fa-la-la refrains. It developed from the *balletto*, an Italian instrumental or vocal dance of the 16th century.

Structure

Sing We at Pleasure has a **binary** structure, consisting of two repeated sections, each ending in a fa-la-la refrain:

➢ Section A (bars 1–22), which is repeated unchanged

➢ Section B (bars 22–53), which is then repeated in varied form in bars 53–85.

The second section is longer because it contains four lines of text before the refrain, rather than two. Its repeat is written out in full because the two sopranos exchange parts for the second time through this section.

Rhythm

The dance style is brought out by word setting that is almost entirely **syllabic** (one note per syllable) and lively triple-time rhythms. Most of these are dotted ( ) and are immediately repeated in another voice part.

The rhythm is given added spice with **syncopation** (e.g. alto bars 7 and 12) and **hemiola** (e.g. bars 20–21). The latter gives the effect of the music moving into duple metre, as shown *right*, where bars 20–21 have been barred in $\frac{2}{4}$ time to illustrate the effect.

Harmony and tonality

The style is **consonant** and all of the chords are root-position or first-inversion triads, most of them major. The only on-beat discords are:

➢ **Suspensions**, some written in crotchets (alto, bar 52, shown *right*) and some in quavers (alto, bar 7³). Both are associated with syncopation and give impetus to the dancing rhythms that prevail throughout the ballett

➢ Unprepared **tritones** between the outer parts (at the end of bars 10, 13 and 16) – these are one of the fingerprints of Weelkes' style.

Despite the lack of key signatures these chords, both consonant and dissonant, clearly define the key of G major and suggest passing modulations to D major (bars 9–11²) and C major (bars 15³–17). However, the idea of using related key centres was still relatively new at this time, and the lingering influence of the modal system is apparent when Weelkes uses a triad of F major on the last beat of bar 14.

Textures

The ballett divides into a number of sections that correspond with phrases of the text. Each verbal phrase has its own characteristic melodic shape which is either treated in **imitation** or used as the top part in a brief **homophonic** passage (bars 22–25, 30–35 and 61–65).

Sometimes these sections overlap, as when 'Sing we at pleasure' overlaps with 'content is our treasure' on the third beat of bar 3. Every section ends with a perfect cadence in G major, except for 'All shepherds in a ring', which ends with an imperfect cadence in the same key. Some of these cadences mark a break in the flow of the music and a change of texture (as in bar 22, where the counter-point of the refrain ends and the first homophonic passage begins).

Weelkes' textures are very fluid. The opening is treated imitatively in the soprano parts while the other parts provide homophonic support. After less than four bars a second **imitative point** begins ('content is our treasure'). It is announced by soprano 2 and tenor in 10ths, and imitated by soprano 1 and bass also in 10ths. When the fa-la-la refrain starts in bar 8 the imitation is shared between three parts: bass and both sopranos, while alto and tenor have **contrapuntal** but non-imitative lines.

Weelkes unites the voices in homophony for the start of 'Sweet love shall keep the ground', but this is immediately followed by very close imitation for 'Whilst we his praises sound' where the entries tumble in only one beat apart.

The voices again come together in homophony and simple root-position triads at 'All shepherds in a ring'. The word underlay of 'Dancing' places the second syllable on an unstressed quaver, giving a syncopated effect, and this tripping dotted rhythm accompanies the word whenever it appears. Notice how the sopranos ascend a seven-note scale to top G as they 'ever sing' in imitation with one another.

> Try performing NAM 34 with your fellow students. It will not matter if you have to replace some of the parts with instruments – the Elizabethans would sometimes do this, too. The pitch of the recording matches the score, but most scholars believe that pitch at this time was about a tone lower than it is today, so it may be appropriate (and it may be more comfortable for singing) to transpose the piece down. Remember that the most important element of the ballett is its lively, dancing rhythm.

Bars 43–53 introduce another new texture. The most remarkable feature of this refrain is the canon between the two top parts. The second soprano sings the same notes as the first soprano but one bar later until the end of bar 51. The almost continuous quavers shared between the tenor and bass propel the joyful counterpoint forward, but the alto has to be satisfied with an inner tonic **pedal** lasting 7 bars.

Exercise 5

1. In which country did the madrigal originate?

2. What are the main features of a ballett?

3. How and where might *Sing We at Pleasure* have been performed in Elizabethan times? Mention the number of singers you might expect to be involved.

4. What term describes the rhythm of the tenor part in bar 9?

5. Briefly explain the difference between a homophonic texture and a contrapuntal texture, and give an example of each from this work.

6. Which of the following is true about the soprano 2 part in bars 69–72?
   (a) It imitates the soprano 2 part of bars 36–39.
   (b) It imitates the soprano 1 part of bars 38–41.
   (c) It imitates the soprano 1 part of bars 67–70.

7. Where does a canon occur on page 352 of NAM?

8. With what sort of cadence does the madrigal end?

9. *Sing We at Pleasure* was published in 1598, one year before Holborne's Pavane and Galliard (NAM 13). What similarities in style can you find between these two works?

Der Doppelgänger (Schubert)

By the early 19th century, most well-to-do households had a piano which formed the focus of domestic music-making. Singing with piano accompaniment was a popular pastime for family and guests, and composers wrote vast numbers of songs to supply this market. Some examples, such as NAM 37, are light and inconsequential, but Schubert was prepared to explore much deeper emotions in many of the 630 *Lieder* he wrote in the course of just 18 years.

Schubert wrote *Der Doppelgänger* (The Ghostly Double) in 1828, when he was 31 and knew that he had only a short time to live. It is a setting of poem by Heine, one of the most important German poets of the time, that had been published the previous year.

In the poem, the narrator walks at dead of night to a house where the woman he loved once lived. There he sees a man in agony, overwhelmed with grief. In the moonlight he realises with horror that this man is himself, gone mad with torment.

Although the poem has three verses (starting at bars 5, 25 and 43), Schubert doesn't repeat the same music for each of them. His setting is **through-composed** – the music develops throughout the song. However, it is based on a four-bar **ostinato** figure which is heard in its original form five times during the course of the work.

Der Doppelgänger makes its initial impact from its very slow (*Sehr langsam*) tempo and minor key. The stillness of the night is represented by the extremely low dynamic level, the very static rhythm of the accompaniment and by the F♯ which forms an inner **pedal** on the dominant of B minor throughout the first 40 bars. Schubert creates a sense of obsession by beginning and ending every one of the singer's two-bar phrases on this pitch in the first verse.

The opening bars suggest B minor, but the triads are incomplete and the bare 5ths in bars 1, 4, 5 and 8 suggest the empty loneliness of the poet, as does the halting and fragmented vocal line. As the poet fills in details of the scene, so the tolling piano chords fill out until the singer gradually starts to break free of the fateful F♯ in the second verse. But the piano retains the F♯ and the rising melodic line returns to F♯ in the first climax of the song, marked to be played as loud as possible in bar 31 and underpinned by the chromatic dissonance in the next bar.

The ostinato resumes in bar 34, but this time the tenor claws his way up from F♯ to reach G, the highest note of both the vocal and piano parts. It is at this second climax (bar 41) that the pianist at last relinquishes the dominant note and it is here that the poet realises that the man he saw is a horrifying reflection of himself. He knows that he is doomed, for the person who meets their other self is, according to legend, about to die.

Now begins one of the most remarkable harmonic progressions that Schubert devised. While the voice revolves hopelessly around F♯, the piano rises chromatically from B to D♯, retaining an F♯ in every one of these bleak chords. The chromaticism leads to a modulation to D♯ minor, and this unusual and remote key is affirmed by

Context

NAM 38 (page 361)	CD3 Track 16
Peter Schreier (tenor)	
András Schiff (piano)	

The German word *Lied* means a song. The term *Lieder* (songs), pronounced 'leeder', is often used in English to refer to German songs of the Romantic period. Many, like this *Lied*, are settings of words of literary quality. A translation of Heine's poem appears on page 539 of NAM.

Structure

Commentary

alternate tonic and dominant hammer blows in bars 47–50. This is the only passage not in the key of B minor – it is as if the poet has already gone and his mocking ghost has triumphed.

Another chromatic dissonance (bar 51) at a stroke returns the music to B minor and the last climax of the song, in which the poet recalls the torment of love in days gone by. From this point the singer sinks exhausted back to the tonic. Finally the ostinato returns, but this time its fourth chord is changed to C major. In the context it seems enigmatic and questioning – the major chord certainly sheds no ray of hope. The piano postlude ends with a plagal cadence and **tierce de Picardie** – and no ray of hope is shed by that either.

> A postlude is a closing section. The term usually refers to a passage for piano alone at the end of a song.

Exercise 6

1. How does the introduction set the mood for the song that is to follow?

2. What is an ostinato? What effect is created by the use of an ostinato in parts of this song?

3. There is a **false relation** in bar 13. What does this term mean and which two pitches in this bar form the false relation?

4. How does Schubert illustrate the terror of the poet in bar 35?

5. The climax of the poem occurs when the poet realises that the face he sees is his own (*eig'ne Gestalt* 'own being' or 'self'). How does Schubert reflect this in his music?

6. Describe the texture of this song.

7. Listen carefully to the recording. What do you notice about the tempo?

Symphony of Psalms, movement 3 (Stravinsky)

Context

> NAM 31 (page 307)   CD3 Track 9
> Choir of Westminster Cathedral
> City of London Sinfonia
> Conducted by James O'Donnell

Stravinsky's *Symphony of Psalms* is a three-movement work that was commissioned to celebrate the 50th annual season of the Boston Symphony Orchestra in the USA. It was actually first performed in Brussels, but the American premiere in the Boston Symphony Hall followed six days later, on 19 December 1930.

The words are taken from the Latin version of the psalms, although the work is intended for the concert hall. Stravinsky's omission of some of the text and repetition of other parts out of order, along with the very large orchestra, makes it unsuitable to use in a church service. The composer himself explained the role of the text:

> It is not a symphony in which I have included Psalms to be sung. On the contrary, it is the singing of the Psalms that I am symphonizing.

Surprisingly for an orchestral commission, there are no parts for violins, violas or clarinets. However, there are still 14 woodwind, four horns in F (sounding a perfect 5th lower than printed), a trumpet in D (sounding a tone higher than printed), four more trumpets, three trombones, tuba, timpani, bass drum, harp, two pianos, cellos, double basses (the latter sounding an octave lower than printed) and an all-male four-part choir (although it is often sung by mixed voices). The hard-edged timbres and variety of clear textures that Stravinsky achieves with these forces are as vital to his concept of the piece as the notes themselves.

Despite these formidable resources the *Symphony of Psalms* is an understated work. Stravinsky shuns the obvious opportunities for **word-painting**. For instance at 'Praise him in the sound of the trumpet' (bars 87–94) the trumpets are very much in the background. When the text mentions 'timpano' in bar 152 Stravinsky studiously avoids using drums, and the 'cymbalis' (cymbals) sung about in bar 165 are not even included in his orchestra. Similarly when Stravinsky interpolates the word 'Alleluia' he sets it softly for unaccompanied voices: the effect is one of rapt adoration rather than the great outburst of joy with which composers usually treat this word.

Stravinsky himself identified two ideas that are central to this movement. The first is the two linked 3rds heard on trumpet and harp in bars 29^4–30^3 (G–B♭ and A♭–C). This motif recurs at different pitches and on different instruments, for example piano 2 in bars 109–112. It also unifies the movement in less obvious ways. For instance in bar 38 the notes of the motif are presented in a different order in the trombone and piano parts – the first and last notes make the 3rd C–A♭, while the middle two make the third B♭–D.

By a similar reordering Stravinsky constructs the whole melody of bars 4–11, the outer notes of 'laudate' being D–B♭, the next phrase using C–E♭. The opening melody, suggesting the key of E♭ major, is accompanied by a bass part outlining a triad of C major, giving an impression of **bitonality**, a device frequently used by Stravinsky. These dissonances wonderfully resolve to a pure major 3rd on C (the tonic of the entire movement) in bar 7 – significantly on the capitalised Latin name for God.

The second of Stravinsky's ideas that dominate the whole movement is the six-note rhythm first heard in bar 24. This is used to generate excitement as it steps up in the horns from a C major triad (bars 32–36) to a D major triad (bar 37) then an E major triad (bars 40–43). Stravinsky wrote of bars 40–47, which culminate in the massive D major chords (with bass G♯) of bars 48–49. that he

> was inspired by a vision of Elijah's chariot climbing the heavens …
> never before had I written anything quite so literal as the triplets …
> to suggest the horses and chariots.

In bar 65 the six-note rhythm is shifted forward a quaver to form the setting of the key words of the movement ('Laudate Dominum', 'Praise the Lord). Stravinsky then combines this idea with other motifs from the opening section, reaching a climax in bars 87–98.

In the recapitulation (which begins at bar 99) the six-note rhythm is sung to a series of chords that rise from C major (bars 114–121) through E major (bars 126–128) to B♭ major (bars 132–133). The triplets return in bars 126–132, now overlapping with the rhythmic 'Laudate Dominum' motif. This time, propelled by the higher-rising chords, they culminate in massive E major chords (with bass A♯) in the main climax of the movement at bars 144–146.

Another important element in the movement, and one that helps account for its hypnotic effect, is the measured tread of slowly evolving **ostinato** patterns. The first of these is the three-note figure heard in the bass of bars 14–19, but much more memorable is the four-note ostinato in the **coda**. Starting at bar 163 this pattern o 4ths, played by timpani, harp and pianos, is heard more than 3 times, underpinning the exquisitely balanced dissonances of thi final section. The 'alleluia' returns one more time at bar 205, to b followed by the complete resolution of all tonal tension in the plai C major triad with which the *Symphony of Psalms* ends.

Exercise 7

1. What is an ostinato?

2. The time signature of the coda (bar 163) indicates three minim beats in a bar. What effect does thi metre have on the four-beat length of the ostinato figure?

3. In bar 65 do the altos and tenors sing in harmony, in octaves or in unison?

4. (i) From what is the soprano motif in bar 150 constructed?
   (ii) How does the bass entry in the next bar relate to this?
   (iii) What do you notice about the part played by the double bassoon and bass trombone throughou bars 150–156?

5. What is unusual about the instrumentation of this work?

6. What do you notice about the voicing (that is, the spacing and layout) of the final chord of the work (The cor anglais sounds a perfect 5th lower than written.)

7. Check that you know the meaning of all of the terms used in the score – use a good music dictionary o the internet to work out any that are unfamiliar.

I'm Leavin' You (Howlin' Wolf)

Context

NAM 51 (page 471)   CD4 Track 10
Howlin' Wolf (vocal, harmonica)
Hosea Lee Kennard (piano)
L. D. McGhee (guitar)
Hubert Sumlin (guitar)
S. P. Leary (drums)

While the wealthy inhabitants of Boston were celebrating the 50t anniversary of their symphony orchestra, the great depression o the 1930s saw vast numbers of unemployed farm workers mov north to industrial cities such as Chicago in search of work. Mos were African-Americans and with them came their music, includ ing gospel and the blues.

As they settled, the blues changed from a rural type of music to a harder urban style. Rhythm and blues, which emerged in th 1940s, invested the traditional blues style with the rhythms of jaz and, as it started to be performed for dancing, the tempo becam faster and the rhythm became tighter, with an emphasised **backbeat** Because rhythm and blues was often played in large inner-city hall for dancing, the sound had to be loud, leading to the introductio of the drum kit, electric guitar and saxophone, and the vocalis needing amplification to balance. All of which points to the fac that rhythm and blues would later become one of the key influence in the development of rock music.

Chester Burnett (1910–76) was a black American blues singe guitarist and harmonica (mouth organ) player who worked unde the name Howlin' Wolf and was famous for keeping alive th impassioned vocal delivery of the Chicago rhythm-and-blues style *I'm Leaving You* was recorded in Chicago in 1958, and released as single and as a track on the album *Moanin' in the Moonlight*.

The form is typical of rhythm-and-blues songs of the 1950s – six repetitions of a 12-bar blues in G, without modulation, and with the singer replaced by an instrumental solo in the fourth repetition. There is a two-bar introduction and the song finishes with a coda that fades out (what we would now call an outro – the counterpart to an intro). The fade-out indicates that the song was conceived more for recording than for live performance (it also rather nicely illustrates the final words).

The order in which the score is played is shown *right*. Rather confusingly, repetitions of a blues pattern are known as choruses, but because each of the first three have different words, they are marked as verses in the score. The important thing to remember is that this is not verse-and-chorus form. There is only one main section, played six times, and so this is **strophic** form.

The 12-bar blues progression follows the standard format of four three-bar phrases, based on chord I, IV and V:

$G^{(7)}$	G	G	$G^{(7)}$	C^9	C^9	G^7	G^7	D^7	C^9	G^7	G^7
$I^{(7)}$	I	I	$I^{(7)}$	IV^9	IV^9	I^7	I^7	V^7	IV^9	I^7	I^7

However, it is important to note that in blues-based styles, these chords don't function in the key-defining way we saw in works such as Haydn's *Lamentatione* Symphony. In this song, chord I generally includes a 7th (F♮), chord IV^9 includes a B♭, and D^7 leads to IV, not directly to I as a dominant 7th would normally do.

F♮ and B♭, along with the D♭ used in the lead-guitar and harmonica solos, are **blue notes**, each a semitone lower than their equivalent pitches in G major. They are marked * in the first example *right*. Flat thirds and fifths appear in close proximity to the natural forms of these notes in the solo lines, creating the characteristic blues sound. The pianist's opening improvisation is based on the minor **pentatonic** scale on G (shown *right*) which is closely related to the blues scale.

Most of the vocal melody is based on the figure heard at the start – a decorated falling triad of G minor (D–B♭–G). In classic blues fashion this isn't transposed when the chord changes. So in bar 7 a similar G minor figure is heard over a chord of C. Notice how the structure of the vocal line overlaps the four-bar units of blues harmony – the first phrase is five bars long, and is followed by three two-bar phrases, plus a rest to complete the 12-bar period. The numerous small differences in the melody line of each verse are a clear indication that it is essentially improvised around a basic composed structure. The texture is underpinned by a simple bass part confined to the root of each chord.

In the first verse the accompaniment is based on the **swing quavers** of shuffle rhythm. The alternation of 5ths, 6ths and 7ths by the rhythm guitar is characteristic of rhythm and blues. The drummer plays the shuffle rhythm on a hi-hat cymbal, adding bass drum on the strong beats and snare drum on the backbeats (the latter are not prominent on CD4). Simple drum **fills** at the ends of verses help to move the song forward.

Structure

Bars		
1–2	Introduction	
3–14	Verse 1	Six
15–26	Verse 2	choruses
27–38	Verse 3	of a
39–50	Instrumental	12-bar
15–26	Repeat of verse 2	blues in
27–36	Repeat of verse 3	G major
51–52	new ending for verse 3	
53–58	Coda (fade-out)	

Harmony

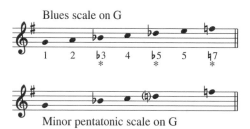

Blues scale on G

1 2 ♭3* 4 ♭5* 5 ♮7*

Minor pentatonic scale on G

Melody and rhythm

Commentary

The lead guitar is silent in bars 3–5 to highlight the entry of the vocal, and then improvises short **licks** in **dialogue** with the singer, filling in rests in the vocal line and sometimes overlapping with it. The piano starts with the shuffle pattern, but soon breaks into improvised passages of continuous triplets, based around the chord progression.

The accompaniment in verses 2 and 3 offers contrast by opening with isolated chords ('**stop time**') that allow the solo lines to cut through the backing. The drummer's continuous triplets in bar 18 herald a busier texture in the rest of the chorus, with some lead guitar work in a very high register in bars 19–22, and with **cross rhythms** in bar 31. Notice how one of the band occasionally joins in with the vocal line at the lower octave – another indication of the essentially improvised nature of the recording.

The fourth chorus (starting at bar 39) features a lead guitar solo, in which the typical heavy reverberation of the time is particularly evident. The band keep in the background for most of this chorus. Howlin' Wolf adds some simple vocalising in the first few bars, then switches to harmonica (mouth organ) for the rest of the chorus.

After the repeat of verses 2 and 3 the coda features the descending blues scale played by the lead guitar at the end of the instrumental chorus, followed by a play-out based on the vocal motif from bar 7 accompanied by a short guitar **riff**.

When Howlin' Wolf recorded *I'm Leaving You* he was 48, and much younger white singers were already starting to achieve success with rock and roll. Rhythm and blues was more earthy and, being played mainly by black musicians, was considered to be a less commercial style. However, Howlin' Wolf's work was well known to inquisitive rock musicians and was very influential in shaping British rock and roll in the 1960s and 1970s. Bands that recorded his songs include the Rolling Stones, the Yardbirds, the Grateful Dead, Cream, Little Feat, the Doors and Led Zeppelin.

The score

The musicians at the original recording session played without notation. They would have been thoroughly familiar with the 12-bar blues progression and well experienced in improvising within the framework it provides. The score in NAM is a transcription from the recording, made many years later and omitting some of the fine detail. Nevertheless, it does indicate some of the performance techniques heard in the recording:

➢ A curved line (as in bars 9 and 10) represents a **pitch bend**

➢ A diagonal line (as in bar 42) represents a **glissando**

➢ The word **fill** in bar 17 indicates a short improvisation that has not been notated.

Exercise 8

1. Why could *I'm Leaving You* be described as a strophic song?

2. How is the last chord of the 12-bar blues progression decorated in bar 14? Where is this type of decoration first heard in the song?

3. What do you notice about the direction of most vocal phrases in this song?

4. Explain the meaning of 'stop chorus' in bar 15 and state the purpose of the ⅙ sign in this bar.

5. Look at the lead guitar solo in bar 49. Which are the blue notes in this bar?

6. Name the type of melodic decoration shown by the sign ⌇ in bars 53 and 55 of the lead-guitar part. How is this ornament played? (Revise pages 37–38 if you are not sure.)

7. What suggests that some aspects of this song were improvised at the recording session?

You Can Get It if you Really Want (Jimmy Cliff)

It was rare for anything other than British and American music to appear in the charts during the 1960s, but in 1969 the Jamaican singer Desmond Dekker (1941–2006) had a number one hit in the UK with his song *Israelites*. The style, like that of his 1970 hit *You Can Get It if you Really Want* (written by Jamaican singer and song-writer Jimmy Cliff, born 1948), is an early version of reggae known as rock steady. Like reggae, there is a clear **backbeat** (see the drum part from bar 5 onwards) and a concentration on short repeated patterns based on a limited number of chords. Also like much reggae, the lyrics allude to a struggle against poverty and oppression, although here they are set in the context of irresistibly tuneful dance music.

The accompaniment reflects the rich mix of influences in Jamaican music. The close-harmony vocals of the backing group are a legacy of 1950s doo-wop music (which remained very popular in Jamaica), the high trumpet riffs are a feature of music from nearby Cuba and Mexico, while the tight rhythmic style of the song betrays Latin-American influences. The two guitars have a subsidiary role. The first is used mainly as a rhythm instrument, its picked semiquaver patterns giving an almost calypso-like feel to the texture, while the second provides background chordal support in partnership with the electric organ (an instrument often used in the Jamaican styles of ska, rock steady and reggae).

Much of the track's character comes from the bass part. It is often low, prominent in the mix, and centred on the root of each chord. From the end of bar 4 onwards, the bass part forms a four-note **riff** – a repeating pattern that changes with the harmony but that retains its basic character throughout most of the rest of the song. Its heavy, steady nature reflects the name given to this style of Jamaican music – rock steady – and differentiates it from reggae in which the bass is usually syncopated and often silent on the first beat of the bar.

The influence of reggae (which was just starting to appear around 1970) is thus not seen at all in the bass part, although it can be felt in the prominent backbeat of the drum part. Most of the snare drum part, except for the fills, is played cross stick. This involves resting the tip of the stick near the edge of the drum head and striking the main part of the shaft on the opposite rim of the drum, producing a dry percussive click. The drums are supplemented by the fast tambourine pattern notated in bar 5, although this is so far back in the mix that it is often inaudible on CD4.

Context and forces

NAM 55 (page 496)   CD4 Track 13
Desmond Dekker and the Aces

Melody

The lead vocal opens with a **hook** (a short, memorable phrase) formed by decorating a stepwise descent to the tonic (F–E♭–D♭, the pitches 3–2–1 in D♭ major). Since this is set to the title words of the song, it is known as the title hook, but it appears in so many bars that it becomes almost as riff-like as the bass part. It gradually extends to other pitches, but mainly keeps to notes of the major pentatonic scale (D♭–E♭–F–A♭–B♭). Much of the lead vocal stays within a range of a 6th, the high falsetto notes in bars 25, 43 and 56 being all the more effective for their rarity. Backing vocals also keep to a narrow range, although their parts are not pentatonic.

Harmony

The harmony is based mainly on two chords, another feature that anticipates reggae. The hypnotic alternations of chords I (D♭) and IV (G♭) are occasionally supplemented with other closely-related chords, such as the dominant (A♭) or dominant 7th (A♭⁷) near the end of the choruses and during the verses.

The only harmonic surprise occurs in the instrumental, where the unrelated chord of E major appears (bar 37) followed by a descent down part of a **whole-tone scale** in bar 39. When the effect is repeated four bars later, the wind section harmonise this scale fragment in parallel triads. However, these are only moments of chromatic colour, as are the brief chromatic note (E♮) in the bass part of bar 21 and the chords of C which chromatically lean up to D♭ in the introduction. Despite these, the song remains in the key of D♭ major throughout.

Structure

You Can Get It if you Really Want is in verse-and-chorus form. After a brief introduction the chorus, starting with its title hook, is heard before the first verse. An instrumental takes the place of a third verse, and the song ends (like the previous one we studied) with a fade out. The complete structure is shown *left*.

Form

1–3	Intro	3 bars
4–13	Chorus	10 bars
14–25	Verse 1	12 bars
26–13	Chorus (repeat)	10 bars
14–25	Verse 2 (repeat)	12 bars
26–35	Chorus	10 bars
36–43	Instrumental	8 bars
44–53	Chorus	10 bars
54–57	Outro (repeat to fade)	

Play the recording, listening particularly to the bass and chords. Did you notice that the choruses are built in two-bar units? The progression I–IV occurs three times in bars 4–9, followed by I–V–IV–V⁷ (with one chord per bar). Ending on a dominant 7th allows the choruses to flow straight into the verses that follow.

The verses are similar to the chorus, but two bars longer since they start with four appearances of the I–IV pattern. This time they end with the progression iii–IV–V–V⁷, the dominant-7th chord again serving as a link between sections. Notice Desmond Dekker's brief use of falsetto for the high D♭ in bar 25 at the end of the verse.

Exercise 9

1. What is meant by a title hook?

2. How does the trumpet motif in bars 1–2 of the introduction relate to the song's title hook?

3. The lead vocal part is mainly pentatonic. What does pentatonic means?

4. Where does Dekker sing a pitch outside the pentatonic scale?

5. What do you notice about the rhythm of the part played by the organ and second guitar throughout the song?

6. In which two bars is the bass part syncopated?

7. At the start of the drum part it is explained that much of the snare drum part is played cross stick. What does this mean?

8. Briefly describe the tonality and the texture of this song.

9. Compare the structures of *You Can Get if you Really Want* (NAM 55) and *I'm Leavin' You* (NAM 51). What similarities and differences are there?

Sample questions

To gain practice in working Sections A and B of the Unit 3 paper, answer the following questions without refering to any notes or to the scores in NAM. In the actual examination, the two extracts for Question 1 will be supplied on a special CD that will be played in the exam room.

Part A: Listening   Answer *both* questions

1.   INSTRUMENTAL MUSIC

Find the recording of Holborne's Pavane and Galliard on CD2 track 1 of NAM, and play the passage from timing 01:13 to 02:23 five times as you answer the questions *below*. Allow a pause of one minute between playings and five minutes after the last playing. Bar numbers in the questions relate to those in the skeleton score printed *below*.

a)   Name the type of stringed instruments playing this music.   .... **(1)**

b)   How many of these instruments are playing in this excerpt?   .... **(1)**

c)   Name the harmonic device heard on the first beat of bar 3.   .... **(1)**

d)   Describe as precisely as you can the pitches of the melody in (i) bar 9 ....

and (ii) bar 12 .... **(4)**

e)   Complete the blanks in the following sentence.

The rhythm of the melody in bar 15 is .... and the extract ends with

a(n) .... cadence in the key of .... **(3)**

f)   When the music is repeated, the melody is ornamented. Describe as precisely as possible how bar 7 is decorated in the repeat.

.... **(2)**

g)   Put a cross in the box next to the word which describes the texture of this music:

⊠ Monophonic   ⊠ Heterophonic   ⊠ Polyphonic   ⊠ Homophonic   **(1)**

h)   This extract comes from Holborne's Pavane, 'The image of melancholy'. Name two features of a pavane that you can hear in the music.

(i) ....   (ii) .... **(2)**

i)   From which section of the pavane is this excerpt taken?   .... **(1)**

(TOTAL: 16)

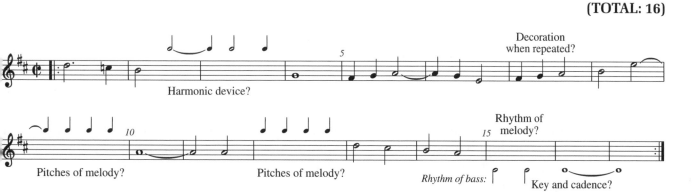

2. VOCAL MUSIC

Find the recording of Schubert's *Der Doppelgänger* on CD3 track 16 of NAM, and play the passage from timing 00:57 to 02:21 five times as you answer the questions *below*. Allow a pause of one minute between playings and five minutes after the last playing. Bar numbers in the questions relate to those in the skeleton score printed *opposite*.

(a) Name the type of voice singing on this recording. .... **(1)**

(b) Give the meaning of *Sehr langsam* in bar 1. .... **(2)**

(c) What is unusual about the tonic chord played by the piano in bar 5?

.... **(1)**

(d) Name the ornament sung at the place marked **1** in bar 7. .... **(1)**

(e) How does the note marked **2** relate to the harmony in bar 9? .... **(1)**

(f) Identify the interval marked **3** in the vocal part of bar 18. .... **(1)**

(g) The chord in bars 18–19 is a(n) .... **(1)**

(h) Complete the blanks in the following sentence.

A dominant .... is heard in the piano part throughout every bar of this extract.

The chord progression in the last four bars of the extract is the same as that heard in bars ....

to .... The extract ends in the key of ...., and Schubert decorates the final chord

with a(n) .... in the vocal part. **(4)**

(i) Put a cross in the box next to the word which describes the texture of this music:

☒ Monophonic ☒ Heterophonic ☒ Polyphonic ☒ Homophonic **(1)**

(j) Briefly describe *two* ways in which the music reflects the mood of the words in this extract. A translation of the German text is printed beneath the skeleton score.

....

.... **(2)**

(k) Put a cross in the box next to the statement that is true:

☒ The excerpt is the opening section of this song.

☒ The excerpt is from the middle of this song.

☒ The excerpt is the final section of this song. **(1)**

(TOTAL: 16)

Remember that in an actual examination, you will be given the titles and composers of the works from which each recorded excerpt has been taken, but you will not be told from which part of the CD track they come. Think carefully about how you could work out the answers to questions on the location of the excerpt without this information.

Translation: [My love] left the town long ago but her house still stands in the same place.
A man is standing there, staring up and wringing his hands in pain.
I shudder when I see his face …

Part B: Investigating Musical Styles

Answer *either* Question 3(a) *or* Question 3(b). You must answer both parts of the question you choose. You should spend no more than 45 minutes on this part of the paper. Remember that you are not allowed to consult recordings, scores or notes while answering the questions.

3(a) INSTRUMENTAL MUSIC

(i) Describe the stylistic features of the Symphony No. 26 (first movement) by Haydn which show that this music was composed in the early Classical period. **(10)**

(ii) Compare and contrast the harmony and structure of the Piano Quintet in F minor (third movement) by Brahms and *Pour le Piano*: Sarabande by Debussy. **(18)**

OR

3(b) VOCAL MUSIC

(i) Describe the stylistic features of Stravinsky's *Symphony of Psalms* (third movement) which show that this is an example of 20th-century music. **(10)**

(ii) Compare and contrast the harmony and structure of *I'm Leaving You* by Howlin' Wolf and *You Can Get It if you Really Want* by Jimmy Cliff. **(18)**

(TOTAL: 28)

Set works for 2015

Instrumental music

Brandenburg Concerto No. 4, movement 1 (Bach)

Context

A concerto is a large-scale composition for contrasting musical forces, most commonly a soloist (or group of soloists) and an orchestra. The basic design of three movements in a fast–slow–fast pattern was established in the early 18th century and widely used by late-Baroque composers such as Bach and Vivaldi.

> NAM 1 (page 7)   CD1 Track 1
> Northern Sinfonia of England
> Directed by George Malcolm

There are two main types of Baroque concerto. The solo concerto features one instrument with orchestra – Vivaldi's set of four violin concertos called *The Four Seasons* are well-known examples. The concerto grosso (large concerto) features a group of solo instruments with orchestra. Bach's fourth *Brandenburg* concerto is of this type.

Bach's six *Brandenburg* concertos were written between 1717 and 1722 for the small but very competent court orchestra of Cöthen, one of the many states into which Germany was then divided, and where Bach was then director of music. He later presented a score of the six works to the ruler of the much larger state of Brandenburg, hence their title. It is not known if the concertos were ever played at Brandenburg, but most were forgotten after Bach's death in 1750. Even after the rediscovery and publication of Bach's manuscripts in the 19th century performances were rare. It was not until the 20th century, when recording made the Brandenburg concertos available to a wide audience, that they became established as some of the best-loved instrumental works of the Baroque period.

Forces

In this concerto the group of soloists, or *concertino*, consists of a violin and two recorders while the orchestra consists of strings. The size of the string ensemble depends on the number of players available – at Cöthen Bach seldom had more than four violinists, plus one player for each of the three lower parts. Whatever the numbers used, the word *ripieno* at the start indicates that these staves are not solo parts.

> The recording on CD1 uses flutes instead of recorders. Try to compare it with one of the many recordings that uses recorders and period string instruments.

A harpsichordist accompanies both groups with chords that are improvised, in accordance with the conventions of the time, from the music on the stave marked **continuo** (the name reflecting its near-continuous role in the music). On CD1 the notes on this stave are also played on a solo cello.

There is a clear distinction in this movement between the **virtuoso** solo-violin part and the less taxing recorder parts. The violin is allowed some long, sparsely accompanied solos (bars 83–102, for instance), but the recorders nearly always play together, often in parallel 3rds or 6ths. This distinction is most noticeable in the extrovert violin solo in bars 187–209, where the recorders supply unobtrusive accompaniment figures in 6ths and 3rds (bars 187–192) that are little different from the duet for ripieno violins in the next six bars.

> Almost all Baroque music, apart from solo pieces, includes a continuo part – a bass part, often with figures below the notes to indicate chords. The bass notes are usually played by at least one bass instrument such as a cello, sometimes with double bass and bassoon. At least one harmony instrument (such as a harpsichord, organ or lute) also plays from the part, using it as the basis for improvising a chordal accompaniment. These instruments are often referred to as the continuo section.

Listen to the movement and try to work out how it is put together. It starts with a long opening section (bars 1–83) that begins with a I–V–I chord progression heard four times in the first 12 bars in order to firmly establish the tonic key of G major. This first section ends with the syncopated rhythms and perfect cadence in bars 79–83. Listen to the recording without the score, but use these two features as markers in order to identify what happens in the rest of the music.

Although there are no dynamic markings, you probably noticed that contrasts in dynamics come about because of the changes in texture between the concertino and the ripieno: loud when all are playing (**tutti**), quieter when only the concertino is playing. These clear contrast in level between soft and loud, without the use of crescendo or diminuendo, are known as 'terraced dynamics' and are a characteristic of late-Baroque style.

Did you notice that between the solo sections parts of the opening music return in different keys, and that all of the opening music is repeated in the tonic key at the end? This is known as **ritornello** form. Ritornello means 'a little return' and refers to the use of shortened repetitions (between contrasting **episodes**) as a structural device. It is a musical form that was widely used in the Baroque period, not only in concertos but also in vocal music, such as the last movement of NAM 28. This structure is summarised in the table *right* – we have given timings since this may help you follow the music without needing to use the score.

Structure and tonality

Bars	Structure	Key	Timing
1–83	Ritornello 1	G	0:00
83–137	Solo 1		1:23
137–157	Ritornello 2	E mi	2:14
157–209	Solo 2		2:36
209–235	Ritornello 3	C	3:28
235–323	Solo 3		3:55
323–344	Ritornello 4	B mi	5:21
345–427	Ritornello 1	G	5:44

The solo episodes do not stay in one key. Instead they modulate from the key of the previous ritornello to the key of the next. Notice how small fragments of the ritornello punctuate these sections, as in bars 89–91. Because this fragment consists of chords I–V–I Bach can use it as a perfect cadence to highlight the most important keys through which the music passes, as in bars 103–105 where they appear in the dominant, D major. However the orchestra mainly takes a background role during the solo episodes, as can be seen in the sustained A in bars 125–128. Sometimes the accompaniment is provided by just the continuo. Listen to the harpsichordist's improvisation starting at bar 114 and say how this relates to the violin solo that it accompanies.

Rhythm and metre

The time signature of $\frac{3}{8}$ indicates simple triple metre ($\frac{3}{8}$ is not a compound metre like $\frac{6}{8}$ and $\frac{9}{8}$). However, if you tap your foot in time to the recording you will find that at this speed the pulse is felt as one dotted-crotchet beat per bar, not three quaver beats.

The dance-like Allegro is enlivened by the syncopated rhythms of the recorders in bars 4, 6, 15, 17, 43–47 and so on, and by the use of **hemiola** – for example, the continuo in bars 79–80 effectively goes into one bar of $\frac{3}{4}$ time, as shown *right*. These bars contain the most joyful and complex rhythms of the whole movement. The upper strings accentuate the second, first then third quavers of each bar (and are thus out of phase with the hemiola), while recorders accentuate the intervening quavers (and are therefore in phase with it). But all of the parts agree on the characteristic syncopated rhythm at the cadence, where the second quaver of bar 82 is given particular

emphasis because the chords change at this point. Bach uses this startling collection of syncopations elsewhere in the movement, always to signal the end of an important section, thus underlining the structure of the music.

Melody   Bach's melodic lines often include arpeggio figures that outline the underlying chords. For example, the second recorder's arpeggios in bars 1–2 clearly trace the triads played by *ripieno* strings (chords I and V). Variants are two-a-penny: for instance, a triad of E minor is as clear in the upper string parts in bar 14 as it is in the second recorder's arpeggio in the same bar. Such harmonically charged melodic lines are particularly obvious in the extended violin solos. For instance, the unaccompanied violin in bar 84 clearly changes the G major triad of bar 83 into the dominant 7th of C major. Even when Bach writes scale-based figures, as in bars 187–208, the harmonic implications are almost as clear. For instance, in bar 202 the violin part changes the underlying G major triad into the dominant 7th of C major and so initiates the lead into C major for the third ritornello (starting at bar 209).

An important feature of late-Baroque style is the spinning out of short motifs to form longer melodic lines, often by using sequence and varied repetition. For example, the second recorder's triadic figure in bar 1 is repeated a 4th lower to form a sequence in bar 2. The scalic figure in bars 3–4 is then repeated in sequence a step lower to form bars 5–6. Next the recorders exchange parts, but with the second now an octave lower, for a repeat of the first six bars. The solo violin then introduces an ascending scale (bar 13) followed by a descending arpeggio (bar 14).

These four tiny cells, along with the figures introduced by the recorders in bars 35–36 and 43^3–44^2, form the melodic material for virtually the entire movement. Look at the recorder parts in bar 69 – which of our small cells is this? Which other motif is heard in **counterpoint** with it, played by the solo violin? Do you see how it has been treated in rising sequence and how, at bar 75, it leads seamlessly into a transposed return of bars 13–14? We then hear just the second of these two bars in descending sequence, leading to the syncopated cadential figure that signals the end of the first ritornello.

Harmony   Chords I and $V^{(7)}$ not only play a vital role in asserting the tonic key in the long outer ritornellos, but they fulfil the same function in establishing the keys of the shorter inner ritornellos. Other chords are mostly root-position or first-inversion triads, sometimes decorated with suspensions, but brief chromatic colour appears with the use of a **Neapolitan 6th** before some minor-key cadences – for instance, on the first beat of bar 155.

Try to hear the **harmonic rhythm** of the movement by listening to the recording rather than studying the score. Its variety helps give the music its buoyancy: one chord per bar at the start, but two or three in busier passages, especially when a cadence is due, and occasionally calmer passages, such as bars 125–136, where each chord lasts for four bars at a time.

Tonic **pedals** help to reinforce tonal centres, although they are all quite short – for instance, G in bars 83–89, D in bars 105–111 and B in bars 325–329. Bach also makes use of one of the most common harmonic progressions in tonal music: the **circle of 5ths** in bars 97–103 modulates from G to D major by passing through chords whose roots are G–C–F♯–B–E–A–D.

Texture

Bach is famous for his skill in **counterpoint**. We have already noted the contrapuntal combination of motifs in bar 69, but there are countless other examples throughout the movement, such as the counterpoint of bars 165–174. Although contrapuntal textures predominate, they are highly varied. For instance, in bars 187–208 lower strings playing detached chords while recorders play the motif from bars 3–4 in combination with the virtuoso violin solo, then the accompanying roles are reversed in bars 194–197.

The key to such contrapuntal ingenuity lies in the harmony. By having a clear chord progression in mind, Bach could devise several different melodies to fit the same chord pattern, each of which makes musical sense on its own or when combined.

Exercise 1

1. Name one chordal instrument and one bass instrument that might be used to play a continuo part in Baroque music.

2. Explain the difference between the ripieno and the concertino.

3. In ritornello form, what is an episode?

4. How does Bach ensure that the recorders (flutes) can be heard in the first 12 bars, despite the fact that everyone is playing?

5. How does Bach make bars 69–83 sound exciting? Comment on the rhythm of the solo violin part in the section immediately after this (bars 83–136).

6. What are the main differences between the recorder (flute) parts in bars 125–156 and their parts in bars 165–186?

7. Identify the chord on the first beat of bar 341 (the key is B minor).

8. For what type of musical texture is Bach most famous?

Piano Sonata in B♭, movement 1 (Mozart)

By 1783, when Mozart wrote his Sonata in B♭, K. 333, the late Baroque contrapuntal style of Bach had given way to the elegance of the Classical style, and the piano had started to replace the harpsichord as the keyboard instrument of choice in both concert hall and home. Although the 18th-century piano was lighter in tone than a modern instrument, it was sufficiently powerful for Mozart to be able to show off his virtuosity in the piano concertos he wrote for the purpose and it was also capable of delicate dynamic effects, making it ideal for domestic performances of the series of piano sonatas that he wrote for himself and his amateur pupils. This work was first published in Vienna in 1784, as one of three sonatas (two for piano, and one for violin and piano), all by Mozart.

Context

NAM 22 (page 253)   CD2 Track 12
Alfred Brendel (piano)

K. 333 is the number of this work in the catalogue of Mozart's compositions compiled in the 19th century by an Austrian scholar named Köchel.

Structure

Like many Classical sonatas, this work has three movements in the order fast–slow–fast, of which we are to study the first. It is in **sonata form**, a structure as closely connected with Classical style as ritornello form is with late-Baroque style. It has three main sections, each defined by key:

The **exposition** begins by establishing the home key of B♭ major with a theme called the first subject (1–10). The next 12 bars move towards the contrasting key of the dominant (F major). Starting in bar 23 Mozart presents the first of several ideas in this key (the second subject group). The exposition ends with a **codetta** (bars 50–63) in which F major is affirmed by a succession of perfect cadences (bars 53–54, 57–59 and 62–63).

In minor-key sonata-form movements the second subject is usually in the relative major rather than the dominant: see the diagram on page 55.

The development (bars 63⁴–93³) is characterised by a wider range of keys. It begins with the first subject in F major but soon veers off to pass through the keys of F minor, C minor, B♭ major and G minor until Mozart signals the imminent return of the home key with seven bars of **dominant preparation** starting in bar 87.

Bars

1–63   An **exposition** of the main themes, grouped into two contrasting tonal centres (tonic and dominant: B♭ and F)

63–93   A **development** of these themes passing through several related keys (including C minor and G minor)

93–165   A **recapitulation** of the principal themes in the tonic

The recapitulation (bar 93⁴ to the end) sees the material of the exposition return, but now centred on the home key of B♭ major. The conflict of keys has been resolved in a perfectly balanced sonata-form structure (summarised *left*).

Style

The Classical style of this movement stands in marked contrast to Bach's contrapuntal spinning of motifs in NAM 1. Some of its key features are:

Periodic phrasing – pairs of equal-length phrases sounding like questions and answers. For example, the eight-bar phrase starting at bar 23 ends with an imperfect cadence in F major, and the eight-bar answer starting at bar 31 ends with a perfect cadence in the same key. However, Mozart is often ingenious in avoiding the predictability of periodic phrasing. The work opens with a four-bar phrase, but it is answered by a phrase that is extended to six bars in length, ending on the third beat of bar 10.

Melody-dominated **homophony**. The chief focus of the music is the ornate right-hand melody supported by the broken chords of the left-hand accompaniment. The melodies include frequent use of non-chord notes, especially **appoggiaturas** – both **diatonic** (such as the first B♭ in bar 88 which clashes with the dominant-7th chord beneath it) and **chromatic** (C♯ in bar 110).

Thin, crystal-clear textures. The first 22 bars use an almost entirely two-part texture. When full chords are used they draw attention to the beginnings or endings of important sections (as in bar 23).

Broken-chord accompaniments. These are evident in the first four bars where Mozart achieves a delicate effect by beginning each left-hand pattern after the first beat of the bar. Elsewhere (notably bars 71–80) he uses an **Alberti bass** accompaniment.

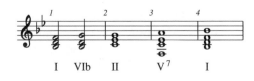

Clear harmonic progressions with regular cadences to define keys. Mozart starts with the chords shown *left* and reaches a perfect cadence in B♭ major in bar 10. The modulation to the dominant

F major) in bars 11–22 is equally clear – notice how E♮ occurs with
ncreasing frequency in these bars.

Much of the harmony is based on simple triads, especially tonic
and dominant in various keys, but chromatic harmony appears in
the development: **diminished-7th** chords in bars 67 and 69, the
minor version of chord IV (E♭ minor) in bar 76, and **augmented-6th**
chords on the last beats of bars 80 and 82. The augmented 6th in
these is the interval E♭–C♯; the E♭ leans down to D in the next bar
and the C♯ leans up to D, in a section that sounds for all the world
like dominant preparation for a recapitulation in G minor. After six
bars Mozart cheekily moves up a 3rd and begins proper dominant
preparation for the return of B♭ major, as expected.

The movement includes two of the most characteristic harmonic
features of the Classical style:

➤ The **cadential** $\frac{6}{4}$ – chord Ic used as the approach to a perfect cadence, forming the progression Ic–V$^{(7)}$–I. The example in bars
57–59 is preceded by a spectacular scalic descent from top F,
the highest note on Mozart's piano.

➤ Accented dissonances on the final chord of a perfect cadence,
as in bars 63 and 165, where the upper notes in the right hand
are appoggiaturas and the lower ones are suspensions.

Exercise 2

. In bars 1–10 which are the only bars that do *not* start with appoggiaturas or accented passing notes?

. Where does Mozart use an Alberti bass in the exposition?

. What do you understand is meant by dominant preparation?

. State the key of the second subject in (i) the exposition, and (ii) the recapitulation. (It is this difference that would enable you to give the location of the second subject if it occurred in an exam extract.)

. Identify the harmonic progression in bars 159–161[1].

. Unlike NAM 1, the mood of this music seems to change rapidly. Choose a section of about 24 bars and explain some of the techniques Mozart uses to create such lively variety without the music sounding disjointed.

Sonata for Horn, Trumpet and Trombone, movement 1 (Poulenc)

Francis Poulenc was a 20th-century French composer who achieved considerable success in such diverse areas as music for stage and film, church music, songs and **chamber music**. The last of these includes a number of sonatas and other works for wind instruments, of which NAM 19 (the first movement of a three-movement work) is among the first.

It was written in late 1922 and first performed on 4 January 1923 at a concert of contemporary French music in Paris. The work was published in 1924, but Poulenc subsequently produced a revised version in 1945. The technical difficulty of the parts indicates that this is concert music for professional performers.

Context

NAM 19 (page 242)   CD2 Track 8
Nash Ensemble

Movements from Poulenc's flute and clarinet sonatas are often studied by young woodwind players. If anyone in your AS group is learning one of these it would be an ideal opportunity to get to know more about Poulenc's music.

Style   Much of Poulenc's early music is light and witty, like that of the other five young French composers in the group dubbed *Les Six* by a critic in 1920. They disliked the influence that the nostalgic styles of previous generations were having on contemporary music and sought a new clarity and simplicity in their own work. They were inspired by the music of Erik Satie and by popular music of the day, and often tried to be deliberately provocative, like the artists of the Dada movement that flourished in Paris at the time.

Poulenc greatly admired the music of Stravinsky, whose ballet *Pulcinella* (see NAM 7) had received its first performance in Paris in 1920. *Pulcinella* draws on the music of Baroque composers but Stravinsky reinterpreted this material with syncopated rhythms, pungent 'wrong notes' and unusual instrumentation.

The influence of this **Neoclassical** style on NAM 19 is evident in:

➢ Simple **diatonic** melodies (opening trumpet theme)

➢ **Syncopation** (bars 13–14)

➢ Tonal harmonies (chords I, IV and V in bars 1–4)

➢ **Discords** that spice-up conventional progressions (see *left*)

➢ Humour, in short-winded phrases that constantly change metre and tempo (the recording on CD2 brings this out particularly well – listen to how the brass make a headlong dash towards the first cadence in bar 4)

➢ Classical-like periodic phrasing (bars 1–4 end with a perfect cadence in the tonic and are answered by bars 5–8 which end with a perfect cadence in the dominant).

Of course, the piece cannot be mistaken for Classical music. The first cadence includes a 'wrong note' and the second ends in the wrong place (on the weak fourth beat of bar 8). The frequent changes of metre and speed and the surprising changes of key are nothing like Classical music – nor could an 18th-century trumpet or horn play music of this kind. Poulenc noted that the audience at the first performance were amazed, and greeted the work with a huge roar of laughter – just the reaction that the composers of *Les Six* hoped to provoke in their early, Dada-esque works.

Forces and textures   Poulenc's choice of a horn, trumpet and trombone as his trio was highly unusual, and he admitted that it caused him problems of balance. Notice how he addresses this in bar 30 with detailed instructions and differentiated dynamics.

Music for brass ensemble is usually written for at least a quartet of instruments, to avoid chords being incomplete and to give each player a chance for an occasional rest while the others continue. With a trio, all three players have to be used almost constantly, apart from where a few very brief unaccompanied solos provide a short break for the other two parts.

The texture mainly consists of melody-dominated **homophony**. The tune is often in the trumpet part, but the horn takes the lead in bars 30–33 and 40–47, and becomes the bass instrument in bars 74–81. The horn is in F and so sounds a perfect 5th lower than written.

The movement is in **ternary form** – an outline of the structure is shown *right*. The opening trumpet figure, based on the tonic triad of G, is bold and diatonic, and it forms the start of two balancing four-bar phrases that modulate to the dominant (D major). Shorter phrases at a quicker tempo and with changing time signatures follow. The trumpet announces a new two-bar idea, starting on the last quaver of bar 17, but the answer to this phrase is the same tune played an octave lower and it slows to a halt in bar 21 as quickly as it began.

The opening triadic figure returns in bars 21^4–25, but it too has lost all its energy (and its accompaniment), and even its shape, as it fragments among the trio. The horn gets the rhythm of the first two notes 'wrong' (quavers instead of semiquavers) and the trombone slows it down further by augmenting this rhythm to crotchets. They then try it more quietly in G minor. Exasperated, they give up any further development for the moment and instead embark on the middle section of the ternary form.

The contrast of key and speed at bar 26 is matched by a change in style, with quiet dynamics and legato phrasing, but this mood is suddenly disrupted by the loud outburst and wild trumpet leaps in bars 36–38. A downward scale for trumpet in free time leads to a dramatic pause, followed by a fast and staccato variation on the opening melody of the movement. This time the horn has the melody, but Poulenc retains the pattern of two balanced phrases, ending in F major in bar 47. A succession of shorter phrases brings the B section to an end with an unaccompanied downward scale for trumpet, repeated in sequence by the horn. The latter ends on D, the dominant of G, ready for the return of G major and a varied repeat of the first section of the movement.

Poulenc begins this with the first eight-bar phrase (bars 58–65) but he then interpolates material from the B section (bars 66–71 are taken from bars 48–53) before continuing with the rest of the A section (bars 73–85, which are taken from bars 9–21). Both of these last two passages are transposed, re-scored and re-harmonised. The coda (bars 86–89) consists of an obstinate B♭ against a *très discret* (very unobtrusive) chromatic scale, followed by a cheeky reference to the opening notes of the movement.

Commentary

Bars		
1–25	A	G major (modulating to the dominant and back)
26–57	B	Mainly in B♭ major (at first slow, but fast from the last quaver of bar 39)
57^4–89	A¹	G major (varied repeat of section A with a reference to section B in bars 65–72)

Exercise 3

1. Check that you understand all the directions in French (translations are on page 537 of NAM).

2. Which of the three instruments is given the smallest share of the melodic material?

3. What sort of scale is heard in the trombone part of bars 86–87?

4. What are the sounding pitches of the last three notes played by the horn? How do these pitches relate to those played by the other instruments in the last bar?

5. What term describes the texture of bars 22–25? How would you describe the texture in most of the rest of this movement?

6. Explain the meaning of Neoclassical and indicate which aspects of this movement refer to older styles of music and which are clearly 20th century.

String Quartet No. 8, movement 1 (Shostakovich)

Context

NAM 9 (page 163)   CD1 Track 11
Coull Quartet

While Poulenc's choice of instruments for NAM 19 was highly unusual, Shostakovich wrote this work for the most common of all chamber music groups, the string quartet. Works for string quartet have been popular since the second half of the 18th century, and Shostakovich contributed 15 such works to the **genre**.

This quartet is in five movements, played without breaks between of which we are to study the first. It was given its first performance in Leningrad (now known by its original name of St Petersburg) on 2 October 1960. The performance was given by the Beethoven Quartet, with whom Shostakovich had worked closely for many years in the preparation of almost all of his string quartets.

Shostakovich lived all his life in Russia, where he was one of several prominent composers who periodically suffered harsh criticism from the communist state. His opera *Lady Macbeth of Mtsensk* was denounced in 1936 (possibly by Stalin himself) as a representation of 'chaos instead of music' and banned for its decadent western modernism. Shostakovich toed the party line by supplying suitably heroic and wholesome music to glorify the state – only to be denounced again in the cultural purges of 1948. 'I know the party is right,' he humbly replied, 'I am deeply grateful for the criticism.'

Shostakovich's relations with the all-powerful state became easier after Stalin's death, but he was deeply humiliated by being forced to join the Communist party in 1960 – the price he paid for the removal of the ban on some of his earlier works. In July that year Shostakovich visited Germany where he saw the remains of the beautiful and historic city of Dresden after its intensive bombing in the Second World War. It is said that this experience inspired his eighth string quartet, completed in just three days and dedicated to the 'memory of the victims of fascism and war'.

This dedication may not be as clear-cut as it seems – the words have the potential double meaning that many Russian dissidents used under Communism. They had long referred to the Communists as 'fascists' and they would have understood that Shostakovich's 'victims of fascism' did not necessarily refer exclusively to those persecuted by the Nazis. It is likely that the composer saw himself as one of those victims, and intended the eighth quartet to be his final work. 'When I die,' he wrote to his friend Isaak Glickmann 'it's hardly likely that someone will write a quartet to my memory. So I decided to write it myself.' He later wrote to another friend 'One could write on the frontispiece: "Dedicated to the author of this quartet".'

The cipher and the quotations

Russian is written in the Cyrillic alphabet and this can result in inconsistency when names are transliterated. You may find books refer to 'Dimitri' and German scores that call the composer Schostakowitsch.

The personal nature of this work is evident in Shostakovich's use of quotations from earlier works, almost as if he is looking back on his life, and in his use of a cipher – a group of letters with a hidden meaning. It is first heard in the opening cello notes: D–E♭–C–B♮. In German these pitches are known as D–Es–C–H and, since Es sounds like the letter 'S', they transliterate to D Sch(ostakovich), a musical encryption of the German version of part of the composer's name. He used this motto in other works, but in the eighth quartet it permeates the music, giving the work a powerful sense of unity.

The first movement of the quartet is in **arch form**, which we can represent as $ABCB^1A^1$. In other words, the last two sections are modified repeats of the first two sections, with their order reversed, as shown *right*. When using bar numbers, notice that the movement begins with an anacrusis (an up-beat), so bar number 1 starts with the second note of the opening cello solo (E♭). Although the time signature is shown as $\frac{4}{4}$, Shostakovich's metronome mark ($\downarrow=63$) suggests a slow minim beat. So, when we have added superscript figures to bar numbers in the following account, they refer to the first or second *minim* beat in the bar.

Listen to the first 27 bars of the movement and comment on the way the DSCH motto is introduced by the four instruments. You probably noticed that the rhythms are very simple and that each instrument enters in turn, low to high, with the same motif, but starting on different pitches in a series of **imitative** entries. What do you notice about the **tessitura** of the string parts? Do you agree that the tessitura helps make the opening sound sombre?

At the end of bar 11, DSCH is heard in an entirely different texture - three parts in octaves against a viola G. In the first-violin part, the last note of the cipher (B♮ in bar 13) becomes the first note of a quotation (in greatly expanded note-lengths) of the opening theme from the composer's first symphony, the work that had established his reputation some 34 years earlier. Beneath it, the second violin announces DSCH as a solo (bar 15). The decoration of the third note of the cipher by a quaver D in bar 17 is the point at which the quotation from the symphony moves down to the second-violin part. The quotation returns to the first violin at bar 19^2 and comes to an end in bar 23^1. DSCH then returns, this time in a **homophonic** texture and terminating in a perfect cadence (bars 25–27) that seems to make the C minor tonality totally clear, even though the tonic chord lacks a 3rd.

Did you get the impression that the tonality seems very unclear before this final part of section A? It should not be surprising – Shostakovich has used all 12 pitches of the chromatic scale by bar 7. Further ambiguity follows in bars $13–16^2$ where, beneath an inverted **pedal** on B♮ in the first violin, the lower strings shift chromatically through triads of E minor, E major, E♭ major, D major and back to E♭ major). But the textbook-like harmonisation of DSCH in bars $23^2–27$ seems to create order out of the foregoing tonal obscurity.

From here on, the tonality remains anchored to C minor with long dominant and tonic pedal points. Sometimes Shostakovich prefers major 3rds to minor 3rds in chord I, and sometimes no 3rd at all. But neither the chromatic writing nor a short excursion to A minor (starting in bar 86) suggest that this is anything other than a profoundly tonal movement.

Most of section B (bars 28–50) is accompanied by a long double pedal on tonic (C) and dominant (G). This drone is played by all three lower parts, while the first-violin has a falling, then rising, chromatic line. This leads to an expressive figure in bars $32^2–33$ that Shostakovich modifies in various ways over the next ten bars.

Structure

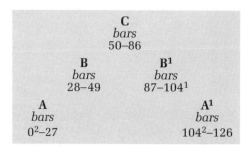

Commentary

As the drone ceases, another reference to DSCH (cello, bar 46) marks the end of Section B.

At the start of the central C section, a simple idea introduced by the first violin (bar 50) is transferred to the second violin two bars later, and developed into a **countermelody** to the long, slow first violin theme that begins in bar 55. This begins with a quotation from the first movement of Shostakovich's fifth symphony – one of his most famous works (see *left*). This violin duet is accompanied throughout by more long pedals, this time in octaves, first on C then on G, and finally back to C. The section ends, like the previous two sections, with DSCH at its original pitch (starting in bar 79) followed by a perfect cadence in C minor. Here the motto is heard in **augmentation**, and the texture is not just homophonic but strictly **homorhythmic** for the four notes of the actual cipher. They are harmonised with three simple but unrelated root-position triads (C major, Eb minor and F major) and then two biting dissonances in bars 82–83.

Section B¹ (bars 87–104¹) is a restatement of material from the first B section, but with a number of changes. It begins with the only extended passage in the movement to completely break free of the fateful key of C minor. Violin parts in 3rds give the music greater warmth and below them the cello plays the chromatic melody that was allocated to the first violin when it first appeared in bar 28. Another ray of sunshine permeates the gloom with the appearance of very quiet root-position triads of C major and F major in bar 95, but chromatic lines soon return. This is the only one of the five sections of the movement that doesn't finish with a statement of DSCH at its original pitch – instead, the cipher is used to open the final section in the second half of bar 104.

Instead of beginning with the imitative entries of DSCH that we heard at the start of the work, the motto at the start of section A is played in octaves. Its first note (and accompanying dominant pedal in the viola part) is a continuation of the last note of section B¹ for the three lower parts, providing a seamless join in bar 104. The omission of the opening imitative section of the movement results in the theme from the first symphony starting in bar 106 (11 bars earlier than before), where its first note overlaps with the last note of DSCH. The music from section A is then restated almost exactly until a brief extension (bar 114) leads to a final appearance of DSCH (bar 118², second violin), again leading to a perfect cadence in C minor. All of the instruments sink to their lowest notes and the second violin briefly refers to the motif from the central section (bars 122–123). On the last repetition of this, the Ab is notated as G♯ (known as an **enharmonic** change) to form a link to the second movement, which is in the remote key of G♯ minor.

Shostakovich's life was at a low ebb in 1960 when he wrote this work. He had been diagnosed with an incurable illness (although he was to live for another 15 years) and was feeling suicidal after being forced to join the Communist Party that he so loathed. This may help to explain the gloomy mood of this work, but can you see how it is achieved in musical terms? The instruments are used in a low register throughout, often playing on just their lowest strings.

Shostakovich wrote his popular fifth symphony, cringingly subtitled 'A Soviet artist's reply to just criticism', after his opera *Lady Macbeth of Mtsensk* was banned and the premiere of his fourth symphony was cancelled. Music from the opera itself is quoted in the last movement of this string quartet.

NAM 9 is one of Shostakovich's most sombre works. To get a more rounded picture of his long and varied output, listen to his music for the 1955 film *The Gadfly*, which includes one of the most famous and beautiful melodies ever written for the cinema, his Suite for Jazz Orchestra, which reflects popular music styles of the 1930s, and his dramatic fifth symphony.

The melodies are slow moving, and mainly conjunct, and there is no use of pizzicato, tremolo or other effects. The gloom of C minor is intensified by long pedals on tonic and/or dominant, and the dynamics are mainly very quiet, only rising in level for the homophonic statements of DSCH at the ends of sections A and C.

Exercise 4

1. What are the only two pitches played by the viola in bars 50–79?

2. Compare bars 87–92 with bars 28–33.

3. What effect do you feel the long pedal notes and low tessitura of the strong parts have on the character of this music?

4. Briefly describe some of the different types of texture used in this movement.

5. What examples would you choose from NAM 9 to show that the music is essentially tonal?

Vocal music

Ohimè, se tanto amate (Monteverdi)

A madrigal is a musical setting of a poem for several solo voices, usually unaccompanied but sometimes supported by a plucked string instrument such as a lute. This type of work originated in 16th-century Italy, although it spread to other countries such as England (see page 62).

NAM 35 was published in Venice in 1603, as part of Monteverdi's fourth book of madrigals, and is typical of a late type of serious Italian madrigal in which composers sought to express every nuance of the text in what became known as the 'representational style'. Understanding the meaning of the poem by Guarini, one of the major Italian lyric poets of the period, is therefore essential. This includes realising that the word *Ohimè* can mean either the same as the Shakespearean 'alas!' or it can refer to the sigh of a lover. It is also important that in both Italy and England in this period the verb to die (Italian *morire*) was also a euphemism for sexual release. So the poet might die of love withheld or, if his lady chooses, she might accede to his requests and hear ten thousand ecstatic sighs.

The music is written for five solo voices, the part labelled *Canto* (melody) being for first soprano and that labelled *Quinto* (fifth part) being for second soprano. The vocal technique required to perform NAM 35 suggests that it was not written for amateurs to sing at home, like NAM 34, but for trained singers to present in private concerts to audiences of wealthy and educated connoisseurs in the sophisticated courts of the Italian nobility.

Ohimè, se tanto amate is through-composed: each phrase of the poem has new music, the structure being determined by the text, although the falling 3rds of *Ohimè* act as a unifying device.

Context and forces

NAM 35 (page 353)   CD3 Track 13
The Consort of Musicke
Directed by Anthony Rooley

A translation of the poem by Walter Shewring appears on page 539 of NAM. In it he comes as near as possible to Guarini's punning text with a rhyming paraphrase which, of its nature, cannot be a line-by-line, let alone a word-by-word, translation.

Structure

Commentary

The importance of the text in the representational style can be seen in all of the following aspects of *Ohimè, se tanto amate.*

The setting is almost entirely **syllabic** to give maximum clarity to the words.

Extremely irregular rhythms change with each new phrase of the poem and closely follow the rhythms of the Italian verse. For example, in bars 5–6 the accented second syllable of *a-ma-te* (love) falls on the strong third beat of the bar. Throughout the madrigal Monteverdi constructs his music to mirror the speech rhythms of spoken Italian.

Expressive melodic lines reflect the meaning of the words. Sometimes these take the form of reflecting the way the voice rises or falls when speaking. Thus the falling 3rds of *Ohimè* (Ah me) suggest the way the voice falls on these syllables when spoken. In bars 49–52 this falling 3rd is repeated over and over in sequence to express the thousand sweet 'Ahs' of the lovers.

Melodic lines include intervals which were almost never heard in previous styles (a **tritone** in the canto part of bar 12 and a 7th in the bass part of bar 16). **Chromatic** writing was also rare at this time (C–C♯–D in the quinto part of bars 16–17).

G minor: V⁷ –   I (major)

tierce de Picardie

Extreme dissonance reflects the mock agony of the poem. The unprepared 9ths between bass and quinto in bars 2 and 4 sound harsh even to modern ears. The same is true of the dissonances in bars 16–17 (A against G, A against B, and C♯ against B and D). Other dissonant effects are more typical of late-Renaissance music. Thus the **false relation** formed between the B♮ in the **tierce de Picardie** of bar 38 and the B♭ in bar 39 (see *left*) was a cliché of many 16th-century styles. But the whole chain of false relations in bars 49–51 is unparalled in earlier music. The Consort of Musicke on CD3 wonderfully underlines the pleasure and pain of these thousand 'deaths' the lover hopes to experience with his mistress.

Contrasts in texture are exploited to the full, again in the service of the words. In the first four bars, for instance, two pairs of voices engage in a dialogue that suggests the sighs of the two lovers. Monteverdi's use of **imitative** textures also springs from the text. In bars 23–27 the 'sad Ah me' is reflected in grinding dissonances (for example D, C♯ and E all sounded simultaneously) that are a product of a deliberate use of imitation in such a way that discords are bound to arise.

Contrasting passages of **homophonic** texture predominate towards the end, either for three parts (two sopranos plus bass contrasting with the three lowest parts) or for all five parts. Melody and rhythm become as simple as possible for the ten thousand sighs, and the final cadence is preceded by a long **dominant pedal**, starting in bar 61³. The last two chords form an unusual variant on a perfect cadence – chord IIIb of G minor (with B♮ rather than B♭) is used instead of V, and the final chord contains another tierce de Picardie (so B♮ appears again). The result allows both soprano and tenor a final, weary falling 3rd on *Ohimè*, leaving the listener to guess whether the poet was unsuccessful in his advances or just totally exhausted by his efforts.

The main key of the madrigal is G minor and today this would normally be notated with a key signature of two flats (B♭ and E♭). Monteverdi uses just B♭ in the key signature and adds E♭ where needed – this was common practice in minor-key movements until the 18th century. Monteverdi gives no tempo, dynamics or other performing directions in his music. This was normal in music at his time, matters of interpretation being left to the performers. Listen carefully to the recording and note the performing decisions that have been made, especially for the ending.

Notation and interpretation

Exercise 5

. Is the word setting in NAM 35 **melismatic** or **syllabic**?

. Which two notes in bar 56 form a false relation?

. Why is the change from D major in bar 19 to D minor in bar 20 *not* a false relation?

. Describe the texture of the phrase starting in bar 20.

. How does Monteverdi express the change of mood in bar 39 at the words *Ma se cor mio volete che vita* (but if, my love, you wish to let me live)? Consider both rhythm and tonality.

. Explain the meaning of **tierce de Picardie** and give an example of its use on page 354 of NAM.

. Give three examples of the way in which Monteverdi's music reflects the meaning of Guarini's poetry.

Après un rêve (Fauré)

Après un rêve (After a dream) is a type of song known as a *mélodie* – in this context meaning a French art song of the Romantic period. It was published in 1878 as the first of a set of three songs by Gabriel Fauré. Like its German counterpart the *Lied* (see page 65) it could have been sung at home, or to small gatherings in the fashionable salons of Paris and other cities.

Context

NAM 39 (page 363)   CD3 Track 17
Janet Baker (mezzo-soprano)
Geoffrey Parsons (piano)

The text is by Fauré's friend Romain Bussine, who was professor of singing at the Paris Conservatoire of Music. It is based on an anonymous Italian poem, and its message of longing for a return to lost dreams of love had special meaning for Fauré, who almost certainly set the words to music shortly after his fiancée broke off their engagement in late 1877.

A translation of the poem appears on page 540 of NAM.

A **strophic** song is one which uses the same music for each verse of the text. In NAM 39 Fauré uses similar music for the first two stanzas of the poem (verse 2 starts in bar 17), but the third verse (starting on the last beat of bar 30) has different music to reflect the poet's awakening from the dream. We should therefore refer to this as *modified* strophic form.

Structure

To give musical expression to the dream images of the poetry, Fauré is deliberately ambiguous in both key and rhythm. Keys are normally defined by perfect cadences in which the seventh note of the scale rises to the tonic (B♮–C in the case of C minor). Here the vocal melody begins by outlining the tonic chord of C minor but the piano

Verse 1

introduces B♭ as early as bar 2, accompanying the singer with richly chromatic harmonies, full of 7ths and 9ths.

The first vocal phrase ends on B♭ in bar 4 and the next phrase (bar 5–8) introduces D♭ and more chromatic chords. Even when we reach a perfect cadence in C minor (V⁷–I in bars 7–9) the B♭s of the singer pull against the B♮ in the piano to produce false relations.

> This conflict arises in the scale of C melodic minor, which has B♮ when ascending and B♭ when descending. But Fauré was a church musician interested in modes, and you could say that the B♭s in the vocal line are modal while the piano accompaniment exerts a more tonal influence with its B♮s.

But underpinning this complexity is a simple and strong harmonic device – a **circle of 5ths** that begins on C in bar 1 and moves from middle C through F, B♭, E♭, A♭, D♮ and G in the left hand of the piano part before returning to C in bar 9.

Similarly Fauré uses subtlety of rhythm to enhance his dreamy atmosphere. The triplets with which the singer approaches all of the cadences cut across the rhythm of the piano, producing delicate **cross-rhythms** which not only reflect the accents of the French language but which also help to blur the symmetry of the continuous quavers in the accompaniment.

Verse 2

With a return to C minor in bar 17 comes a repeat of the opening melody, set to the words of the second verse. However, after the first nine bars Fauré writes a new ending, based on the previous triplet figures, that leads to an imperfect cadence in F minor (the subdominant of C minor) at the end of the verse in bar 30.

Verse 3

The final verse begins without any break, on the last beat of bar 30 as the dream suddenly ends. The music is new, although still based on the familiar triplet figures, and immediately heads further in the subdominant direction to B♭ minor (bars 31–32). The conventional secondary key for a minor-key piece is the relative major, which tends to have a brightening and uplifting effect. Modulations in the subdominant direction – and we've now had two in succession – have the opposite effect, but just what is needed for this 'sad awakening from dreams'.

The first four-bar phrase (bars 30³–34²) begins with the song's climax and is balanced by four bars (34³–38¹) that end with an imperfect cadence in the home key of C minor. The rising 4th from the start of the verse aptly returns (a 4th lower) for the impassioned plea 'Return' in bars 38³–39² and the radiance of the dream is recalled by an unexpected E♭-major chord at *radieuse* in bar 41. The final vocal phrase is extended to five bars, coming to rest with a definitive if sombre perfect cadence in C minor.

Vocal and piano writing

Fauré's vocal phrases are long and linked to form a continuous melodic line. The only rest for the singer is in bar 16, between the first two verses. Nevertheless, singers enjoy performing the song because of Fauré's gratifying balance of conjunct movement and expressive leaps. Many of the phrases are broadly arch-shaped except at the start of the third verse, where the climactic top note comes on the second note. Fauré also skilfully reflects the nuances of the French language, for example by a falling interval to a weak beat on the final syllable of a line (as in bar 15). Most of the setting is **syllabic**, with **melismas** to express important words, such as *mirage* (bar 7), *splendeurs* (bar 27) and *mystérieuse* (bars 45–46).

The range of the vocal part is from middle C to F an 11th higher – there are no extremely high or low notes. The piano part is purely supportive and entirely in a mid-to-low register. While it includes some richly expressive harmonies, it is no more demanding than the vocal part, all of which points to the suitability of the song for domestic performance by accomplished amateurs.

A comparison of the score of NAM 39 with the score of NAM 35 will show that by the late 19th century composers were including detailed dynamic markings in their music, as well as indicating the tempo and, with the word *dolce* (sweetly), suggesting how the vocal line might be interpreted.

> The best way to get to know this music is to sing it for yourself, even if you do so in a small group and perhaps with a melody instrument to double the vocal line. Alternatively, see if someone in your study group has learned to play *Après un rêve* – it has been arranged for a wide variety of instruments.

Exercise 6

1. What is the total vocal range of this song? Where is the hightest note in the voice part?

2. Fauré marks the vocal part *dolce*. What does this mean?

3. What is a false relation? Where does one occur in bars 17–23?

4. What is a circle of 5ths and where is one used in this song?

5. The performance on CD3 is sung by a mezzo-soprano. What type of voice is this?

6. How does the rhythm of the piano accompaniment differ from the rhythm of the vocal part?

7. Briefly list some of the ways in which Fauré establishes a dream-like mood in this song.

The Lamb (John Tavener)

Tavener's music became increasingly popular in the final years of the 20th century, and the performance of his *Song for Athene* that brought the funeral of Princess Diana to its moving close in 1997 resulted in him becoming one of the best-known British composers of contemporary art music.

> NAM 32 (page 344)   CD3 Track 10
> Westminster Abbey Choir
> Directed by Martin Neary

Context

The Lamb is a sacred song written for four-part choir and set to an 18th-century poem by William Blake. Tavener wrote the work in 1982 for his nephew's third birthday and records that 'It was composed from seven notes in an afternoon'. In the poem Blake appears to speak as a child ('I a child' in bar 17), but in reality the poem deals with the destiny of the human spirit. The subject of the setting is Jesus (referred to in the Bible as 'the lamb of God') who 'became a little child' (bar 16).

Because of this reference to the birth of Christ, *The Lamb* was first sung at a carol service in Winchester Cathedral on 22 December 1982 and was broadcast two days later as part of the famous Christmas Eve carol service from King's College, Cambridge. It is also sometimes sung as an anthem at the end of the Anglican service of Evensong.

Structure

Bars 1–10 form a setting of the first verse of the poem, bars 11–20 are the setting of the second verse. Although Tavener uses a fuller texture in the second verse, the music is essentially the same and so we can describe the overall form as **strophic**.

The ear tends to notice that the melody of bars 1–2 returns in bars 7–10, giving the impression that verse one is a ternary structure (ABA¹) in which section B is formed by bars 3–6. This is then repeated in verse 2 (A=bars 11–12, B=bars 13–16, A¹=bars 17–20).

Rhythm and word setting

There is no time signature. Although some bars have a distinctly $\frac{4}{4}$ feel, others are much freer. As Tavener indicates at the start, the rhythm is always guided by the words and not by a regular pulse imposed on those words, as occurs in NAM 39, for example. The barlines simply mark the ends of lines in the poem, being given as reference points for rehearsals (and for exams!).

The word setting is largely **syllabic**, although occasionally two notes are slurred together to draw attention to important words. The combination of outward simplicity and underlying sophistication reflects the dual nature of the text – an innocent little lamb, but a lamb who was to be slain as a sacrifice for the sins of the world. This explains the bitter-sweet dissonances, particularly the Am⁹ chord that appears at the words *such*, *all*, *Lamb* and *know* in bars 7–10 (and all four chords with a tenuto dash in bars 17–20). Tavener refers to it as his 'joy–sorrow' chord, and it certainly adds pathos to these passages.

Melody and texture

The opening bar is **monophonic** and uses just four notes from the scale of G major, giving the question it poses a very childlike sense of innocence. Tavener constructs the entire work from this bar.

The addition of the altos in bar 2 creates a two-part **homophonic** texture – we could also describe it as homorhythmic since both parts have the same rhythm. Compare the alto part in bar 2 with the opening melody. Can you see how it is formed? Every interval of the soprano melody has been reused in **inversion**. The soprano part is in G major, its mirror image in the alto is in E♭ major. The simultaneous use of a melody and its own mirror image is used to express the rhetorical question asked of the lamb – 'Dost thou know who made thee?' – the only possible answer is shown to be reflected in the question itself.

The monophonic melody in bar 3 starts with the soprano pitches of bar 2 (G major) and ends with the alto pitches of bar 2 (E♭ major) – these are the 'seven notes' mentioned on the previous page.

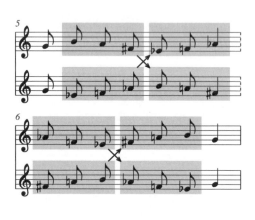

Bar 4 is a **retrograde** version of bar 3 (i.e. the pitches are reused in reverse order), allowing the music to return to G major.

In bars 5–6 the long melody of bars 3–4 is accompanied by its **mirror inversion** (see *left*). Notice how this manipulation allows soprano and alto to exchange three-note cells of the pitches between the surrounding Gs.

In bars 7–10 the opening melody is presented four times in a homophonic texture in which all four parts are heard for the first time. What do you notice when you compare the rhythm of bar 10 with that of bar 9? This is called **augmentation**, and it gives this last repetition of the bar a sense of finality for the end of verse 1.

Verse 2 (bars 11–20) is simply a re-scoring of verse one. Instead of unison sopranos, the first bar is sung by the full choir in octaves, giving weight to the instructional tone of the words ('Little Lamb, I'll tell thee'). Octaves appear for the monophonic statement of bars 13–14, while pairs of voices in octaves (soprano/tenor and alto/bass) are used instead of just sopranos and altos in bars 12 and 15–16. The setting of the final four lines of the second verse is exactly the same as the setting of the final four lines of the first verse. The devotional style of the music arises in part from the very restricted range of the soprano's melody (an augmented 5th, from E♭ to B♮) as well as from the limited dynamic range (*pp* to *mp*).

Harmony and tonality

The four pitches in bar 1 all come from the key of G major and the phrase begins and ends on G. Bar 2 is **bitonal** – the sopranos stay in G major while the inversion of their melody in the alto part suggests E♭ major. However, the resulting clashes are not highly dissonant, and the two keys are reconciled by starting and ending on the same note (G). The phrases in bars 3–4 and 5–6 are similarly anchored to G as starting and ending notes.

However, new light is thrown on the opening melody when it is given a four-part harmonisation in bars 7–10 – all the notes are from the aeolian **mode** on E (E–F♯–G–A–B–C–D–E). Every note of this mode is contained in these bars – there is no sharpening of the 7th degree in the dominant chords (the penultimate chord in each of these bars) and so all of the cadences are modal. Tavener has deliberately exploited the ambiguity created by an idea based on just four pitches to suggest major keys, bitonality and modality within the space of just ten bars.

> Could the ambiguity that can result from basing a piece on a very limited set of pitches be a technique that you could use in your own composing?

Modal writing for unaccompanied four-part choir might seem to hark back to a much older era, as might Tavener's conventional approach to his 'joy–sorrow' chord, which he treats as a double suspension, with the dissonance prepared and resolved in the soprano and alto parts each time it occurs. And yet the resulting rich succession of 9th and 7th chords is not like early music, nor is his use of consecutive 5ths between soprano and tenor on the word 'tender' (and in seven similar places). The resulting mix of old and new is typical of the postmodernist style of this piece, while the repetitive nature of bars 7–10 and 17–20 suggests the influence of minimalism.

Exercise 7

1. What is the total range of the soprano part? On what pitch does every two-bar phrase in the soprano part begin and end?

2. Explain the terms bitonal, monophonic and strophic.

3. How does Tavener ensure that the words are heard clearly?

4. State two ways in which bar 20 is given a more final quality than bar 19.

5. Name the mode in which the *The Lamb* ends. Why can the final cadence be described as modal?

6. Which aspects of the music identify this as a 20th-century work?

7. What were the original performance circumstances of this piece?

Waterloo Sunset (Ray Davies)

Context and forces

NAM 53 (page 483)   CD4 Track 12
The Kinks

Like most British groups of the 1960s, the Kinks began by playing blues-influenced music, but under the direction of singer, guitarist and song-writer Ray Davies they became one of the few groups to resist copying everything American. Davies' lyrics draw on very ordinary aspects of British culture such as afternoon tea, London sunsets, commuters and the taxman, using them as themes for a series of wry miniatures which were still very influential 30 years later in the Britpop style of the 1990s, especially in works such as Blur's album *The Great Escape*.

Waterloo Sunset was released as a single in May 1967. It rose to number 2 in the UK charts and was also included on the album *Something Else* by the Kinks later that year. The song is often described as a rock ballad – a song that tells a story.

The band came from north London and at the time consisted of Ray Davies (lead vocals and acoustic guitar), his brother Dave (lead guitar and backing vocals), Pete Quaife (bass guitar and backing vocals) and Mick Avory (drums). Ray Davies' first wife Rasa is also heard on the recording as one of the backing singers.

The roles of the main vocal and instrumental parts are clearly defined and maintained throughout the song, although the lead guitar has some chordal work in addition to its solo passages and its short **licks** played in dialogue with the singer.

Commentary

Bars		
1–8	Intro	8 bars
9–24	Verse 1 (AABA)	16 bars
25–32	Middle eight ...	8 bars
33–34	and turnaround	2 bars
	Verse 2, middle eight and turnaround (formed by a repeat of bars 9–34)	
35–50	Verse 3 (AABA)	16 bars
51–60	Outro (fade out)	10 bars

'Double-tracked' (bar 8) means that after the vocal solo was recorded, it was sung again and the new recording was mixed with the previous one to create a thicker sound.

The form of the ballad is shown *left*. It is basically strophic, but the three verses are each separated by linking passages and the song starts with an introduction and ends with an outro (or coda).

The main musical ingredient of *Waterloo Sunset* is the five-note **hook** first sung to the words 'Dirty old river' (bars 8–9). This motif is repeated in descending **sequence** for 'must you keep rolling' and again, slightly varied, for 'flowing into the night'. This third appearance of the motif is extended to complete the four-bar phrase we have called 'A'. The downward direction of both motif and phrase echoes the imagery of the lyrics, but right from the start there is a contradiction between such apparent melancholy and the bright key of E major at a fairly fast tempo. We shall explore the effect of this combination later. Phrase A is then repeated to the second line of lyrics, the frequent repetitions of the hook nicely reflecting the words 'makes me feel dizzy'.

Each of the three verses is in 16-bar popular song form – an AABA structure that rose to prominence in the music of Gershwin, Porter, Berlin and other song-writers of the 1920s and 1930s. In this very traditional form the third phrase (B) normally contrasts with the A phrase in melody and harmony. We can see this in bars 16–19 of *Waterloo Sunset* – the hook line is dropped, the lyrics suddenly become defiantly positive ('But I don't need no friends'), the melodic line heads for an aspirational top G♯ on 'need' and the first use of chromatic harmony appears in bar 18. Finally, the verse ends with a return to phrase A, modified at the end, starting in bar 20.

The melody of phrase A is pentatonic (E–F♯–G♯–B–C♯) but the harmonisation makes the E-major tonality totally clear through the use of the three primary triads of that key (I, IV and V). In contrast, the B section (known as the 'bridge' or 'release') introduces chord II (F♯m) and the major version of chord VI (C♯):

A				A				B				A			
E	B⁷	A	A	E	B⁷	A	A	F♯m	C♯	F♯m	B⁷	E	B⁷	A	A
I	V⁷	IV	IV	I	V⁷	IV	IV	II	VI^#3	II	V⁷	I	V⁷	IV	IV

This 16-bar verse is followed by two more structural features that hark back to the popular songs of the early 20th century. The first is a middle eight (bars 25–32) which, following convention, briefly modulates to a related key (the dominant, B major, in bars 25–27). Notice how the bass shadows the lead vocal in a different rhythm – a type of **heterophony**. The second familiar feature is the two-bar extension in bars 33–34. This is known as a turnaround, as it prepares (by means of the extended V⁷ chord) for the return of the main theme and tonic key at the start of each succeeding verse. All three verses use essentially the same music, with just slight differences in the backing tracks.

The introduction is purely instrumental, and begins by defining the key of E major through four bars of dominant 7th below which the bass, in repeated **straight quavers**, descends stepwise from upper dominant to lower dominant. As this all resolves on to a tonic chord of E major in bar 5, the lead guitar plays through the opening A phrase of the song. The descending bass pattern below a B⁷ chord is used again in bars 31–34, becoming an extension of the falling bass in the middle eight. It fulfils the same purpose of introducing the main A phrase, while also serving to unify this turnaround section with the introduction.

The outro reverses the order of events in the introduction. Here the instrumental version of phrase A comes first (starting in the second half of bar 50), accompanied by a more sustained descending bass pattern. It is followed by repeated dominant 7ths in the fade-out bars which match those of the opening (although now the bass remains on the dominant throughout).

With the exception of the two-bar turnaround, all phrases are four-bars in length. Such intensely regular phrasing can make a song sound predictably sectional, but this is disguised by the long pick-up (or **anacrusis**) of the hook, which crosses the gap between sections, and by the guitar licks which fill gaps in the vocal line, as in bars 11, 15 and 23.

The lyrics centre on a person who views the world from his window as a series of images – the dirty old river, the confusing crowds, the dazzling lights, the lovers Terry and Julie meeting at Waterloo station each Friday. He wants no part in the frenzied crowd, he needs no friends and is content to gaze on the sunset. It seems a sad story – a recluse who views the world as an outsider. But the bright tempo and major key of the music seem to tell a more positive tale. And that is one of the ways in which this perfect vignette works its magic – the suggestion in the music that perhaps it really is better indoors than out, that perhaps there really is nothing better

Lyrics

Waterloo is home to one of London's busiest commuter railway stations. It is close to the Thames, which was a very dirty river when this song was written. In 2004 Ray Davies revealed that Terry and Julie were not, as had long been presumed, two well-known actors of the day, but simply two friends of his.

than gazing out of the window at the sunset, that perhaps pride in self is the thing that really matters.

This was very different from the 'boy meets girl, boy loses girl' content of many pop songs of the day. The characteristically British notion of being happy with your lot in life, the very specific references to London, and the ironic juxtaposition of music and lyric all help explain why this song (like most by the Kinks) was not successful in America, but why it has appealed to generations of British listeners, becoming a primary source of inspiration for the Britpop revival of the 1990s.

Damon Albarn, formerly lead singer of the Britpop group Blur, recorded *Waterloo Sunset* (which he described as one of his favourite songs) as a duet with Ray Davies on *The Songs of Ray Davies and the Kinks* (2002).

Exercise 8

1. Explain the meaning of the terms hook, lick and turnaround and give examples of their use in *Waterloo Sunset*.

2. Describe the rhythm of the hook.

3. What is the total range of the lead vocal part?

4. Which of the following statements about the lead vocal is true for the entire song?
    (i)   It is entirely pentatonic.   (ii)   It is entirely diatonic.   (iii)   It is sometimes chromatic.

5. How does the bridge differ from the other three phrases in the verses?

6. In which key does the middle eight begin? How is this key related to the tonic key of E major?

7. What do you notice about the **harmonic rhythm** in most of this song?

Tupelo Honey (Van Morrison)

Context and forces

Van Morrison grew up in Belfast, although he has lived most of his life in America where he developed a unique style of nostalgic music that combines elements of rhythm and blues (which he played in Ireland), rock, jazz, soul and Irish folk music. *Tupelo Honey* is from Van Morrison's 1971 album of the same name. The title refers to a particularly fine honey from Florida and reflects the sweet and mellow style of the mainly autobiographical set of songs on the album.

NAM 56 (page 501)   CD4 Track 14
Van Morrison

Morrison plays acoustic guitar and sings the lead vocal, recorded live with the accompanying studio band (the backing vocals were dubbed on later). In addition to the parts printed in the score, a vibraphone can just be heard in the background – listen for it in bar 36. The rhythmic freedom of song, and especially the vocal line, is influenced by soul, a style that developed in America during the 1960s from a combination of gospel music and rhythm and blues. Look at bars 5–12 to see the extent to which the melody of verse 1 is displaced and adapted in verse 2.

Structure

Tupelo Honey has a fairly standard verse-and-chorus form (with an introduction, an instrumental, a middle eight and a coda). It looks complicated because there are many repeats in the score and neither of the two sections marked 'Coda' is actually a structural coda. Also, you may find the score a little difficult to follow because there is little melodic or harmonic difference between the sections.

The table printed *right* unpacks the repeats and explains the form, but you will need to get used to following the score in NAM while listening to the recording.

Morrison has a reputation for bucking commercial trends, and *Tupelo Honey* is no exception being, at almost seven minutes, very long for a 1971 pop song. The score in NAM is a transcription, made by notating the music from the recording, and it cannot realistically show all the rhythmic subtleties. However, the many syncopations should be obvious, as well as the **cross-rhythms** in bars 33–35, where the acoustic guitar's triplets constantly cut across the electric guitar's semiquavers.

Other features of the song are more straightforward. The vocal line is **pentatonic** (Bb–C–D–F–G), possibly revealing the influence of Irish folk music in Van Morrison's work. Remove the complex rhythms and the basic melodic outline of the start of the chorus (bars 13–16) is shown in the simple pattern *right*.

Do you feel that the music has a hypnotic quality? One reason is that the entire song is constructed from repetitions of the chord pattern heard in its first two bars: | I   IIIc | IV   I | in Bb major. This progression is played four times in each eight-bar section of the song, with the last of these chords changed to V on the second of its four cycles. This chordal **ostinato** anchors the music to the key of Bb major throughout. The song is almost entirely **diatonic**, with just an occasional chromatic passing note in the bass, and there are no modulations.

The hypnotic effect is reinforced by the similarity of the vocal phrases, which mostly have a descending shape and end on notes of the tonic chord. Variety comes from Van Morrison's adaption of this basic material to new contexts. For instance, the start of the middle eight (bar 37) features a climactic top Bb, the highest note in the lead vocal (repeated in the coda, which is based on the middle eight), while the final chorus (bars 45–52) is marked out by frequent returns to a high G. Further variety comes from variations in the bass part and in the guitar **countermelodies**, while the instrumental introduces a texture of free but dense four-part **counterpoint**.

NAM 56 has an improvisatory quality, and yet the texture seems too complex for true improvisation. The reason for this can be found in the way that arrangements of this sort were developed. Mark Jordan, the piano and organ player in this recording, explained the process in a 1972 article for *Rolling Stone* magazine. Because Van Morrison doesn't read music, he plays his melodies to the rest of the band on guitar. They pick up the tunes by ear and by watching his fingers, and then 'flesh out' the material, adding their own suggestions for Van Morrison's approval.

Essentially, then, the arrangement was developed in a cooperative manner by the members of the band. Particular specialist contributions, such as the flute and saxophone solos, were credited to their performers on the original LP record. This method of working meant that details of the song were often changed in live performance, although the version refined in the studio for this recording can reasonably be regarded as definitive.

Bars		
1–4	4 bars	Introduction
5–12	8 bars	Verse 1
13–20	8 bars	Chorus
5–12	8 bars	Verse 2
13–20	8 bars	Chorus
21–36	16 bars	Instrumental
5–12	8 bars	Verse 3 (= verse 2)
13–20	8 bars	Chorus
37–44	8 bars	Middle 8, played as
		‖: 37–40 :‖ 41–44 :‖ 37–40 :‖
5–12	8 bars	Verse 4 (= verse 1)
13–20	8 bars	Chorus
45–52	8 bars	Chorus (varied repeat)
53–56	4 bars	Coda (repeat to fade)

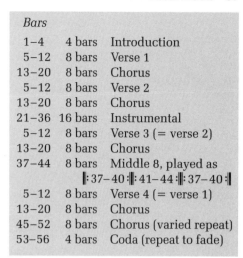

Notice the notation Dm/A for chord IIIc in the score. This is known as a 'slash chord' and indicates that the chord of D minor should be played with the note A in the bass, in other words, as a second-inversion chord.

The arrangement

The inclusion of a short flute solo at the beginning is unusual, al though the flute appears in a number of other Van Morrison song and reflects the composer's roots in Irish folk music. Here it is use to introduce a two-bar hook, played twice, variations of which per meate the song – compare it with the second-verse vocal in bar 7–8, for instance, or compare its second, third and fourth note with the first three notes of the chorus.

The lead guitar is used as a melody instrument for much of th song, largely in the upper part of its range. Initially it is in dialogu with the flute or voice, but from bar 21 it takes part in a comple web of improvised counterpoint with saxophone, high acousti guitar and bass. The wide stereo separation of the recording help to differentiate between the two different types of guitar sound.

There is a gradual build-up of dynamics and texture through th song, and the decoration of its one basic pattern becomes increas ingly impassioned – especially in the instrumental, but also in Va Morrison's increasingly elaborate vocal decoration (culminating i top B♭s at the start of both the middle eight and the coda). The hig tessitura of the vocal and guitar parts, set against a low bass an with piano in the middle, gives the song its warm, rich texture

Exercise 9

1. Explain the terms pentatonic, diatonic and cross-rhythm.

2. Give an example of a chromatic passing note in the bass part.

3. What does the sign ✗ in bar 2 of the drum part mean? (Listen to the recording if you are unsure.)

4. Briefly describe the harmonic rhythm of this song.

5. Compare the styles of bass playing in *Tupelo Honey* and *Waterloo Sunset*, referring to differences in th ways that chords are decorated in both songs.

6. To what extent do differences in dynamics help provide contrast in this song?

7. How is the fade-out (bars 53–56) related to the introduction?

Se quema la chumbambá (Familia Valera Miranda)

Context

NAM 63 (page 534)   CD4 Track 21
Familia Valera Miranda

The large Caribbean island of Cuba was colonised by the Spanis in the 16th century. As a result of the slave labour they importe from Africa to work on the land, new musical styles graduall emerged from the interaction of African and Spanish cultures.

Se quema la chumbambá, recorded in 1994, is a *son* – a type o traditional Cuban music sung to accompany dancing and that i the foundation of modern salsa. This particular type of *son* is calle a *son montuno*, a term referring to its origins among farm worker who sang in call-and-response style. The leader improvised phrase on a *pregón* (a street cry) to which the other workers (the *coro*, o chorus, in the score), responded with an unchanging refrain. Whe the *son montuno* started to be used for social dancing rather tha work, a simple and repetitive chordal accompaniment was adde along with instrumental solos.

You may see *Se quema la chumbambá* described as salsa, but *son* is an earlier style that lacks the saxophones, brass instruments and more complicated harmonies that are normally found in modern salsa.

NAM 63 reflects this structure as well as the fusion of African and Spanish elements that is so characteristic of Cuban music. The maracas, bongo and claves are typical of Latin-American styles, but were developed from African instruments. Also from Africa comes the lively syncopation and the use of call-and-response between soloist and chorus. But the use of the (mainly harmonic) minor scale, tonic and dominant chords, and the inclusion of the *cuatro* (a type of guitar) and double bass, all reflect European (and specifically Spanish) influences.

The most important rhythmic element in *son* is the clave pattern seen in bars 6–7 of NAM 63, which provides the timing for all the musicians. This is known as '3:2 son clave' because there are three notes in the first bar of the pattern and two in the second (in some pieces the order of the two bars is reversed, to give '2:3 son clave'). This repeated, syncopated pattern is often heard in African drumming, from which the son clave originally developed, and all the musicians fit their riff-like parts around it, as shown *right*. In fact, son clave is so pervasive that the players feel its presence, even when the claves are not playing (as in the opening *cuatro* solo).

Another important aspect of the rhythm is the silence in the melodic parts on the first down-beat of alternate bars. This gives the singers a chance to take a breath and in all parts it gives life to the rigid two-bar patterning of the piece. Related to this is the 'anticipation bass', common in much modern *son* and salsa. Look at bars 7, 9 and 11: the last bass note in each of these bars belongs to the chord in the *next* bar – these notes are anticipated a crotchet early, leaving a silence on the following downbeat.

The most European aspect of NAM 63 is the **functional harmony** of its recurring chord pattern: Gm–D⁷–D⁷–Gm, a chordal ostinato based on the most key-defining progression of all: V⁷–I.

The son clave and chord pattern remain all-pervasive, but variety comes from the improvised variations on the *pregón* that begin in the second verse and by the *cuatro* and bongo improvisations in the central section. Both players become increasingly adventurous in moving away from the son clave ostinato, but they occasionally resynchronise with it, as in bar 11 of the *cuatro* solo.

Commentary

A translation of the words appears on page 540 of NAM.

Clave is pronounced 'clah-vay', but the percussion instrument called claves (two hardwood sticks clicked together) is often pronounced to rhyme with raves in English. Although illogical, this can help distinguish between the rhythm pattern and the instrument that often plays it!

3:2 Son clave

Cuatro (bars 1–2)

Pregón (bars 13–14)

Pregón (bars 15–16)

Double bass (bars 9–10)

Exercise 10

1. Why is son clave so important in *Se quema la chumbambá*?

2. Define what is meant by syncopation, giving an example from this song.

3. Which other song that you have studied for this paper features a chordal ostinato?

4. Name the chord outlined by the *cuatro* in bar 2.

5. How would you describe the texture of this song?

6. What makes this style of music so suitable for dancing?

7. Show how NAM 63 reveals a fusion of musical cultures.

For an idea of the type of questions that are set in Section A of the paper, see pages 73–75. Obviously, th
two extracts to be used in 2015 will come from the set works you have studied in this chapter, rather tha
the two printed on those pages. Here are some sample questions for practice in answering Section B of th
paper.

Part B: Investigating Musical Styles

Answer *either* Question 3(a) *or* Question 3(b). You must answer both parts of the question you choose
You should spend no more than 45 minutes on this part of the paper. Remember that you are not allowe
to consult recordings, scores or notes while answering the questions.

3(a)   INSTRUMENTAL MUSIC

(i)   Describe the stylistic features of Poulenc's Sonata for Horn, Trumpet and Trombone (first movement
which show that this music was composed in the 20th century.   (10

(ii)   Compare and contrast the structure and tonality of *Brandenburg* Concerto No. 4 in G (first movement
by Bach and the Piano Sonata in B♭, K. 333 (first movement) by Mozart.   (18

OR

3(b)   VOCAL MUSIC

(i)   Describe the stylistic features of Fauré's *Après un rêve* which show that this song was composed ir
the Romantic period.   (10

(ii)   Compare and contrast the harmony and structure of *Waterloo Sunset* by the Kinks and *Tupelo Honey*
by Van Morrison.   (18

(TOTAL: 28

Rhinegold Education publish a book of practice tests covering sections A and C of this paper, *Edexcel AS
Music Listening Tests*. More practice questions for section B are in the *Edexcel AS Music Revision Guide*.

Set works for 2016

Instrumental music

Sarabande and Gigue from Partita in D (Bach)

Context

One of the most popular types of keyboard composition in the late Baroque period was a set of dance movements known as a suite. These works were not intended for actual dancing, but to be played at home, usually on the harpsichord (the most common keyboard instrument of the time).

NAM 21 (page 249)   CD2 Tracks 10–11
András Schiff (piano)

The two dances in NAM 21 are the fifth and seventh movements of such a suite, published by Bach in 1728 under the Italian title of *partita*. On CD2 they are played on the piano rather than the harpsichord. Bach had a reputation as a great keyboard player and teacher in his day, but his compositions received little attention until scholars rediscovered his surviving works during the course of the 19th century. Now he is appreciated as one of the greatest composers of the late-Baroque era.

The score

Performance directions are rare in music of the Baroque period and earlier. Here there are no dynamics or marks of articulation, and Bach did not even specify speeds since it would have been assumed that musicians would know from experience that sarabandes are played slowly and gigues are fast movements.

The ∿ sign above the last beat of bars 1, 13 and 29 in the sarabande is an upper mordent and implies the rapid alternation of the printed note with the note above. The small C♯ on the first beat of bar 20 is an appoggiatura, played on the beat and then resolving to B. Baroque performers would frequently add their own ornaments, in accordance with the conventions of the time, especially when a passage was repeated. See how many ornaments you can hear in András Schiff's repeats on CD2, track 10.

Structure

As in most Baroque suites, the stylised dances in NAM 21 are in the same key (D major) and each is in **binary form**. This consists of two repeated sections, the first (in both movements) ending in the dominant (A major), and the second passing through other related keys before ending in the tonic. It is convenient to think of the structure as ‖:A:‖:B:‖, but note that the letters A and B don't represent contrasting themes: the initial musical ideas and mood are maintained throughout each movement, as they are in much Baroque music.

Sarabande

The history of the sarabande goes back nearly two centuries before Bach wrote this movement. By 1728 it had long ceased to be used for dancing and had become a stately, if not solemn, movement in triple time, often with a stress or long note on the second beat of the bar. Bach only fleetingly refers to this feature (the minims in bars 1–2) before embarking on a series of complex rhythms that sound as free as an improvisation.

The first section consists of three four-bar phrases, the first ending with a perfect cadence in D, the second with an imperfect cadence in A major (the dominant), and the third with a perfect cadence in A major. Apart from G♯, accidentals indicate chromatic notes.

The longer second section begins with a reworking of material from the first section modulating through the relative minor (B minor bars 19–20) and E minor (bars 21–24) before returning to the tonic key for the last ten bars (see *left*). In these final bars Bach recapitulates most of the first section: bars 29–30 are the same as bars 1–2 and bars 31–32 and 36–38 are slightly modified and transposed versions of bars 6–7 and 9–12 respectively. Movements like this that are rounded off with material from the opening section are described as **rounded binary form**.

The texture is mainly two part, with melodic interest in the right hand and a supportive bass in the left, but is thicker at important structural moments (the beginning and ending of the two main sections plus the return of the first section at bar 29). Bach creates an extraordinary sense of unity by constructing almost the entire movement from motifs heard in its opening few bars.

‖: D - A :‖: Bm - Em - D :‖
   I   V   vi   ii   I

Gigue

The French word gigue is related to the English word jig and is pronounced with a soft initial 'g': *zheeg*.

As was customary in Baroque suites Bach ends with a rollicking binary-form gigue in compound time. The unusual time signature of $\frac{9}{16}$ indicates that there are nine semiquavers per bar, grouped into three very fast dotted-quaver beats.

As in many Baroque gigues, the first 21 bars are in a **fugal** texture. The opening melody is known as the fugal subject and is followed by a fugal answer (the same tune as the subject, but transposed down a 4th) in the left hand of bars 7–12, above which the right hand part is known as the countersubject. After a passage of free **counterpoint** the subject is stated again (left hand, bars 16–21). However, Bach does not intend this to be a full-blown, serious fugue. As early as bar 20 counterpoint gives way to a whirling semiquaver melody accompanied by two-part chords.

Bach introduces what sounds like another entry of the subject in bar 27, but it evaporates after only a bar. A version of the subject reappears in bars 36–41, but the opening arpeggio is turned upside down. The end of this version of the subject guides the music to the expected key of A major and the perfect cadence that marks the end of the first section.

The second section begins with a new fugal subject (bars 49–54). It is answered a 4th higher by the right hand in bars 55–60, beneath which Bach ingeniously fits a complete restatement of the first fugal subject from the start of the gigue. After this the second fugal subject is heard in modified form in bars 64–69 and 74–77 (the latter without its ending) and the final entry of the first fugal subject (without its first two bars) appears in the left hand of bars 86–89.

Unlike the sarabande, the two sections of the gigue are of equal length, but the tonal plan is similar – the first section ends in the dominant and the second passes through a variety of related keys before ending in the tonic.

Exercise 1

. What form did Baroque composers most often use for each of the dances in a suite?

. Name another feature that is normally common to all the dances in a Baroque suite.

. On what instrument might Bach have played this music?

. What sort of dance is (a) a sarabande and (b) a gigue?

. Look at the motif on beat 1 of bar 17 in the sarabande. How is this motif treated in beats 2 and 3 of that bar? Where was this motif *first* heard in the sarabande?

. What happens at bar 29 in the sarabande?

. What melodic feature is common to bar 2 of both dances in NAM 21?

. Look at bar 3 of the gigue. How is this melody treated in bar 4? In which bars of the countersubject does Bach use the same technique?

. Describe what is meant by a fugal texture.

String quartet 'The Joke', movement 4 (Haydn)

For much of his life Haydn was director of music to the Hungarian Prince Esterházy at a magnificent palace 50 kilometres south-east of Vienna. Here he had musicians at his disposal to supply the court with a huge variety of music, ranging from operas, church music and orchestral works, to intimate pieces of chamber music in which the prince himself often took part as one of the performers.

Haydn established the string quartet as the most successful and long-lasting of all **genres** of chamber music. The combination of two violins, viola and cello proved ideal. The instruments blend superbly well and can offer full four-part harmony in a wide variety of textures. By the time Haydn wrote the movement in NAM 16 he had completed at least 30 string quartets, gradually developing a style in which all four instruments are treated as equally important. He had also settled on a four-movement format, typically in the order fast – slow – minuet – finale. The last of these is usually the fastest of the four movements and is often (as here) cast in the form of a jolly **rondo**.

In 1781, after Haydn had completed the six quartets published as his opus 33, he wrote to potential purchasers describing them as 'written in a new and special manner'. Although this statement was perhaps just a marketing ploy, the way in which Haydn provides musical interest in all four parts was certainly a feature that would appeal to the increasing number of amateur musicians who were playing string quartets at home, purely for their own pleasure.

These works are also lighter in style than some of Haydn's earlier quartets and often deliberately humorous. NAM 16 is the finale of the second quartet of the set. It is nicknamed *The Joke* for reasons that will become apparent, but all six quartets contain many appealing features, including melodies that are frequently folk-like in their dancing simplicity.

Context and forces

| NAM 16 (page 202) | CD2 Track 5 |
| The Lindsays | |

Structure

As in many of Haydn's finales, the form of NAM 16 is a rondo, a structure in which a main section in the tonic, called the refrain, alternates with contrasting sections, usually in related keys, called episodes. It is unusual in that the refrain gets shorter each time it appears, and that the second episode is in the tonic key. Although we've used the letters A, B and C to show the structure, the themes in these sections are closely related and so sound very similar.

The refrain (A) has a structure of its own – one that is familiar from our study of Bach's sarabande, since it is in rounded binary form. Its first section is eight bars long and ends with a perfect cadence in the tonic key of E♭ major. It is repeated. The second section (B, bars 8–28), remains in E♭, but is distinguished from section A by:

➤ A slower **harmonic rhythm** at the start (V for two bars, then I for two bars) and a more sustained style of accompaniment

➤ Prominent **appoggiaturas** at the ends of the third and fourth two-bar phrases (bars 14 and 16)

➤ A long dominant **pedal** (bars 16–28) supporting some chromatic colouring (A♮ and G♭, both resolving by step, one to the root and the other to the fifth of chord V).

Bars	Section	Key
0–36	‖:A:‖:BA:‖	E♭ major
36–70	C	A♭, Fm, E♭
71–107	ABA	E♭ major
107–140	C1	E♭ major
140–172	A (Adagio) A¹	E♭ major

These final bars of B form a dominant preparation for the exact repeat of A in bars 28–36, after which the entire second section is marked to be repeated (see *left*).

The first episode (C, bars 36–70) focuses on A♭ major in bars 36–47 and F minor in bars 48–53, but neither key is established with a root-position tonic chord. Haydn then returns to E♭ major for bars 54–70. The **harmonic rhythm** speeds up after the last pedal resolves to chord I of E♭ major (bar 59). This progression includes a sequential rise from tonic to submediant (I–IV–II–V–III–VI in bars 59–61). This creates tension which is released when VIIb of V (the second chord of bar 63) resolves to another dominant pedal of E♭ major in bars 64–68.

The entire rounded binary structure of the refrain (ABA but without any repeats) then returns in bars 71–107.

The second episode (bars 107–140) is a modified repeat of the first episode, so we'll call it C¹. It stays in the tonic key throughout, and ends with yet another another dominant pedal (bars 128–140).

The final refrain is shorn of its B section. It starts with a repeat of just section A in bars 140–148, but then Haydn surprisingly adds a short Adagio that begins with a melodramatic dominant major 9th (bars 148–149) and ends with another perfect cadence in the tonic key.

G.P. in bar 155 and later stands for General Pause. This indicates that everyone is silent in these bars, not that there is necessarily any pause in the pulse. The figure 3 along with the rests in bar 167 indicates that the last of these general pauses extends through three complete bars.

Section A returns, but it is now chopped up into its constituent two-bar phrases by silences (see *left*). The perfect cadence in bars 165–166 seems to be the end – Haydn follows it with three bars of silence to tempt a premature round of applause, but he's playing a joke. Suddenly the refrain starts up again! Before the audience has time to work out what's going on, it fizzles out after only two bars – another joke, since that really is the end.

Nearly all of the thematic material derives from motifs in the opening theme of the refrain. which is underpinned by strongly functional harmony:

Harmonic sequence

In the theme itself motif *y* is inverted (*y¹ above*) then repeated to form the rising scale in bar 6. In bars 9–13 chromatic notes are added to both motifs, and in bars 22–24 the middle note of motif *x* is shortened to produce playful slurred quavers. This new version of *x* is then repeated to form the chromatic **sequence** in bars 24–27.

Many more manipulations of this material occur throughout the movement – try to spot some for yourself.

The nickname for this work should be 'the jokes' for there are more than just the two at the end of the movement. For example, at bar 16 the cello begins a dominant **pedal** that lasts for 13 bars, creating expectancy for a terrific musical event. What actually follows is the tiny eight-second musical squib of the refrain (bars 28–36).

The jokes

The central episode begins with another dominant pedal, this time in the key of A♭ major (bars 36–47). But instead of resolving to chord I in bar 41 the music gets stuck on chord Ic, not once, but four times. Every time this happens chord Ic is marked **sf**, as though Haydn were venting his fury at being unable to find the root position. Haydn then moves down to F minor with a similar lack of success (bars 48–53). Having failed to establish either key, he gives up and returns to E♭ major and, after two abortive attempts (bars 55 and 57), Haydn at last achieves a perfect cadence in bars 58–59. To celebrate his success he uses motif *y* in a rising sequence which leads to … another dominant pedal (bars 64–68)!

By the time we get to the second episode, 54 out of 107 bars have featured prolonged dominant pedals so it is a relief to hear a tonic pedal (bars 107–111) and what sound like some conclusive perfect cadences (bars 120–123). But Haydn hasn't finished – he continues to another dominant pedal (bars 128–141) and some fun with a truncated version of motif *x*. A total silence and melodramatic appoggiaturas (bar 139) lead to a dominant 7th (note the pitch of the viola in bar 140). After another dramatic silence that catchy refrain sneaks in yet again.

Could this be the end? No! A loud dominant 9th ushers in the Adagio almost as if we're in for an extra slow movement, just when we thought it was all over. But all movement stops and the wretched refrain starts up yet again. But this time it is in its death throes – chopped into pieces by the general pause that interrupts every two bars. After the silence has expanded to a total of more than four bars (a long time when you are trying not to giggle) Haydn pulls his last rabbit out of the hat in the shape of the first two bars of the movement which, we now discover, already contain the perfect cadence with which the work abruptly ends.

The score   Note that the viola part is in the alto C clef throughout, and that the *sf* accents in bars 41 and 43 are emphasised by **double-stopping** in the first violin part. Notice also that in the 50 or so years since Bach published his partita, composers had started including much more performance detail in their scores, including dynamic and articulation marks (staccatos, slurs and *sforzandi*).

Style   NAM 16 is typical of the Classical style in many of its features. **Periodic phrasing** – pairs of equal-length phrases sounding like questions and answers – is seen in the example printed on the previous page. This also shows the Classical preference for clear harmonic progressions, centred on chords I and V^7, with regular cadences to define keys. Progressions such as II–V^7–I in bars 35–36 are a feature of the style, as are appoggiaturas both chromatic (B♮ in bar 161) and diatonic (G in bar 165). Finally, the texture of melody-dominated **homophony** (although with plenty of interest in the accompanying parts) is typical of much Classical music.

Exercise 2

1. In harmony, what is a pedal? In which bars does a pedal occur (a) in the viola part, and (b) in the violin 1 part? How do these differ?

2. What is double-stopping? Where is it used on page 206 of NAM?

3. What is meant by harmonic rhythm? In what way is the harmonic rhythm in bars 9–28 different from that in the first eight bars?

4. Which note in the first-violin part of bar 5 is chromatic?

5. In a rondo, what is the difference between the refrain and an episode?

6. Explain the precise meaning of the letters G.P. and the figure 3 in bars 167–169.

Quartet Op. 22, movement 1 (Webern)

Context and forces   Webern's Quartet, completed in 1930, could not be more different from the quartet by Haydn we have just discussed. It is scored for the contrasting timbres of violin, clarinet, saxophone and piano, rather than for the homogenous sound of four string instruments; it is **atonal**, not tonal; and it is contrapuntal, not homophonic.

NAM 8 (page 160)	CD1 Track 10
Jacqueline Ross (violin)	
Ruth MacDowell (clarinet)	
Jan Steele (saxophone)	
Mark Racz (piano)	

The clarinet and saxophone are transposing instruments, but their parts are thankfully printed at sounding pitch in NAM, making it easier to read this complex score. We saw that Haydn, unlike Bach, included a good range of performing directions in his score, but Webern marks almost every note with some kind of instruction. Terms in German can be looked up on page 537 of NAM.

The work has only two movements, although Webern at one stage planned a third, and is most likely to be played by professional musicians at specialist concerts of modern music.

Style   One of the features of late 19th-century music was a tendency to fire up the emotional tension by using successions of chromatic dissonances over complex chords that seldom resolve on tonic harmony. Some early 20th-century composers, such as Schoenberg, continued to develop this style, their dissonances becoming longer and their resolutions ever briefer, until familiar signposts such as tonic and dominant chords became rare. By 1908 Schoenberg realised that by abandoning the concept of key entirely he could use expressive dissonance as freely as he wanted. Without key centres to act as focal points this atonal music at first proved difficult to structure and it was sometimes hard to prevent one particular note sounding like a home note. To help avoid this problem Schoenberg in the early 1920s adopted a technique known as serialism, in which a series of notes replaces tonality as the most important element of the music.

Serial music

The basis of serialism is the arrangement of the 12 pitches of the chromatic scale into a particular series called a tone row. Each note can appear only once in the row, thus helping to avoid the sense that any individual pitch is more important than the others. The row can be used forwards, backwards (known as retrograde), in melodic **inversion** or in retrograde inversion. It can be transposed and in addition any note may be used in any octave. However in strict 12-tone music the pitches must always appear in one of these predetermined patterns – and that is what gives such 12-tone (or dodecaphonic) music its sense of unity and order.

Although the concepts behind serialism sound mathematical, they produced some highly concentrated, expressive, but very dissonant music. The technique was used by Schoenberg's pupils, Berg and Webern, and by other 20th-century composers, such as Stravinsky (in the later part of his life), Boulez and Stockhausen.

Schoenberg, Berg and Webern all lived in Vienna and are collectively known as the Second Viennese School – the first including composers such as Mozart and Haydn who worked in and around Vienna in the Classical period. The word 'school' in this context refers to similarities in style and not to any sort of educational establishment!

Webern was particularly interested in contrapuntal techniques and in his mature works he avoided anything which hints at Romanticism, so do not expect to find sequences, familiar chords or lyrical melodies – his preference was for angular leaps of 7ths and 9ths. Webern's compositions are highly condensed and very short, and often written for unusual combinations of instruments, as in this quartet.

Structure

It takes time to get to grips with Webern's sound-world, but when you listen to the movement can you identify its overall shape? The music doesn't really seem to get going until bar 6, as if the first five bars are just an introduction, and the middle section (bars 16–23) seems to be differentiated by more activity, louder dynamics and wider leaps. At the end of bar 22 the five octaves between the violin's high C and the low C in the left hand of the piano forms the widest range of notes anywhere in the piece – it is clearly a central climax. If you compare bar 28 with bar 6 you might spot that there are similarities – in fact the final part is a varied repeat of bars 6–15.

This gives us the structure shown *right* – an introduction followed by what is basically a **ternary form** (ABA). The three sections marked * all use related material. In fact a more precise (if rather less obvious) description of the structure would be a modernised version of **sonata form**. The main parts of this are labelled in the diagram: the principal ideas are presented in an exposition, they are manipulated in various ways in a development, and then they

Bars	Structure	
1–5	*	Introduction
6–15	A	Exposition
16–23	B	Development
24–27	*	Link
28–39	A	Recapitulation
39–43	*	Coda

Prime, bars 6–10:

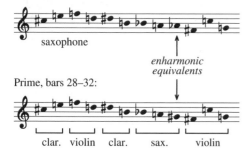

Prime, bars 28–32:

Inversion:

return in altered form in a recapitulation. This is a structure found in Classical music, although in that style sonata form essentially concerns the relationship between different keys and that is clearly not the case here.

Next take a look at the rhythm. Can you spot that almost every rhythm is derived from the three shown *left*?

The first of these rhythmic cells is played in bar 1 by the saxophone, and is immediately repeated by the violin in bar 2. The second is introduced by the left hand of the piano in bar 3 and is immediately repeated in the right hand. The third starts at the end of bar 3 in the violin and is immediately repeated by the saxophone and then the clarinet. While the rhythms themselves sound very modern the technique of basing a piece on a small number of repeated rhythms is very common in the music of J. S. Bach and many other Baroque composers. Another more subtle reference to Bach comes in the length of the piece. NAM 8 appears to show 43 bar numbers, but Webern himself numbered the second-time bars on the last page as variants of the first-time bars, giving 41 bars in all. The significance of this and the potential homage it pays to the name of J. S. Bach is shown in the margin note, *left*.

Now let's turn our attention to the note row. The basic series of 12 pitches (called the prime order) is most easily seen in the saxophone part of bars 6–10. The pitches are printed *left* (but without the changes of octave). This is the melodic material from which the entire work is constructed, but be aware that **enharmonic** notation is used for some notes as the piece unfolds.

The row returns in bars 28–32, at the start of the recapitulation, but here it is split between the instruments so that the tone colour is constantly changing. This sort of melody of differing tone colours is known in German as *Klangfarbenmelodie* (*Klang* = sound or tone, *farben* = colour, *melodie* = melody). The texture of the whole movement is very sparse – tiny groups of notes appear from out of the many rests as tiny dots of colour. This is sometimes described as pointillist – a word used in art to describe paintings formed from tiny dots of colour.

The stave *left* shows the inversion of the row (D♭ at the start is the enharmonic equivalent of C♯). Where the original series rises a minor 3rd, then a semitone, then drops a minor 3rd, the inversion replicates all the intervals in the opposite direction – it falls a minor 3rd, then a semitone, then it rises a minor 3rd … and so on. It can be seen in bars 1–5, divided among the instruments shown on the lower stave *below*:

Prime (transposed):

Inversion:

Do you recognise the pattern on the top stave in this example? It is the original prime order of the note row, transposed down by a tone. The combination of the two versions results in a type of **canon** known as a mirror canon because all of the intervals on the bottom stave are reflected on the other stave by the same intervals moving in the opposite direction. This is another technique found, in an entirely different musical context, in the music of Bach and it is a technique that Webern uses throughout this movement.

Earlier we mentioned that the tone row and its inversion can both be used backwards in serial music. Both of these versions occur in the link passage (bars 24–27), which is essentially a retrograde version of the introduction. Notice how the saxophone pitches in bar 27 are the reverse of those in bars 1–2, and how the violin pitches in bars 26–27 are the reverse of those in bar 2. The following staves shows the complete retrograde versions (and the way they are laid out) and indicates how they compare with versions in the introduction (octave displacements have again been ignored):

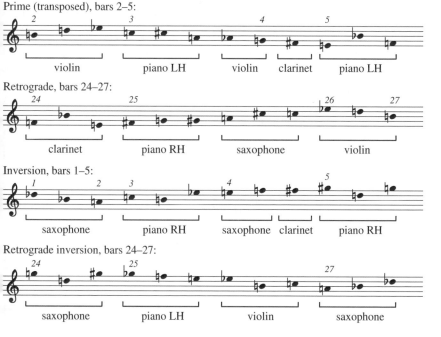

With typical attention to symmetry, Webern reworks this passage one more time to form the Coda (bars 39–43). Be aware that in many editions there is a missing treble clef before the last two saxophone notes.

We have touched on only a few of the complex interrelationships in this movement. Every note is derived from various forms of the tone row, every rhythm from the basic rhythmic cells, and canonic structures permeate the entire, intensely concentrated work.

Exercise 3

1. What is meant by the terms (a) atonality and (b) mirror canon?

2. Explain what is meant by a tone row and describe how it can be transformed in serial music.

3. How does Webern achieve rhythmic unity in this movement?

4. Give the meaning of *mit Dämpfer* in bar 1 and *Dämpfer auf* in bar 24.

5. What is this texture of this music and where would you most likely hear the work performed?

Concerto for Double String Orchestra, movement 1 (Tippett)

Context and forces

NAM 6 (page 120)   CD1 Track 6
Academy of St Martin-in-the-Fields
Conducted by Neville Marriner

The English composer Michael Tippett wrote this work for the South London Orchestra, a group formed in the 1930s to provide performance opportunities for unemployed professional musicians, particularly those who had worked in cinema orchestras in the days of silent film. He conducted them in the first performance of the work at Morley College, Lambeth on 21 April 1940, during the early months of the Second World War.

Although the term concerto usually refers to a work in which one or more soloists and an orchestra are heard together and apart, here Tippett uses it for a piece in which two identically-sized string groups are heard separately and in combination.

The players at his disposal would have been proficient, since the work is technically demanding, but Tippett requires few unusual effects. In only three bars does he require **double stopping**, nowhere does he use solo strings or extreme registers, and special performance techniques are limited to a few pizzicato bass notes and a passage beginning at bar 113 marked *sul tasto poco a poco Naturale* (bowed over the fingerboard then gradually reverting to the normal bowing position).

Rather than employing unusual timbres, Tippett concentrates on the two elements that characterise this concerto – **counterpoint** and **syncopation**. However, although the score looks dense, Tippett often doubles his melodies at the octave above and/or below. Look carefully at the first eight bars and you will discover that they are in lean two-part counterpoint, with each part doubled in octaves and galvanised by syncopation. Throughout the movement, Tippett doubles important melodic lines in octaves to give them clarity and emphasis within the overall string sound.

Notice that the viola parts have an alto C clef, with a treble clef for higher passsages, and be aware that double basses sound an octave lower than written. Tippett includes bowing marks in some places: ⊓ indicates a down bow, and ∨ means an up bow.

Tonality

Although the work is dissonant, it is not atonal. Tippett's use of modes and keys is shown in the diagram *opposite*, but they don't form a hierarchy of related keys as they do in the works by Bach and Haydn that we have studied.

We saw how Webern applied old techniques, such as mirror canons, to new music in his Quartet. Tippett, too, was influenced by aspects of earlier music, although in his case it was modality, which he sometimes uses as a substitute for tonality. He even uses ancient devices such as the **phrygian cadence** (IVb–V in a minor key) in bars 20–21, something we will encounter in the next set work to study (which dates back to at least 1600).

Rhythm

Syncopation makes the music sound jazzy, but do you agree that at the start (and for most of the rest of the movement) there is no clear sense of a regular pulse, as in most types of jazz?

Instead we hear 'additive rhythms' of a type that composers such as Stravinsky and Bartók often used. In this type of rhythmic organisation there is a constant unit of time (the quaver in Tippett's concerto) which is too fast to be perceived as a pulse. These quavers are gathered into irregular units that deny a regular beat. At its simplest such units can produce the type of 3+3+2 rhythms that are found in Latin-American dances (as in bar 15 and other bars marked 'Beat 3'). At a more complex level, additive rhythms can ride rough-shod over the barlines, as in the melody in the second orchestra during the first four bars. It is the contrapuntal combination of two or more rhythmically independent strands that gives this movement its tremendous vitality and excitement.

Tippett's interest in music of the past is also reflected in the structure of the movement. On a small scale there is, embedded within the two contrasting contrapuntal strands of the first four bars, a number of motifs from which most of the rest of the movement is constructed – a method we saw in our study of Bach's dances and Haydn's quartet. Take, for example, the oscillating two-pitch figure of the first four notes. In bars 8–12 it becomes a sequence (violins) that is imitated in **inversion** by violas and cellos. In bars 21–30 this syncopated figure becomes an accompaniment to a new motif (marked *scherzando* – jokingly). On a larger scale the two-note figure, and the motif introduced by the second orchestra in bar 1, help us recognise the start of a section (bars 1–20) that recurs in whole or in part in bars 68–71, 129–146 and 194–197, rather like the ritornellos in Baroque **ritornello form**.

But listen again and you will hear that these sections signal the starting points for something that seems more like **sonata form**, the structure that also influenced Webern. The exposition in Classical sonata form typically consists of a first subject (theme) in the tonic, followed by a transition to a second subject in a related key. Motifs from these themes are manipulated in a development section, after which the exposition returns, with both subjects now in the tonic key. The movement is often rounded off with a coda.

All of these features are present in NAM 6, with the important exception that Tippett doesn't use related key centres (see *right*). The first section that we identified earlier (bars 1–20) corresponds with a 'first subject' and bars 33–67 serve as a 'second subject'. The 'development' (bars 68–128) does indeed manipulate motifs from the first part of the movement, but it is marked by a passage in which additive rhythms give way to simpler rhythms (sounding more like $\frac{2}{2}$ time) starting at bar 95. Look at the first-orchestra staves and compare the violin parts in bars 95–96 with the cello and and bass parts two bars earlier. Do you see that the violins are playing the inverted theme in **augmentation** at bar 95? Now look at the cello and bass parts of bars 99–102. Can you say how this inverted theme has been changed again?

Eventually forward propulsion begins again and additive rhythms return in bars 107–112 until we reach the recapitulation. Almost the whole of the 'first subject' is repeated in bars 129–146 (compare them with bars 1–18) and the 'second subject' in bars 159–193 (which is a transposed and slightly modified repeat of bars 33–67).

The final section, beginning in bar 194, forms a coda in which a new lyrical cello melody (bars 202–208) is combined with earlier motifs, and the descending triadic figures of bars 15–16 are inverted to form the ascending figures in bars 210, 212 and 215. The movement concludes with a contrapuntal fireworks display that ends with a cadence on the note with which the movement began.

Structure

Exposition (bars 1–67)
First subject (bars 1–20)
tonal centre A
Transition (bars 21–32)
aeolian on A and lydian on C leading to …
Second subject (bars 33–67)
tonal centre G

Development (bars 68–128)
Unrelated tonal centres such as A (bars 68–75), C♯ major (bars 80–89) and A♭ major (bars 107–112)

Recapitulation (bars 129–193)
First subject (bars 129–146)
tonal centre A
Transition (bars 147–158)
modified to maintain A as the chief tonal centre
Second subject (bars 159–193)
tonal centre A

Coda (bars 194–232)
more unrelated tonal centres but ending with a cadence that features the two chief tonal centres: G (now lydian in bars 228–231) and A (with a bare-5th chord in the last bar)

Exercise 4

1. In what way does NAM 6 differ from most works described as a concerto?

2. Why does Tippett use $\frac{8}{8}$ and not $\frac{4}{4}$ as the time signature?

3. Compare the music played by the three lowest parts of the first orchestra in bars 5–6 with the music the first orchestra plays in bars 1–2.

4. How is the opening motif from bar 1 treated when it returns in bar 8?

5. What is the significance of the instruction 'Beat 3' in bar 15?

6. Explain the meaning of *sotto voce* (bar 148) and *cantando* (bar 213). Use a music dictionary or the internet to help if you are not sure.

7. Briefly mention some of the variety of string-orchestra textures that Tippett uses in this work.

Vocal music

Flow my tears (Dowland)

Context and forces

NAM 33 (page 347)   CD3 Track 11
James Bowman (countertenor) with
David Miller (lute) and Mark Caudle
(bass viol).

This work began life as a pavane for solo lute, a plucked string instrument with frets like a guitar, written by the English composer John Dowland in the late Renaissance, probably around 1594. The pavane was a slow processional dance in duple time, and Dowland called his work the *Lachrimae Pavan* (tearful pavane) to reflect its sad mood.

Melancholy was all the rage in Elizabethan England, and Dowland's piece became the hit of its day. Many composers arranged it and Dowland himself produced two later versions, one of which is NAM 33, in which he 'texted' the music (that is, added words) to turn it into a lute song – a song with lute accompaniment.

The song was published in 1600, as part of a collection of 22 songs by Dowland, which was circulated widely. It would have been performed by amateur musicians at home, and by professional musicians at court. Dowland himself was employed as a royal lute player, first to the King of Denmark and later to King James I of England. The influence of *Flow my tears* can be seen in a number of early 17th-century works based on Dowland's original, including the keyboard variations by Sweelinck in NAM 20.

In the 1600 publication the song is printed with the lute part in tablature. This showed the player where to stop each of the strings of the lute (rather like the 'tab' used by some modern guitarists). The vocal part was printed above the lute tablature since the same person usually performed both parts. Alongside this is a bass part for either a second singer or (as used on CD3) a bass viol – a low-pitched, bowed-string instrument. This part was printed at 90 degrees to the tablature so that both performers could sit at a table and read their parts from the same book.

The vocal part on CD3 is sung by a countertenor – a man trained to sing falsetto in a range higher than a tenor (a voice sometimes described as 'male alto').

The song is divided into three repeated sections by the three main cadences in A minor:

➤ Bars 1–8, which end with a perfect cadence

➤ Bars 9–16, which end with an imperfect cadence

➤ Bars 17–24, which end with a perfect cadence.

Both perfect cadences have a **tierce de Picardie** (the C♯ in the chord of A major). Both are also decorated with **suspensions** (shown *right* in undecorated form). This type of suspension is called a 4–3 suspension because of the intervals it forms above the bass note. Another very common type of suspension is heard at the start of bar 2, where the lute holds a 7th (E) above F in the bass, and then resolves this dissonance by falling to D, a 6th above the same bass note. This is known as a 7–6 suspension for similar reasons.

Bars 15^4–16 feature a **phrygian cadence**, a type of imperfect cadence that consists of the progression IVb–V in a minor key.

Dowland uses **false relations** as an expressive device. For example, in bar 5 the lute's G♮ followed by the vocal G♯ creates a particularly poignant effect to reflect the sad words.

All of the features mentioned *above* (suspensions, false relations, phrygian cadences and the tierce de Picardie) are characteristic features of late-Renaissance music and help to identify the style.

The key is A minor, defined by the three main cadences we have described. However, the descending melodic minor scale introduces a G♮ in falling phrases (such as those in bars 1 and 9). This note is sometimes harmonised by a chord of C major (bar 9) or G major (bar 5^3), the latter adding a touch of modality to the music each time it appears.

Rhythm is used flexibly to give a declamatory character to the text. In the first phrase the word 'fall' seizes the attention through the use of syncopation, as does 'infamy' in bar 6. The word setting is almost entirely **syllabic**, but on CD3 James Bowman adds a little embellishment in the repeat of bar 15 and in bar 23.

The vocal melody has a fairly narrow range of a 9th but features some expressive leaps, such as the minor 6th in bar 1. What is most remarkable is the way Dowland, taking his cue from the poetic image of falling tears, unifies the whole song by a falling 4th figure. This 'tear motif' is first heard as a scalic descent of a perfect 4th, from tonic to dominant (bar 1). It is immediately repeated with much greater anguish, caused by starting a 3rd higher, on an off beat (bar 1^4), and descending through a diminished 4th from C to G♯. Elsewhere the falling 4th is heard unadorned (bar 3) and in sequence (bars 20–21). See how many other examples of this figure you can find.

Although the texture can correctly be described as melody and accompaniment, the lute part is often more contrapuntal than homophonic. In bars 12–14 notice how the vocal solo is imitated by the lute in a rising-3rd motif, the rests perhaps expressing the poet's gasping for air between his 'teares, and sighs, and grones'.

Other examples of **word-painting** include the reservation of the highest note of the song for 'Happie' in bar 20 and the unusual interval of a diminished 4th following the word 'hell' in bar 22.

Scholars believe that pitch in the late Renaissance was lower than it is today, which is reflected by the fact that the performance on CD3 is a tone lower than the music printed in the score.

Exercise 5

1. What is a tierce de Picardie? Where does one occur on page 348 of NAM?

2. Explain what is meant by a phrygian cadence and give an example of one in the first eight bars of this song.

3. Give the bar and beat numbers on which you hear suspensions in the middle section (bars 9–16).

4. The first syllable of the word 'Happie' in bar 20 is set to the highest note in the vocal part. How else does Dowland draw attention to this word?

5. In bar 22, G♮ in the bass is followed by G♯ in the melody (on the word 'hell') and then G♮ in the lute part. What term describes this sort of tonal conflict?

6. Briefly describe how the sound of the lute on the recording differs from the sound of a modern acoustic guitar.

7. On the recording this song is sung by a counter-tenor. Describe this type of voice, and explain why the recording of the song on CD3 is a tone lower than written.

Locus iste (Bruckner)

Context

NAM 30 (page 305)   CD3 Track 8
Christ Church Cathedral Choir Oxford
Conducted by Stephen Darlington

Locus iste, written in 1869 by the Austrian composer Bruckner, is a motet – a short piece of sacred music with Latin words to be sung *a capella* (unaccompanied) by a choir. The text of this motet ('This is a place that God has made') is traditionally sung to celebrate the dedication of a church. It was composed for the cathedral of Linz in Austria, where Bruckner was organist from 1856 to 1870. Begun in 1855 (and not finished until 1924) it is thought that *Locus iste* was first sung in 1869 at the opening of one of the chapels in the gigantic new cathedral.

Bruckner would have expected the two top parts to be sung by boys. On CD3 the soprano part is sung by boy trebles and the alto part by male altos.

Bruckner ensures that the words can be heard clearly, even in the echoing vaults of a large cathedral, by using a mainly **homophonic** texture in which each phrase of the text is repeated. For the same reason, the word-setting is **syllabic**, apart from bars 40–42 where a **melisma** in all parts highlights the word God (*Deo*).

Bruckner also takes account of the effect of reverberant acoustics by the judicious use of silence – short at the end of bars 4 and 33, longer at the end of bars 20 and 29, and extended to a full five beats after the reference to God in bar 40.

Structure

The motet is written in C major and in **ternary** form (ABA¹). The first A section ends at bar 12¹ with an imperfect cadence. This leads to a central section (B), which ends in bar 29 with another imperfect cadence in C major. The first ten bars are then repeated and extended (A¹) to end with a sustained perfect cadence.

The simple C major melody of the first four bars at first sounds as it is repeated in sequence, but it is subtly varied so that, having passed through G major, it ends back in C.

Commentary

The tonality is more varied in the B section. For the second phrase of the text ('a wonderful mystery') Bruckner devises an aspiring melodic ascent, first to an imperfect cadence in D minor (bar 16), then to the same cadence in E minor (bar 20). Bar 21 introduces a thinner three-part texture of hushed chromatic harmonies returning to an imperfect cadence in the tonic at bar 29.

In the ensuing repeat of the opening, the cadence originally heard in bars 11–12 is chromatically extended – Bruckner marks this passage with a crescendo leading to a loud chord in bar 42 that will echo around large churches in the rests that follow, before the final pianissimo cadence in C major.

Variety comes from contrasting the four-part texture of most of the setting with the three-part texture of bars 21–29, where the basses get a well-earned rest after having started four phrases before the rest of the choir enters. The last two of these are imitated (rather freely) by the sopranos and Bruckner also includes **imitation** by **inversion** between the tenors and sopranos in bars 21–26.

The fact that *Locus iste* is a Latin motet for unaccompanied choir could mislead the casual listener into assuming that it must be from the Renaissance. Indeed, Bruckner was interested in old music and uses some familiar friends that you will remember from our study of Dowland: the B♭ in the bass of bar 13 forms a **false relation** with the B♮ in the soprano part of the previous bar, and there is a **phrygian cadence** in bars 15^4–16^2, albeit spiced up with an **anticipation** on its first chord (E in the soprano) and a **suspension** on its second chord (D in the tenor).

Style

However, the motet has a number of other features which identify it as Romantic music – warmly expressive melodies, dramatic contrasts of dynamics, some unusual melodic intervals (such as the major 7th in the soprano between bars 9 and 10), several chromatic passages, some rich harmonies, unprepared discords (alto, bar 22) and lingering dissonances (soprano and alto, bar 46). But all of these devices are used in great moderation by Bruckner and in a far less flamboyant way than most of his Romantic contemporaries.

Exercise 6

1. What is the total range of (a) the soprano part, and (b) the bass part in this motet? How do these ranges compare with the vocal range in Dowland's lute song?

2. How else does the vocal writing differ from that in Dowland's song?

3. Compare the soprano parts in bars 13–16 and 17–20. What technical device does Bruckner use here?

4. To what extent is imitation used in this motet?

5. Which features of this piece do you feel make it appropriate for use as church music?

Summertime (Gershwin)

NAM 41 (page 366)   CD3 Track 19
Leona Mitchell (soprano)
Cleveland Orchestra and Chorus
Conducted by Lorin Maazel

Context

George Gershwin achieved enormous success as a composer of popular songs, musicals and film scores in America during the 1920s and 1930s. He also wrote several works for the concert hall that combine elements of popular music and jazz with classical genres such as the concerto, most notably in his *Rhapsody in Blue*.

Porgy and Bess, completed in 1935, was another work in which he fused together different traditions: in this case the idea of an opera which sought to portray (albeit through white-American eyes) the lifestyle and music of African-Americans from the south of the USA. The result is often referred to as an 'American folk opera'.

In *Porgy and Bess* the songs are not discrete items separated by spoken dialogue as they often are in musicals. Instead, the dialogue is set to music and each item flows into the next without a break. Thus the introduction in NAM 41 is actually a continuation from the opening chorus and the rests in bar 46 are, in the stage show, filled by chords that crescendo into the next section.

'Summertime' occurs early in the work, forming part of a long opening number. Initially, the image of Clara, a mother singing a tender lullaby to her baby on a sultry summer evening, seems to be just part of the atmospheric 'scene setting' established during the first few minutes of Act 1. However, later in the opera we see both of the child's parents perish in a storm, and a reprise of 'Summertime' is sung to the orphaned baby by another character in the drama, adding great poignancy to the final phrase, 'With Daddy an' Mammy standin' by'.

Structure and texture

The song is in modified **strophic** form – in other words, the music of verse 1 is repeated, with adaptations, for verse 2. The main changes in the second verse are a violin **countermelody** (not heard in the recording on CD 3) and a vocalise (wordless singing) for two and then three-part womens' voices. In both verses there are four four-bar phrases, forming the pattern ABAC. Melodic fragments in the accompaniment fill the gaps in the vocal part so the music is continuous.

The texture of the song is melody-dominated **homophony**, in which the accompaniment has a largely supportive role. The texture is thickened in the second verse by the countermelody and vocalise, although the latter mainly doubles orchestral parts.

Harmony and tonality

The key of the song is B minor, although this is not obvious in the first bar, which is the end of the link from the previous section. The falling minor 3rd (F♮–D), one of the most characteristic sounds of the blues, was heard many times in the opening minutes of the opera, but the replacement of F♮ by F♯ (the dominant of B minor) in bar 2 signals the start of a new number and the new key, which is confirmed by a **dominant pedal** on F♯ in bars 3–7.

Over this pedal, the clarinet part falls in 3rds through every pitch of the descending melodic scale of B minor. The gentle rocking of the child in Clara's arms is suggested by the continuation of the clarinet part as it oscillates between the sharpened 6th and 7th degrees of the ascending melodic minor (G♯–A♯).

Both the dominant pedal and the leading note (A♯) resolve at the double barline to the type of chord that colours the whole song: a bitter-sweet minor triad with an added major 6th. The rocking motion of the lullaby continues with the alternation of Bm^6 and C♯m^6 in bars 8–11. These added 6ths on chords I and II of B minor are repeated in bars 16–19^2 thus supplying the harmony for nearly alf of the verse. The harmony is richly expressive, but if we strip way Gershwin's blue notes, added notes and chromaticism, and lentify just one main chord per bar, the 16-bar blues chord pattern a B minor that supports the melody is revealed (it is much easier o hear on CD3 than to analyse from the score):

bars	8	9	10	11	12	13	14	15	16	17	18	19	20	21	22	23
chord	Bm	Bm	Bm	Bm	Em	Em	F♯	F♯	Bm	Bm	Bm	Bm	D	E	Bm	Bm
	I	I	I	I	IV	IV	V	V	I	I	I	I	III	IV	I	I

he same harmonic progressions are used in verse 2 until bar 40. he B-minor chord in this bar marks the beginning of a **circle of ths** heard against the soprano's sustained **tonic pedal**. Each of the ass notes B–E–A–D–G–C♮–F♯–B) is the root of a triad or 7th hord, except in bar 41^3 (Em^7/A) and bar 43^3 (F♯^{13} = V^{13}). Although his looks complicated, the effect is of a steady march toward the nal perfect cadence.

he extension of the traditional 12-bar blues chord pattern into a nore European 16-bar length, and its enrichment with complex, azz-like harmonies, is just one of many examples of musical fusion hat permeate 'Summertime'. Here are some more:

Style

rom the blues comes the clashing E♮ and E♯ in bars 14^2 and 32^2. n classical music this would be known as a false relation but in the ontext of this work the E♮ is a **blue note**.

rom jazz comes the use of **swing quavers** in the performance. The lotted rhythms of bar 9 are sung approximately as shown *right* Gershwin could have notated them as even quavers but jazz nusicians would still interpret them roughly as shown). Also nfluenced by jazz is the gentle **syncopation**, which is sometimes mprovised ('Fish' in bar 11) and sometimes notated ('Oh yo' daddy's ich' in bars 15–16). Both swing quavers and syncopation are also ometimes notated in the accompaniment (for example, bar 19).

rom black-American folk music such as the spiritual comes the se of the **pentatonic** scale on which the solo melody is based: 3–D–E–F♯–A (the C♯ in bar 14, repeated in bar 32, is the only note n the vocal part outside this pattern). From the same source comes he use of **portamento** (the slides between notes), notated in bar 21 ut added by the singer in bar 10. Her ecstatic embellishment of he ending is an effect often heard in gospel music.

rom popular music of the 1930s comes the lush vocabulary of :hromatic harmony (bars 20–22), chromatic melody (bars 14–15 in he accompaniment) and chords with added 6ths (bars 8–11), 7ths bar 12), 9ths (bar 25) and 13ths (bar 43^2). Also from popular and ilm music comes the added crooning of the women's voices in verse 2.

rom western art music comes the use of an orchestra based on strings, with flute and oboe adding colour, and also the form of the song, in which the ABAC phrase structure of each verse is totally mlike the typical AAB phrase structure of the blues.

Exercise 7

1. What is the form of this song and what is the only non-pentatonic note in its melody?

2. How is the music of bar 5 used in bars 6–7? What is the function of the F♯ in the bass that run throughout these bars?

3. Compare the motif sung by Clara in bar 9 with the motif played by the flute in bar 22. How does the flut motif differ in pitch? How do both of these motifs differ in rhythm from what you hear on the recording

4. Name the type of scale sung by the first sopranos of the backing choir in bars 41–44.

5. Which two motifs heard earlier in the song are used to form the final bass phrase in bars 44–46?

6. Describe as precisely as possible how the singer embellishes her last note.

7. Gershwin describes this song as a lullaby. Which aspects of his music give the song the character o a lullaby?

Sequenza III for female voice (Berio)

Context

The Italian composer Luciano Berio (1925–2003) is particularl remembered for the series of 14 works he wrote between 1958 an 2002 entitled *Sequenza*. Each is composed for a single instrument apart from this one, which is for solo female voice, and each i technically demanding. Berio fully explores the potential of the sol instrument or voice, often through the use of unusual methods o sound production (referred to as 'extended techniques'). Berio sai that the title *Sequenza* is 'meant to underline that the piece wa built from a sequence of harmonic fields from which the othe strongly characterised musical functions were derived'.

NAM 11 (page 171)   CD1 Track 15
Cathy Berberian

Sequenza III is one of a number of works that Berio wrote for hi first wife, the famous singer Cathy Berberian, who performs th piece on CD1. It was written in 1966 and first performed on Radi Bremen in Germany. It is most likely to be heard in concerts an festivals of modern music, although performances are rare becaus of the very specialised nature of the vocal techniques required. I fact, Berio later considered rescoring the work for three voice because he felt that few singers apart from Berberian could manag it alone. Despite this, the work has been performed and recorde a number of times by other singers.

The work includes a strong element of 'performance art' as th composer's opening note on page 171 of NAM makes clear. Th soloist may be a singer, an actor or someone who is both. It als encompasses a vast range of extended vocal techniques, outline on page 172 of NAM. Berio said that he was very sensitive to wha he called the 'excess of connotations that the voice carries'. He hel the view that sounds made by the voice, whether song, speech o just noises, always mean something, and this meaning creates range of associations.

Such associations are intensely concentrated in *Sequenza III*, whic highlights the extreme flexibility of the voice and the way in whic human states (tense, witty, urgent, giddy and so on) can change i a moment. This is reflected in *Sequenza III* by, for example, laughte transforming into operatic high notes, or a cough becoming part o the range of vocal expression. The three main elements of the piece are formed by:

➤ Fragmenting and reordering the text

➤ Using vocal gestures such as muttering, coughing or laughing

➤ Creating a range of expression through abrupt shifts in mood.

The transitions between these, and between the various levels of speech and song, happen very fast – so fast, in fact, that you can get the impression that all occur at once.

Sequenza III is a vocal portrait of a woman's relationship with her voice, but it is also puzzling and disturbing. Are we hearing what is going on inside her head? Is she dreaming aloud? Why do her moods change so rapidly? The first and last identifiable word in the work is 'sing': could *Sequenza III* reflect the woman's experience of finding that song is the best way to articulate her emotions?

The basis of the piece is the poem by Markus Kutter printed on page 172 of NAM. Study the way it is laid out. Are you meant to read it horizontally, vertically or perhaps even diagonally? Berio's treatment of it includes:

Commentary

➤ Using selected phrases ('give me a few words')

➤ Choosing words to make up new phrases ('sing to me')

➤ Splitting words into separate phonemes (so that 'truth' becomes 't – r – uth'

➤ Changing or removing phonemes to make new words (so that 'sing' becomes 'sin' and 'me' becomes 'we')

➤ Interpolating new phonemes into the middle of words (so that 'woman' becomes 'wo – [u] – man'.

Alongside his fragmentation and rearrangement of the text, Berio uses five different types of vocal expression:

➤ Streams of fast, clearly articulated sounds (such as muttering or laughing)

➤ Short vocal or body noises (tongue clicks, coughs, finger snaps, sighs and so on)

➤ Pitched singing (with mouth closed as well as open) and with intervals shown either approximately (on a three-line stave) or more precisely (on a five-line stave)

➤ Sounds that involve changes in timbre (special types of trills and tremolos, or the hand cupped over the mouth)

➤ Pauses (for breath or hesitation).

Berio contrasts these as vividly as possible, to reflect the woman's rapid mood swings. For example, the sustained singing at 0'20" in the score is preceded by tense muttering and mouth clicks.

The work has no sense of metre and is **atonal**. With no cadences or section breaks, plus a setting that doesn't follow the order of the words in the poem, there are no familiar signposts to give the work structure. But it is underpinned by a dramatic scenario that gives shape to the piece and which we can trace using the timings printed in the score:

0'00"   The entrance of the woman
0'21"   Illustrations of her contrasting moods
1'48"   Rather disturbed singing
4'29"   The first anxiety attack
5'16"   Calming down a little, but building to …
6'49"   The second anxiety attack (and climax of the work)
7'26"   A return to a still precarious state of mind.

> The timings listed here relate to those in the score rather than those on CD1, where the performance is a little faster than Berio indicated.

Structures of this type are described as episodic – a series of discreet episodes. Within them, Berio manipulates a series of shorter units, rather like motifs in more conventional music. They correspond with the woman's range of moods and fall into five categories:

A   tense (urgent, nervous, apprehensive, intense)
B   anxious (bewildered, desperate, whimpering, whining, relieved)
C   hyperactive (witty, giddy, ecstatic, excited, coy)
D   dreamy (distant, impassive, wistful, languourous, faintly)
E   serene (noble, calm, joyful, tender)

Let's look at how Berio weaves these into his episodic structure. The work starts with motifs from group A, but D is introduced at 0'21" and, as noted *above*, changes of mood (between A and D) then start to appear, including the combination of A and D ('dreamy and tense') at 1'10". A brief element from C ('giddy', just before 1'30") is sandwiched between more of the tense A emotions, to be followed by the first group B state ('relieved') at about 1'43", just before the end of the second episode.

These mood swings provide contrast but they mostly happen too rapidly and randomly to provide a conventional musical structure. Nevertheless, in the final 50 seconds of the work, it should be clear that the tense and anxious emotions of groups A and B have all disappeared, and the piece eventually ends with the dreamy and serene moods of groups D and E.

The score   Graphic scores became popular in the 1960s. The type used here allows Berio to specify events and timings fairly precisely, so the music is not really aleatoric (music determined by chance), even though the indications of pitch and rhythm are relative and allow the performer considerable freedom of interpretation.

Exercise 8

1. Is *Sequenza III* merely a showpiece for the voice, or does it make more profound statements as a work of art?

2. Why do you think Berio wrote this specifically for a female voice?

3. In what ways might *Sequenza III* challenge an audience used to listening to more traditional music? Do you think that such a challenge to orthodox views can have beneficial results?

4. Cathy Berberian described *Sequenza III* as 'like an X-ray of a woman's inner life'. To what extent do you agree with this view?

You Can Get It if you Really Want (Jimmy Cliff)

This was a set work in 2014, so you will find a discussion of it on pages 71–72 of this guide. When you work the exercise on page 72, omit the final question.

NAM 55 (page 496)   CD4 Track 13
Desmond Dekker and the Aces

Don't Look Back in Anger (Noel Gallagher)

Oasis was formed in Manchester in 1991 by Noel Gallagher (lead guitarist) and his younger brother Liam (vocalist). The band also includes rhythm guitar, bass guitar and drums, the players of which have changed over the years. Oasis rose to fame in 1994 with the release of their first album, *Definitely Maybe*, and quickly became known as one of the leading bands in the Britpop movement of the mid 1990s. Britpop was a reaction against the electronic dance music and American grunge bands that were then in vogue, and found its inspiration in the music of guitar-based British pop groups of the 1960s, such as the Beatles and the Kinks.

Don't Look Back in Anger comes from Oasis' second album, *(What's the Story) Morning Glory*? Released in October 1995, it went straight to number 1 in the UK album charts, and four of its tracks became hit singles, including NAM 57, which was released as a single in February 1996. *Don't Look Back in Anger* has become a much-loved number at Oasis' live concerts, at which the audience is often encouraged to join in singing the chorus. It reflects several important musical features of the Britpop style:

➢ A lyrical vocal melody

➢ Regular four-bar phrasing

➢ Simple root-position chords

➢ A verse-and-chorus structure

➢ An instrumentation based around guitars and drum kit.

The lyrics, too, are characteristic of Britpop, with their nostalgic tale of a relationship that has faded away.

Noel Gallagher's song-writing was influenced by John Lennon of the Beatles, and this song includes two acknowledgements of the debt. Firstly, the alternation of broken chords of C major and F major for piano in the introduction, along with the semiquaver figures at the end of bars 2 and 4, recalls the introduction to Lennon's song *Imagine* (although there are differences in detail). Secondly, the lyric in bars 13–16 refers to Lennon's famous protest against the Vietnam war. He invited the press to photograph him and Yoko Ono during and after their honeymoon, in bed discussing peace.

The texture of the song is melody-dominated **homophony**, in which the voice is supported by a chordal accompaniment on piano, guitars and organ. A dense wall of sound is created by the combination of a busy, low bass part (as in bars 13–24), repeatedly strummed guitar chords (the quaver and semiquaver rhythms in bar 5 form a template for much of the rest of the song), the use of a low register on the piano (both staves are in the bass clef) and a recording that is bass-heavy with a good deal of reverberation.

Context

NAM 57 (page 509)   CD4 Track 15
Oasis

The song's title is possibly an ironic reference to John Osborne's play *Look Back in Anger*, written 40 years earlier and made into a film in 1958. Its portrait of domestic realism was an important influence on 1960s British culture.

Texture and instrumentation

The scoring is reduced from bar 59 onwards, and the heavy bass fades away, resulting in a much more transparent texture for the ending, although all instruments return for the quiet final chord.

From bar 13, the texture is thickened by strings in octaves, and later in four-part chords, again in a low range. These seem to be sampled sounds, played on a **mellotron**, an instrument that uses a keyboard to trigger the playback of sounds recorded on loops of tape.

> The mellotron was used by a number of British pop groups in the 1960s and its presence here is another indication of Oasis' respect for the music of that era.

Variety is provided by the instrumental section in bars 33–34, in which the singer makes way for a lead-guitar solo improvising on the chords of the first half of the chorus. The lead guitar also provides the link (bars 33–35) before the second verse, and often plays short **licks** between vocal phrases, as in bars 14, 16, 18 and 24. The mild distortion on this part is another technique that is more redolent of the 1960s than of the heavily-distorted guitar parts common in the 1970s and 1980s.

The bass-guitar part is entirely functional, being mainly confined to the root of the current chord, with only minimal decoration.

The drums enter in the middle of bar 4 with a **pick-up (anacrusis)** to introduce the vocal. They maintain a steady beat throughout most of the song, with bass drum on beats 1 and 3, and snare drum emphasing the **backbeats** (beats 2 and 4). However, the part is a good deal more complex than the drum part in the score, and both bass and snare drum have additional notes in each bar. Short **fills** on the tom-toms project the music forward at the end of sections (as in bars 12 and 24), and there is a one-bar solo drum **break** in bar 44. Continous semiquavers on tambourine are added to the basic drum-kit part in several sections.

Tonality and harmony

The song is in C major throughout, with a clear sense of tonality resulting from the use of repeated progressions of root-position chords. Each of the four patterns is four bars long, and together they form the building blocks of the entire song:

Pattern A	| C	G	| Am	E	| F	G	| C	Am G |
Pattern B	| F	Fm^7	| C		| F	Fm^7	| C	|
Pattern B^1	| F	Fm^7	| C		| G		| G♯dim	|
Pattern C	| Am	G	| F		| G		| G	|

If pattern A sounds familiar, it is because it is a variant of the chord progression heard 28 times in succession in Pachelbel's famous Canon. Pachelbel's harmonies have, in fact, become a standard chord progression used in many pop songs, most notably in the Farm's 1991 hit, *All Together Now*, revived as England's anthem for the Euro 2004 football cup. Noel Gallagher's version differs from Pachelbel's towards the end and also in his choice of E major rather than E minor as the fourth chord. There are just two other chromatic chords in the entire song: Fm^7 in pattern B is a **substitution chord** for F major, and G♯dim at the end of pattern B^1, which leads nicely into the chord of A minor at the start of pattern C since it is chord VII in the key of A minor (there is no actual modulation to A minor because G♮ returns almost immediately).

All of the other chords are diatonic. Few chords have 7ths or any other sort of added note, but the vocal melody adds frequent passing dissonances.

The four chord patterns we have discussed are arranged as follows to create the modified verse-and-chorus form of the entire song:

Structure

		Bar numbers	*Chord pattern*
Introduction	4 bars	1–4	B (but with chords of F instead of Fm^7)
Verse 1	8 bars	5–8	A
		9–12	A
Pre-chorus	12 bars	13–16	B
		17–20	B^1
		21–24	C
Chorus	8 bars	25–28	A (with new melody)
		29–31	A (omitting 4th bar)
Link	4 bars	32–35	A (last bar of chorus overlaps with start of link)
Verse 2	8 bars	Repeat of bars 5–12 with new words	
Pre-chorus	12 bars	Repeat of bars 13–24	
Chorus	8 bars	Repeat of bars 25–28 followed by	
		29–32	A (now completed in the 2nd time bar)
Pre-chorus (instrumental)	12 bars	33–36	B
		37–40	B^1
		41–44	C
Chorus	8 bars	45–48	A
		49–52	A
Chorus	9 bars	53–56	A
		57–61	A^1 (C G | Am | F | Fm^7 | Fm^7)
Coda	4 bars	62–65	A^2 (C G^7 | Am E | F G♯dim (G$^{7♭9}$) | C)

Because of the way the final chorus merges into the coda, it could equally well be argued that the latter starts with the change to a slower tempo in bar 58.

In the previous choruses the title **hook** (that is, the phrase sung to 'Don't look back in anger') ended over a chord of F major. In bar 60 a modification of pattern A leaves the voice suspended over a chord of Fm^7, the chromatic chord that earlier coloured pattern B. As in bars 13, 15 and 17, it resolves to the tonic chord, but here it is sustained for two full bars at a slow tempo.

The final appearance of pattern A in bars 62–65 is also modified. In the second half of bar 64 the expected chord of G is replaced by G♯dim – the chromatic chord from the end of pattern B^1. But now it is heard simultaneously with a chord of G^7 in the lead guitar, and when the bass enters on a G♮ at the end of the bar, it becomes clear that the two chords together form a dominant minor 9th ($G^{7\flat9}$) in which the minor 9th (A♭) is notated as G♯. This dominant discord gives a poignant twist to the final vocal motif 'least not today' before resolving to the tonic and thus allowing the song to come to rest on a quiet chord of C major.

Melody   The melody is sung by Noel Gallagher (not Liam, who is usually the lead vocalist of Oasis) and the recording of the vocal part is double-tracked to thicken the sound (which is why it occasionally seems as if more than one person is singing).

The vocal melody in the verses uses the **pentatonic** scale on C (C–D–E–G–A). This scale also forms the basis of the melody in the pre-chorus, although Gallagher includes a blues-like E♭ in bars 17 and 20. Notice that in the second verse, the E♭ in bar 20 is replaced by a G♯ which resolves to a climactic top A in bar 21.

> Another feature unique to verse 2 is the pair of short guitar interjections printed on the string stave in bars 10–11. They illustrate the reference to a 'rock and roll band' in the lyrics of the second verse.

The note F is added to the basic set of five pitches in the melody of the chorus, the result being a hexatonic (six-note) scale. However, although the leading-note (B) is avoided throughout the vocal solo, it is firmly embedded in the dominant chords that form the first half of the perfect cadences in the accompaniment (V–I in bars 28^4–29^1 and 31^3–32^1), thus making the tonality crystal clear.

The word-setting is mainly **syllabic** with short falling **melismas** at the ends of many phrases in the verses (on 'mind', 'find', 'play', 'been' and 'seen' in verse 1). Most phrases combine stepwise movement with small leaps and most have a falling contour – a feature that contributes to the melancholic, nostalgic character of the song.

The verses have a narrow vocal range of a 6th, as does the pre-chorus (except for the extension to a top G♯ and A, mentioned earlier, when the latter is repeated).

The chorus is distinguished by the use of a higher **tessitura** and it starts with an aspirational upward leap of an octave (bars 24–25) but after that, even this lyrical melody descends (to the lower dominant, G in bar 28). When the first four bars of the chorus are repeated, the ending is changed to reach higher, to a top A in bar 30, for the title **hook**, 'don't look back in anger' – but again the melody falls back down the scale, this time to the tonic (C).

The lead-guitar melody in the instrumental **break** (bars 33–44) features semiquaver movement and crushed notes (♪). Given the moderate tempo it tends to sound melodic rather than virtuosic, but it covers a range of almost three octaves, moving into the high register in the second half. Like the vocal version of the pre-chorus it is based on the major pentatonic scale of C, with occasional use of the 'blue third' on E♭.

Exercise 9

1. What is meant by the 'title hook'?

2. The opening melody is mainly pentatonic. Where is the first non-pentatonic note in the vocal part?

3. Which percussion instrument, not normally part of a drum kit, features in *Don't Look Back in Anger*?

4. Does the song ever use chords in inversion, or do all of the harmonies consist of root-position triads?

5. Explain how the bass guitarist decorates the root of the chord of F major in bar 22.

6. How does the introduction (bars 1–4) relate to the rest of the song?

7. Compare bars 25–28 with bars 5–8 in terms of melodic material and accompaniment.

Sample questions

For an idea of the type of questions that are set in Section A of the paper, see pages 73–75. Obviously, the two extracts to be used in 2016 will come from the set works you have studied in this chapter, rather than the two printed on those pages. Here are some sample questions for practice in answering Section B of the paper.

Part B: Investigating Musical Styles

Answer *either* Question 3(a) *or* Question 3(b). You must answer both parts of the question you choose. You should spend no more than 45 minutes on this part of the paper. Remember that you are not allowed to consult recordings, scores or notes while answering the questions.

3(a)   INSTRUMENTAL MUSIC

(i)   Describe the stylistic features of Haydn's String Quartet in E♭, Op. 33 No. 2 (fourth movement) which show that this music was composed in the Classical period.   **(10)**

(ii)   Compare and contrast the structure and tonality of the Concerto for Double String Orchestra (first movement) by Tippett and the Quartet Op. 22 (first movement) by Webern.   **(18)**

OR

3(b)   VOCAL MUSIC

(i)   Describe the stylistic features of Bruckner's *Locus iste* which show that this work was composed in the Romantic period.   **(10)**

(ii)   Compare and contrast the harmony and structure of Y*ou Can Get It if you Really Want* as performed by Desmond Dekker and the Aces and *Don't Look Back in Anger* by Oasis.   **(18)**

(TOTAL: 28)

Rhinegold Education publish a book of practice tests covering sections A and C of this paper, *Edexcel AS Music Listening Tests*. More practice questions for section B are in the *Edexcel AS Music Revision Guide*.

Set works for 2017

Instrumental music

Trio sonata in D, movement 4 (Corelli)

Context and forces

Arcangelo Corelli was an Italian violinist and composer whose published works were widely distributed and influential in the development of instrumental music in the late Baroque period.

NAM 15 (page 200)   CD2 Track 4
Fitzwilliam Ensemble

NAM 15 comes from a collection of 12 trio sonatas by Corelli published in 1689. The term trio refers to the three melodic lines printed in the score, but normally four players are required for a trio sonata. The two treble staves are for solo violins, but the lowest stave, known as a **figured bass** because of the numbers and other symbols printed below it, is labelled for violone *and* organ.

The violone was any sort of low-pitched bowed-string instrument (the part is usually played on a cello today, as on CD2). The figuring below the bass part indicates the type of chords to be improvised by the organist in order to fill out the texture between the high violin parts and the much lower bass notes. This practice is known as 'realising' the figured bass.

The music on the lowest stave is known as a **continuo** part, and is found in almost all Baroque music that requires more than one performer. Although the instruments used can vary, a continuo part normally needs at least one bass instrument to play the notes as written and one chordal instrument, such as a harpsichord, lute or organ, to realise the figured bass.

Most of the 12 trio sonatas that make up Corelli's Opus 3 have four movements, in the order slow–fast–slow–fast. NAM 15 is the last movement of the second sonata in the collection. Each work in the set is sometimes described as a church sonata (*sonata da chiesa* in Italian), perhaps because of the suggestion of an organ as a continuo instrument. It is certainly possible that they could have been played during church services, but it is just as likely that they would have been performed for entertainment in the palaces of the nobility, where a small organ suitable for continuo playing could generally be found.

If possible try to perform NAM 15 with your fellow students. If you don't have violinists available it would work very well on two flutes. Experiment with different ways of realising the figured bass, using a piano or a soft pipe-organ voice on a synthesizer.

Corelli's string writing is idiomatic. This means that each part is conceived in terms of the instrument for which it is written – one of the reasons why Corelli's work was so influential. Although he doesn't use the extremes of the violin's range, the first-violin part in bars 34–35 does require the use of third position (with the left hand higher up the fingerboard), and both violin parts exploit the contrast between lively rhythms and sustained notes.

Structure

Although not labelled as such, NAM 15 is in the style of a gigue, a dance in fast compound time, often used by Corelli and many other Baroque composers to conclude a multi-movement composition (see page 102). Like the gigue in NAM 21, this piece is in **binary form**, its two sections being indicated by repeat marks.

Binary form is often depicted as ‖:A:‖:B:‖, but note that the letters A and B don't represent contrasting themes: the initial musical ideas and mood are maintained throughout each movement, as they are in much Baroque music.

Corelli's **diatonic** harmony and cadences help to clarify the binary structure. The movement starts in D major and then modulates to a perfect cadence in the dominant key of A major in bars 10–11, where it remains until the first double bar. The longer B section passes through several related keys before returning to the tonic in the closing bars:

Harmony and tonality

Bar	9		20	22	26	29	32	34	36		43
‖: D major	:‖	‖: A major	:‖‖: A major	D major	B minor	E minor	A major	G major	‖	D major	:‖

The harmony is **functional** – that is, it defines the keys we have identified, chiefly through the use of perfect cadences. Most of the chords are root-position or first-inversion triads, seasoned with dissonant suspensions that usually resolve by step to a consonant note. Thus nearly every 7 in the figured bass (which indicates a 7th above the bass) is followed by 6 – the resolution of the dissonance above the same bass note.

We have already noted that the movement contains rhythmic variety, especially in the violin parts. The dotted crotchet pulse is enlivened further by the rhythmic features in bars 26–27, shown in the example *below*. The first is the **cross-rhythm** in bar 26, where the tie across the middle of the bar results in the first violin sounding as though it is in $\frac{3}{4}$ while the lower parts remain in $\frac{6}{8}$ time. The second is the **hemiola** in bar 27 that results in all three parts sounding as though they are in $\frac{3}{4}$ time. Notice how the positioning of the chord changes in bar 27 reinforces the effect of this rhythmic disruption. An added delight is the **syncopation** caused by the first violin's tie that joins these two bars:

Rhythm

The movement has a **contrapuntal** texture. It begins like a **fugue**, based on the subject heard in the first two bars. This is followed by a real fugal answer played by the second violin ('real' because it is exactly the same melody as the subject, 'answer' because it sounds a 4th below the subject). The third entry comes in the bass at bar 6. At the start of the B section the fugal subject is heard in free **inversion**. The imitative second-violin and bass parts now enter only a bar apart, forming the fugal texture known as **stretto**.

Texture

Most of the melodic material in the movement derives from the quaver and semiquaver motifs in the subject. Although the imitative entries are shared among all three parts, the bass takes on a more functional role after bar 23 (especially in bars 35–38).

The texture is mainly widely-spaced, with the two violin parts often crossing, and placed high above the bass (as in bar 12). The wide gap (which is filled by the organ) is known as a **polarised texture** and is a feature of much baroque music.

Exercise 1

1. Why are four people usually needed to play a trio sonata?

2. Explain the purpose of the figures and other symbols printed below the bass part.

3. What type of dance is reflected in the style of NAM 15?

4. What is a polarised texture?

5. Identify the location of an inverted **pedal** in the second-violin part.

6. At the start of bar 18 the violins create a point of tension by being a tone apart. What is this device called?

7. Complete the blanks in the following: The first violin part in bar 20 is a(n) .... of the melody in bar 1. It is .... by the second violin in bar 21 and by the violone in bar 22.

8. What type of instrument is a violone?

9. Where in bars 28–35 is there a hemiola?

Septet in E♭, movement 1 (Beethoven)

Context and forces

Although Corelli's trio sonata and Beethoven's Septet (a work for seven players) are both types of chamber music, the latter is on a very much larger scale, making it more suited to concert-hall performance. The work has six movements, of which NAM 17 is the first, and it requires three wind instruments as well as four strings.

NAM 17 (page 207)   CD2 Track 6
Berlin Philharmonic Octet

When reading the score, notice that composers of the Classical period, such as Beethoven, supplied many more detailed performance directions than Baroque composers such as Corelli. Also note that:

➤ The clarinet in B♭ sounds a tone lower than printed

➤ The horn in E♭ sounds a major 6th lower than printed

➤ The double bass sounds an octave lower than printed

➤ The viola part is printed in the alto C clef, in which the middle line of the stave represents the pitch of middle C.

Beethoven wrote the work at the end of 1799 and it received its first public performance in April 1800 at a concert in the Royal Imperial Court Theatre, Vienna, where it shared the programme with the premiere of his first symphony. The Septet was well received and it proved to be Beethoven's most popular work for some years to come.

The movement begins with a slow introduction that moves from the opening tonic chord of Eb major to chord V in bar 8. Notice the dramatic contrast between the loud **tutti** opening and the solo violin figures. The four violin notes starting after the rest in bar 8 will dominate much of the rest of the movement. Bars 8–10 are repeated in the tonic minor (Eb minor, bars 10–12). The major mode returns for the ornate violin melody that ends on a dominant-7th chord (bars 17–18), decorated with a very characteristic clarinet arpeggio.

Introduction

The Allegro con brio that follows the introduction is in **sonata form**, the usual choice for Classical first movements. First try to listen for its main features:

Bars	18	53	111	154	188	233
	Exposition		Development	Recapitulation		Coda
	1st subject	2nd subject		1st subject	2nd subject	
Keys	Eb major	Bb major	Various	Eb major	Eb major	Eb major

The harmony is generally simple and **diatonic**, although decorated with chromatic notes such as those in bar 26. The **harmonic rhythm** is often slow, speeding up towards the cadences. This is evident in the first subject (bars 18–29) in which the first four bars are all harmonised with chord I, then the chords change every bar in bars 23–26, then every half bar in the next two bars.

The first subject starts with a version of the four-note motif we noticed in the introduction, treated in **sequence** in bars 18–21. The whole of the ten-bar violin melody is repeated on the clarinet, supported by a **syncopated** accompaniment in the strings.

Exposition

The second subject, which starts at bar 53 in the dominant key of Bb major, initially has a very different character: a **homophonic** texture of three-part strings, at first in minims although when this four-bar phrase is repeated by wind (bars 56–60) the lively quavers are added in the string parts. Another second subject theme appears in bars 61–68, shared between violin and clarinet doubled by bassoon; this is also immediately repeated in a different scoring. Finally Beethoven introduces a third idea (also part of the second subject) – the staccato chordal phrase in bars 86–88. This is repeated in sequence and (in bar 90) at the original pitch but with varied harmony. A **cadential** $\frac{6}{4}$ (chord Ic in the typically Classical progression Ic–V–I) concludes the second subject in bars 97–98.

Bars 98^3–111 form a **codetta** that reinforces the establishment of the dominant key. The one-bar phrase at the start of this section (based on the four-note motif) will later assume considerable importance. It is repeated in sequence over a reiterated tonic pedal (Bb played by horn then double bass until bar 106). The exposition ends with three perfect cadences (bars 107–111).

The development of ideas from the exposition begins with the opening of the first subject and a rapid modulation to C minor. In this key the melody from the codetta is heard on the clarinet (bars 116–120). The same theme is then heard in sequence on the horn and the music starts to modulate through a wider range of keys, as is usual in a development section. At bar 125 Beethoven draws on

Development

another earlier idea (from bar 40) which alternates with the codetta theme until a dominant pedal in bar 140 heralds the imminent return of the tonic key. Over the pedal the codetta theme is combined with a new version of the minim motif from bar 53. Our four-note motif then appears in rising sequence (bars 148–151), climbing up a chord of V^7 (cellos in **dialogue** with viola and woodwind).

Recapitulation   The recapitulation starts with a rescored repeat of bars 18–30, but a sudden modulation to A♭ major in bars 166–172 leads to more development of earlier material until, at bar 182, Beethoven returns to E♭ major for a repeat of bars 47–98 in the tonic key.

Coda   The coda begins at bar 233 with a repeat of the codetta, but it is greatly expanded by further development of the four-note motif (starting in the cello at bar 249). This accompanies a variation of the codetta theme played on the horn, together with a syncopated dominant pedal on the violin. At bar 258 the two melodies swap positions, the four-note motif now in the treble and the codetta theme in the bass, the latter imitated by woodwind in bar 260. Arpeggios and scales lead to a conclusive cadence in E♭ major (bars 276–277). The movement ends with a new trill figure, compressed in rhythm to increase excitement from bar 285, and harmonised by no less than nine perfect cadences in the last 11 bars.

Texture   One of the features that made the Septet so popular when it first appeared is its lively variety of texture. Let's choose some of the most diverse passages and describe them as concisely as possible.

➤ Bars 1–4: tutti chords flank the **monophonic** texture of bar 2

➤ Bars 8–11: alternation of three-part strings and tutti chords

➤ Bars 12–14: melody-dominated **homophony** (tune in violin accompanied by wind and cello, with melodic fragments in the viola)

➤ Bars 47–49: an **antiphonal** exchange between wind and strings

➤ Bars 111–115: **melody in octaves** with harmony sketched in by horn and double bass

➤ Bars 221^3–231^1: a **homorhythmic** texture in which the three-part string chords alternate with the tutti chords

➤ Bars 254–257: **two-part counterpoint** (clarinet and horn in octaves against lower strings in octaves) plus a tonic **pedal** in bassoon and violin

➤ Bars 258–264: **imitation** (the part for cello and bass is imitated by oboe and bassoon in bar 260, which in turn is imitated by cello and bass in bar 262) plus a **countermelody** for violin. The violin and bass parts in bars 258–261 form a contrapuntal inversion of the clarinet and bass parts in the previous four bars

➤ Bars 274–277: a duet for clarinet and bassoon above sustained string chords.

Style   The Classical style of the work is apparent in Beethoven's use of mainly diatonic chords, decorated with melodic chromaticism, and in clear cadence points that define keys. Equally typical of the

Classical style is the **periodic phrasing** that prevails throughout most of the movement. This is created by pairs of equal-length phrases that sound like questions and answers. For example, the melody of bars 116–136 consists entirely of sequential pairs of two-bar phrases. At the start of this passage two of these phrases form a four-bar phrase that ends with a perfect cadence in C minor (clarinet, bars 116–120). This is answered by a four-bar phrase from the horn (bars 120–124) that ends with a balancing perfect cadence in Ab major. The frequent melodic exchanges between instruments are also typical of the dialogue technique used by composers of the Classical era.

Exercise 2

. On what chord does the movement begin?

. Compare bars 2 and 4.

. In bars 161–164 the key is Eb major. Which of these bars are diatonic and which include chromatic writing?

. What is the name of the ornament in the violin part of bar 163?

. What precisely is meant by 'a syncopated dominant pedal' in the description of the coda, *opposite*?

. Compare bars 53–56 with bars 188–191. What is the main difference between these two passages?

. To what extent are the cello and double bass parts independent of each other?

. Which two instruments have most of the melodic interest in this movement?

. Give an example of **double-stopping** on page 207 of NAM.

Harold in Italy, movement 3 (Berlioz)

Hector Berlioz was one of the most original creative talents of the early Romantic period. His *Symphonie fantastique* of 1830 was a new type of work which illustrates a highly personal 'episode in the life of an artist' (the artist being Berlioz himself) using the medium of the symphony. The composer's beloved is represented by a melody that appears in different guises in every one of its five movements, called an *idée fixe* (a fixed idea, but used in French to mean an obsession). Berlioz wrote detailed notes for publication in concert programmes explaining how this 'programme music' expresses his hopeless fixation with a woman, her rejection of him, and the drug-induced nightmare in which he imagines he has killed her and then witnesses his own execution for the crime.

Harold in Italy arose from a commission by the famous **virtuoso** Paganini for a viola concerto. Berlioz actually wrote a symphony, containing only a modest part for solo viola, intended to represent Harold, the hero of a long poem by Lord Byron. In fact, none of the scenes depicted in the symphony's four movements bear much resemblance to the poem and it is obvious that the hero is, once again, Berlioz himself. Paganini was disappointed at the lack of virtuoso display in the viola part and the first performance was given in 1834 at the Paris Conservatoire of Music without him.

Context

NAM 3 (page 42)	CD1 Track 3
London Symphony Orchestra	
Conducted by Colin Davis	

The idée fixe

Although this symphony is far less programmatic than its ver
explicit predecessor, it too has an *idée fixe* – here it is as it appear
near the beginning of the symphony:

It makes an appearance in every movement, but it is not obsessiv
like its counterpart in the *Symphonie fantastique* – it simply turn
up to represent Harold, the vagabond dreamer, as an onlooker i
picturesque Italian locations. The next example shows Harold'
theme as it appears in bars 65–80 of NAM 3 (the viola player need
to use **double-stopping** to produce the octaves):

Finally, this example shows how Berlioz derives the theme (whicl
first starts in bar 34) from the reordered motifs of Harold's theme:

Cor anglais (sounding a 5th lower)

Orchestration

Berlioz is renowned for his superb orchestration. Natural horn
were still common in 1834 and, because these valveless instru
ments could play only a limited set of pitches, he uses four of them
and in three different keys (C, F and E) to cover as many note
as possible. The score also includes three instruments that wer
still uncommon in the symphony orchestra: the harp, the piccolo
(which sounds an octave higher than written) and the cor anglai
(a low oboe which sounds a perfect 5th lower than written). Notic
the orchestral colours Berlioz obtains by, for instance, doubling th
opening oboe solo an octave higher on the piccolo, and accompa
nying it with divided violas.

Commentary

At the start our attention is focused on a realistic impression o
Italian bagpipes represented by a double **pedal** on the tonic an
dominant of C major. Above this, the melody played by the obo
and piccolo uses the rhythm of the *saltarello*, an ancient Italian fol
dance.

To this day, Italian folk musicians still come down from the mountains of the Abruzzi to entertain tourists and city folk at Christmas time with *saltarelli* and other dances.

At bar 32 Berlioz carefully notes that the speed should halve an
the cor anglais introduces the main theme of the movement (notic
the syncopation in bars 37 and 38). The sequel to this melody intro
duces an oboe playing in octaves with the cor anglais and this dou
ble-reed tone becomes even more biting when the bassoon joins i
an octave lower at bar 53. Horns in C (sounding an octave lowe
than printed) take over the first phrase of the cor anglais theme i
bar 59. At bar 65 Harold's *idée fixe* enters (it is shown in the secon
example *above*) and is combined with earlier material.

the music becomes more chromatic and the textures become more complex (although the harp chords that enter at bar 72 helpfully how the basic harmonies). Passages in G major (bars 89–96) and D minor (bars 97–115) provide tonal variety, but are unrelated to the **ternary** (ABA) structure of the whole movement.

Berlioz frames the central section (bars 32–135) by returning to the folk dance style of the start (bars 136–165 repeat bars 1–30). But at bar 166 a final section begins – so vanishingly quiet that it must surely be Harold dozing off into another daydream in the hot Italian sunshine. Berlioz combines solo viola phrases from the main theme of the Allegretto with Harold's *idée fixe* (flute, pin-pointed with harp harmonics), the folk-dance rhythm (on divided violas) and the bagpipe drone (also violas). Gradually instruments drop out to leave isolated fragments of the saltarello melody (bars 194–198) and the bagpipe drone (violas *ppp* at bar 201). Finally everything winds down to the lowest note of the muted solo viola (C, the tonic) and the movement ends with repeated C major triads played almost inaudibly on muted strings.

Exercise 3

. What is an *idée fixe*? How does the term relate to this movement?

. What type of instrument is a cor anglais? What is special about the notation of music for this instrument?

. Name the chord played by the violas on the first beat of bar 1. How does this chord relate to the key of the movement?

. Identify the type of chord used at the start of bar 97 (all of its notes are present in the harp part).

. Summarise the structure of this entire movement in a single short sentence.

. State **two** reasons why Paganini might have found this work unsatisfactory to reflect his talents as a virtuoso string player.

Kinderscenen, nos. 1, 3 and 11 (Schumann)

Romanticism in music was a style of extremes. Berlioz's setting of the Requiem Mass, dating from 1837, requires a minimum of 160 orchestral players, 210 singers and four brass bands. The following year the German composer Robert Schumann wrote a set of tiny piano pieces entitled *Kinderscenen* (Scenes of Childhood), designed to be played in the home. Works of this type are called character pieces (or characteristic pieces) and are intended to express intense emotional experiences in the most intimate manner. They were extremely popular – Romantic composers could hardly keep up with the demand.

Although Schumann wrote the music first and gave each of the 13 pieces an individual title later, he always intended *Kinderscenen* to be a set of reminiscences of childhood that would be played by adults, unlike his *Album for the Young*, written for his seven-year-old daughter (and for all young pianists) to play.

Schumann's titles deliberately encourage us, as we listen or play, to allow memories to float across our minds: images of distant lands

Context

NAM 23 (page 258)   CD2 Tracks 13–15
Alfred Brendel (piano)

and people, a game of blind man's bluff and spooky childhood experiences. These programmatic interpretations are typical of much Romantic music and are quite different from the absolute music of NAM 17, where Beethoven makes no suggestions about how anyone should experience his sonata-form movement – its elegant patterns and musical architecture stand on their own and can be enjoyed in as abstract a fashion as the listener wishes.

Even more characteristic of early Romanticism is the fragmentary, suggestive nature of many of the pieces in *Kinderscenen*. Thus the melody of 'Von fremden Ländern und Menschen' ends inconclusively on the mediant rather than the tonic, and the accompaniment runs on through the final bar, as though the pianist had intended to stop but instead drifted off into a romantic daydream.

The reverse happens in 'Fürchtenmachen' in which the music slides in as though it had been going for some time and had only just become audible. This effect is enhanced by the chromatic writing in the first two bars which disguises the tonic key.

Von fremden Ländern und Menschen

The first eight bars are repeated at the end, after a six-bar middle section, forming the pattern ‖:A:‖:BA:‖ – this is similar to the type of binary form that we saw in NAM 15, except that the second section is rounded off by a return of the opening material. For that reason it is known as **rounded binary form**.

The melody is simple, repetitive and entirely diatonic – features reflecting the style of the innocent German folk songs that so pleased the growing middle classes of the early Romantic period. But while the many repetitions of the opening two-bar phrase and the short **sequence** in bars 9–12 give the *impression* of a children's song, this is an adult's recollection of childhood, so do not be surprised by sophisticated chromatic harmonies such as the diminished-7th chord in bars 1 and 3, the juxtaposition of the unrelated triads of B major and G major in bar 12, and the artful left-hand **countermelody** based on a **circle of 5ths** in bars 9–12.

> Note that the F♯ in bar 11, beat 2 (left hand) should have a down-stem to show that it is part of the bass countermelody and is to be sustained as a crotchet.

Schumann's piano textures are also far from childlike. Notice the way the broken chords are shared between the hands, the contrast between the legato melody and semi-staccato bass at the start, the two-part **counterpoint** between the outer parts in bars 9–14, and subtle nuances such as the sustained notes in inner parts (bars 5–6 and 14). Other points to note are:

➢ The balanced **periodic phrasing** (2+2+4 bars in the first section, shown by the phrase marks) – typical of Schumann's style but also typical of music from the preceding Classical period (as we saw in NAM 17)

➢ An A section that does not modulate and that is repeated almost exactly when it returns in bars 15–22

➢ A central B section (bars 9–14) that is melodically distinct from section A and that makes only fleeting reference to a different key (E minor)

➢ Triplet figuration in the middle part that continues throughout the piece.

The combination of a simple diatonic melody with subtle and sometimes ambiguous harmonic touches, in a texture of melody-dominated **homophony**, is typical of Schumann in his dreamy romantic mode. The effect is enhanced by the frequent rhythmic blurring caused when the dotted patterns coincide with triplets, often tempting the performer to use **rubato** (encouraged by the ritardando followed by a pause in bars 12–14).

By 1838 the piano could be found in middle-class homes throughout western Europe, and Schumann's idiomatic writing exploits some of its most characteristic features. The articulation of the uppermost part as a song-like melody depends on the performer's ability to play it more loudly than the lower parts (despite the fact that the highest notes of the accompaniment must be played with the right-hand thumb). Although it is possible to give a *cantabile* rendition of the melody without the sustaining pedal, Schumann's romantic style demands the sustained resonance that can only be achieved through its careful use. The artful two-part counterpoint between the outer parts in bars 9–14, with continued harmonic filling, is typical of romantic textures that are enhanced by the sustaining power that pianos had by this time achieved.

Hasche-Mann

This is another rounded binary-form movement with tell-tale signs of Romanticism, such as the sudden intrusion of C major into the key of B minor in bars 13–15. Once again a constant rhythm, this time semiquavers, is heard in one part or another right through to the final bar.

The game of blind-man's bluff is evoked by scurrying semiquavers. The first two bars are repeated in sequence, creating a four-bar phrase which is then repeated in bars 5–8. Like the A section of 'Von fremden Ländern', these bars never move out of the tonic key (in this case B minor). The prominent flattened leading note (A♮) in bar 2 comes from the use of the descending melodic minor scale, but A♯ appears in the perfect cadences (V^7–I in B minor) in bars 4 and 8.

The rising sequence of bars 1–4 is balanced by a falling sequence in bars 9–12, which carries the music to the unexpected and unrelated key of C major. Schumann avoids clearly defined tonal centres by the use of interrupted cadences in G major (bars 10–11) and E minor (bars 12–13). Like a disorientated, blindfolded child, the music seems to get stuck on a chord of C (bars 13–15). Indeed, we seem to be in the *key* of C major judging by the alternating C and G^7 chords above the double pedal on C and G. But in bars 15–17 the tonic key is regained by the use of chords V^7 and I of B minor, the home key.

The texture is again melody-dominated homophony, with a difficult leaping accompaniment for the left hand to suggest the jerky, lurching movements of the blindfolded child.

Fürchtenmachen

The ABACABA structure of this piece is known as symmetrical **rondo** form. The A section is called the refrain, while the other sections (B in bars 9–12, repeated in bars 37–40, and C in bars 21–28) are called episodes. Both contrast vividly with the refrain and Schumann emphasises this by marking episode B *schnelle* (faster) in bars 9 and 37. On CD2 Alfred Brendel sensibly extends this idea to episode C at bar 21.

The refrain consists of two soothing four-bar phrases in G major. Both start with the type of chromatic harmony that disguises the true key and is typical of the Romantic style, but both end with clear imperfect cadences in G major. Notice how, when the opening four-bar melody is freely adapted to form the answering melody of bars 5–8, it starts in the left hand (bar 5) and then transfers to the right hand on the second quaver of bar 7.

Both episodes are characterised by syncopated chords. The first two bars of Episode B are in E minor (the relative minor) and are repeated in sequence a third lower (in C major, but ending on an ambiguous second-inversion chord of E minor).

There is no clear tonal centre in the second episode (C) – the shifting chromaticism gives it an unsettling effect – all part of Schumann's hazy recollection of childhood fear. In fact, the 'scare' seems to be no more than a brief flash-back, since the new rhythm pattern, off-beat *sforzandi* and loud dynamic all vaporise after only four bars. The remainder of the episode then wends its way back to the soothing mood of the refrain, while Schumann cleverly avoids an exact sequence when bars 25–26 are varied to form bars 27–28.

Further examples of Schumann's idiomatic piano writing can be seen in his use of a bass melody with right-hand accompaniment in bars 5–6 and 9–12, and in the sudden contrast of dynamic and off-beat accents in bars 21–24.

Exercise 4

1. Name the main key of each of the three pieces in NAM 23.
2. What term is often used to describe short Romantic piano pieces of this type?
3. Describe the texture *and* form of 'Von fremden Ländern und Menschen' using appropriate technical terms.
4. What type of scale occurs in bar 16 of 'Hasche-Mann'?
5. What does diatonic mean?
6. In a rondo, what is the difference between an episode and the refrain?
7. Explain what is meant by idiomatic instrumental writing, and give three examples of ways in which Schumann's piano pieces in NAM 23 are idiomatic.
8. What features of the music suggest that *Kinderscenen* was intended for adults, not children, to play?

Vocal music

Sing We at Pleasure (Weelkes)

NAM 34 (page 349)   CD3 Track 12
Purcell Consort of Voices
Directed by Grayston Burgess

This was a set work in 2014, so you will find a discussion of it on pages 62–64 of this guide. When you work the exercise on page 64, omit the final question.

My Mother Bids Me Bind My Hair (Haydn)

For most of his life Joseph Haydn was director of music to Prince Esterházy at a magnificent palace on the borders of Austria and Hungary. By the 1790s he was widely recognised as one of the leading composers of the day and, with fewer duties at the palace, Haydn was able to travel to England for two extended and highly succesful visits where he presented many new works, including his 12 'London' symphonies.

Haydn was also introduced to London society, where he met the poet and hostess Anne Hunter, and later set some of her poems to music, published in 1794 as *Six Original Canzonettas* (little songs). The second of these has the title 'A Pastoral Song', although it is now better known by the first line of its text, 'My Mother Bids Me Bind My Hair'.

At this time ladies of fashion were expected, among their other social accomplishments, to entertain by singing and by playing the piano, an instrument that had become increasingly popular in the late 18th century. Haydn's songs, with their simple structures and graceful melodies, were aimed at this lucrative market. Although 'My Mother Bids Me Bind My Hair' is less well known today than Haydn's more substantial compositions, it remained very popular with amateur performers for many decades to come.

Anne Hunter's original text for this song consisted of the four stanzas, shown *right*. If you compare this with NAM 37 you will see how Haydn repeats the last pair of lines in each stanza, adding further repetitions of selected words and phrases as he does so. He also combines Hunter's first two stanzas to make the first verse of his song, and then uses the same music for his second verse, which is a setting of Hunter's third and fourth stanzas, again with text repetition towards the end of each stanza.

Because the same music is used for both verses, we describe the form as **strophic**, but this does have some odd consequences for the word setting. For instance, the halting rhythm that suits the words 'alas! I scarce can go or creep' in bars 27–29 of verse 1 works far less well when 'vil - lage' becomes divided by a rest in verse 2. Similarly, the descending chromatic scale in bars 22–24 reflects the crying and weeping in verse 1, but seems ill-suited to illustrate the spinning of flaxen thread in verse 2.

The intended amateur market for the song is revealed in:

➢ The mainly **syllabic** setting of the words

➢ A melody based on simple patterns such as the tonic triad ('My mother bids') and on stepwise movement ('with bands of rosy hue')

➢ A vocal range of only one octave

➢ An introduction that firmly establishes the key for the singer and reminds her of the tune by beginning with an elaboration of the first phrase of the song

➢ An accompaniment that helps the singer to stay on pitch by frequently doubling or shadowing the vocal melody.

Context and word setting

NAM 37 (page 359)   CD3 Track 15
Elly Ameling (soprano)
Jörg Demus (piano)

A pastoral was a type of poem that offered a highly idealised and very unrealistic portrait of rural life. Anne Hunter's poem, printed *below*, stands in a long tradition of such works, as you will know from your study of the text of NAM 34:

My mother bids me bind my hair
With bands of rosy hue,
Tie up my sleeves with ribbons rare,
And lace my bodice blue.

'For why,' she cries, 'sit still and weep,
While others dance and play?'
Alas! I scarce can go or creep,
While Lubin is away.

'Tis sad to think the days are gone,
When those we love were near;
I sit upon this mossy stone,
And sigh when none can hear.

And while I spin my flaxen thread,
And sing my simple lay,
The village seems asleep or dead,
Now Lubin is away.

Style The song displays many of the fingerprints of the Classical style. The texture is melody-dominated **homophony** and often relatively thin. For instance, the second phrase (bars 5–8) begins with just two parts, only thickening in texture at the cadence. In bars 22–26, **heterophony** results from the pianist's decoration of the melody being sung by the soloist.

Equally typical of the Classical style is the **periodic phrasing**, evident in the piano introduction, in which the opening four-bar statement ends with an imperfect cadence and is followed by a four-bar 'answer' which concludes with a perfect cadence. The first four bars of the vocal part are based on the first phrase of the introduction, but when Haydn repeats this vocal phrase (at 'tie up my sleeves') he changes its second half so that he can establish a perfect cadence in the dominant key of E major in bars 15–16.

Phrase lengths are more varied in the central section (bars 17–27) which remains in the key of E major, although with some colourful chromatic writing at the words 'For why, she cries, sit still and weep'. Haydn then returns to four-bar phrases and the tonic key for the final 12 bars.

This clear tonal scheme is also typical of the Classical style, as are such features as:

➢ The ornamentation of the vocal melody by, for example, an **appoggiatura** in bar 12, and a **slide** and **acciaccatura** in bar 15

➢ The simple piano textures, such as the string of parallel 3rds in bars 35–36 followed by broken chords in bars 37–38

➢ **Functional harmony** with the frequent use of imperfect and perfect cadences to define the main keys, sometimes preceded by a **cadential** $^6_4$ (as in bars 7^4 and 15^5)

➢ Short **pedals** on the tonic (bars 1–2) and the dominant (bars 3–4), along with a long passage of 'dominant preparation' in bars 22–27 to prepare for the return of the tonic key in the last section, all of which serve to strengthen the major-key tonality of the song.

Exercise 5

1. How does Haydn establish the tonic key at the start of 'My Mother Bids Me Bind My Hair'?

2. Identify the chord outlined in the first half of bar 6.

3. Do the accidentals in bars 3 and 6 indicate modulations to other keys or are they chromatic notes that colour the harmony?

4. Show how Haydn contrasts the suggestion of weeping in bars 22^6–24^4 with the suggestion of dancing and playing in bars 24^6–26. Also comment on how he illustrates the idea of being 'away' in the last five bars of the song.

5. Explain what is meant by a cadential $^6_4$ and give an example of one in the last eight bars of the song.

6. Which features of this song suggest that it was written for amateur performance?

Symphony of Psalms, movement 3 (Stravinsky)

This was a set work in 2014, so you will find a discussion of it on pages 66–68 of this guide. Remember to complete the exercise on page 68 before continuing.

> NAM 31 (page 307)   CD3 Track 9
> Choir of Westminster Cathedral
> City of London Sinfonia
> Conducted by James O'Donnell

Honey Don't (Carl Perkins)

Rock and roll first became widely known when Bill Haley's *Rock Around the Clock* was included in the 1955 film, *The Blackboard Jungle*. It combined elements of black-American rhythm and blues with a white-American country-music style known as rockabilly. In NAM 52 this fusion of styles is most apparent in:

Context

> NAM 52 (page 477)   CD4 Track 11
> Carl Perkins (vocal, guitar)
> James 'Buck' Perkins (rhythm guitar)
> Lloyd 'Clayton' Perkins (upright bass)
> W. S. Holland (drums)

➤ The singer's use of 'blue notes' (G♮ and D♮ in E major), the adaptation of 12-bar blues harmonies and the inclusion of drums (with a strong **backbeat** emphasised by the snare drum) come from rhythm and blues

➤ The use of a **walking bass** in much of the song and the regular strumming of the acoustic guitar, both of which came from rockabilly country music.

Honey Don't was one of four songs recorded by the Perkins Brothers in late 1955 at Sun Studios in Memphis, Tennessee, where Elvis Presley had recorded his earliest songs. It was released on 1 January 1956 as the B side to Carl Perkins' *Blue Suede Shoes*. Due to the success of the latter, which became a number one hit, the record had sold more than a million copies by May. But by then a serious car accident had brought a premature end to the performing career of the group. Although Carl survived, he was to see his most famous song, *Blue Suede Shoes*, covered by Elvis Presley. *Honey Don't* was also later to be covered by others, including the Beatles in 1964.

The original recording was made live in mono (not stereo) on a single track, since the studio didn't have one of the new multi-track tape recorders that were just starting to appear around this time. It was issued in the relatively new format of a seven-inch vinyl single (playing at 45 rpm) and in the much older, and fast disappearing, format of a ten-inch shellac record (playing at 78 rpm).

The instrumentation is typical of rockabilly and early rock and roll:

Instrumentation and texture

➤ Lead guitar, an electric guitar played with a plectrum ('pick guitar') and a good deal of echo effect

➤ Acoustic rhythm guitar

➤ Plucked double bass (sometimes called an upright bass or string bass to distinguish it from the bass guitar)

➤ Drums, playing predominantly the pattern seen in bar 4 (the sign ✗ in bar 5 and elsewhere means repeat the previous bar).

A distinctive technique used by most bass players in rockabilly was the slap – so common, in fact, that the instrument was sometimes called a slap bass. The string is pulled hard away from the fingerboard and then allowed to snap back, producing the percussive slap represented by the x-headed notes in the string bass part.

Carl Perkins sang the vocal and also played the lead guitar. The distinctive echo on the guitar part was produced by feeding the signal through a device equipped with a loop of tape on which the sound was recorded and immediately replayed via a series of closely-spaced playback heads, producing repeated tiny delays of the original signal.

The lead guitar has a short solo at the start and two solos (starting in bars 30 and 74). Both of these feature patterns in parallel 4ths, played on the two top strings of the guitar (which are tuned a 4th apart). During the verses the lead guitar punctuates phrases, as in bars 7–13. Elsewhere it doubles and elaborates the bass part, as in bars 14–29.

Jay Perkins plays the entirely chordal rhythm guitar part on an acoustic guitar. During the verses it punctuates phrases in parallel with the lead guitar. Elsewhere it fills out the backing with four strums per bar of the current chord.

> The double bass was amplified using a microphone placed close to the body of the instrument. For the recording, another microphone picked up the amplified sound from the bass's loudspeaker, resulting in the rather boomy and unfocused sound heard on CD4.

In the verses, bassist Clayton Perkins plays the roots of the chords in the same punctuating rhythm as the two guitars. Elsewhere, he plays a walking bass in crotchets that outlines the notes of the current chord. Sometimes his part is entirely triadic, as seen in the broken chords of bars 38–45. When decoration is introduced, it is simple and leaves the functionality of the harmony totally clear. For instance, in bars 37–38 the progression from dominant (B) to tonic (E) is filled-in with descending passing notes.

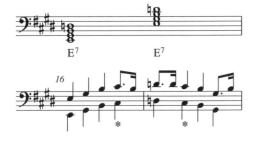

Listen for one of the most characteristic sound of rockabilly and early rock and roll, starting in bars 16–17. The bass outlines each chord, adding a 7th which is approached and quitted by passing notes (marked * in the example *left*), while the lead guitar decorates this walking bass an octave higher. The simultaneous performance of the two different versions provides another example of a simple type of **heterophony**.

> Astonishingly, Holland had never touched a drum kit until the week before the recording, but he went on to become one of the most influential drummers in early rock and was still performing as W. S. 'Fluke' Holland in 2013.

The Perkins brothers were used to performing country music in the traditional way, without a drummer. Shortly before their second recording session they realised that the new rockabilly style would benefit from the sort of drum backing commonly used in rhythm and blues, and so they drafted in W. S. Holland, a friend of Clayton Perkins.

The drum part consists mainly of bass drum on beats 1 and 3, snare drum on the backbeats (beats 2 and 4), and a cymbal pattern that includes **swing quavers** on beats 2 and 4. However, in the verses variety is produced by reserving the bass drum for the first beat of alternate bars and for reinforcing the punctuating rhythm that occurs between phrases (as in bars 7, 9, 11 and 13).

Texture

The texture of the song (excluding the short introduction) can be described as melody-dominated **homophony**, in which variety is achieved by replacing the voice with the lead guitar in the instrumentals and by placing much of verse 3 (bars 49⁴–57³) in a higher vocal register than the first two verses. Otherwise, there is little variety in the texture, with each of the accompanying instruments maintaining similar patterns throughout.

Honey Don't is based on an ingenious version of verse-and-chorus form, in which an eight-bar verse and a 16-bar chorus together form a 24-bar unit that spans two progressions of a 12-bar blues:

	Verse								Chorus			
Bars 6–17 (12 bar blues progression A):	E	E	C	C	E	E	C	C	B^7	B^7	E	E
Bars 18–29 (12 bar blues progression B):	E	E	E	E	A	A	E	E	B^7	B^7	E	E
			Chorus (continued)									

Progression B is a fairly standard 12-bar blues pattern in E major, although the influence of western harmony is felt in the strongly functional progression of the last four bars, where B^7–B^7–E–E is preferred to the V–IV–I–I (B–A–E–E) pattern that would be more typical of a traditional blues.

Progression A is more unusual because a chord of C major replaces the key chord in bars 3–4 and 7–8 of the pattern, between which the harmony returns to E major. C major is chord ♭VI in E major and reflects the influence of American country music, although this chromatic chord also conveniently supports the conventional blue third (G♮) of the melody in these bars.

The blue notes and the chromatic chord simply add colour to the key, which is E major throughout, clarified by the predominance of simple functional harmony (mainly chords I, IV and V^7 in root position). The final tonic chord is coloured by a quiet added 6th (E^6), but this makes no impact on the clear chord progressions in the rest of the song.

The use of eight- and 16-bar sections comes from older styles of western popular music while the 12-bar blues was a structure associated with black music. Perkins' fusion of the two is part of the appeal of this early rock and roll song.

Introduction (bars 1–5)

The lead-guitar solo announces the dominant (B) and tonic (E) in a pattern of 4ths on open strings above a descending chromatic bass (B–A♯–A♮). This prepares for the entry of the rest of the band on the tonic chord in bar 4, who outline the two-bar accompaniment pattern that will later dominate much of the song.

Verse 1 (bars 6–13) and **chorus** (bars 14–29)
The first appearance of the main 24-bar pattern described *above*.

Verse 2 and **chorus** (bars 6–29 repeated)
A repeat of the first verse, with some changes to the vocal melody, mainly to incorporate the different scansion of the new lyrics. Both text and music are repeated in the chorus, which has a slightly modified ending indicated by the 'second time' sign.

Instrumental 1 (bars 30–49)
This section uses a clever contraction of the 24-bar chord scheme: progression A is reduced to eight bars and, by substituting B^7 for C in bar 37, it leads straight into progression B. The solo features a characteristic lead guitar technique – parallel 4ths produced by sliding a finger across the fingerboard while picking the top two strings of the guitar (which are a 4th apart).

Verse 3 (bars 49⁴–57³ and **chorus** (bars 57⁴–73)
The melodic outline of this verse differs from the first two because Perkins creates a climactic effect by centering it around E an octave higher than previously. It is not a simple transposition, though, since Perkins modifies most of the patterns. For instance, in bar 52 he falls a 3rd to C♮ whereas in verse 1 he ascended to a G♮ (bar 8). Verse 3 also differs from verse 2 (although not verse 1) by starting with an **anacrusis** (or 'pick-up') at the end of bar 49 – a feature that Perkins also reflects at the start of the chorus.

Despite these differences, the chords are the same as the earlier verses, and the rhythms are similar, so this section still sounds like a modified verse rather than new material.

Instrumental 2 (bars 74–83) and **coda** (bars 83–96)
These last two sections together span another modified repeat of the paired chord patterns. The instrumental reuses the parallel 4ths idea of the first instrumental and sees progression A reduced to ten bars by omitting the eighth and tenth bars of the chord sequence. The coda uses progression B, with a prolonged final chord. The end of the song is signalled by a brief chromatic descent (B–B♭–A–G♯ in bars 94–95 of the lead-guitar part.

Melody and word setting

The vocal melody is firmly centred on E (the tonic) and is mostly **disjunct** with leaps to and from other chord notes. Much of the melody uses just four pitches: tonic (E), dominant (B) and two blue notes (G♮ and D♮). Perkins occasionally uses the raised form of these last two pitches (G♯ in bars 39–40 and a possibly unintentional D♯ in bar 58). Both C♮ and C♯ also appear, but the second and fourth degrees of E major (F♯ and A) are entirely avoided in the vocal part.

> Notice that Carl Perkins starts the first and second choruses on E, despite the underlying chord of B⁷ in bar 14, but in the third chorus the same harmony pulls him down to D♯ (bar 58).

The vocal part in the verses consists of four two-bar phrases, and the differences between them in each verse suggests that much of the vocal may have been improvised. The guitars and bass play only in the rests between these phrases, in a style known as **stop time** (NAM 51, which is a rhythm and blues song, uses a similar technique – see page 472 of the New Anthology).

The melody in the choruses is fragmentary (mostly one-bar patterns separated by rests) but here the clipped vocal phrases are set against the continuous walking bass, a combination very characteristic of rockabilly and early rock and roll. The tune is even more tightly glued to the tonic in these sections – in the first two choruses, two-thirds of the vocal pitches are E and in the third chorus decoration is removed to produce a **monotone** on E from bar 60 to the first beat of bar 65.

The word-setting throughout the song is **syllabic** (one note per syllable) and the inclusion of nonsense syllables, such as 'ba ba ba' in the third chorus, reinforces the feeling that Perkins improvised some of the vocal part, adapting melodic formulae from the blues to fit the pre-determined chord pattern.

Rhythm

Honey Don't has a clear quadruple-metre pulse, except in bar 83 where a bar of ³⁄₂ time results from the overlap of the end of the in-strumental with the long anacrusis ('Well, little honey') at the start of the coda. The regular pulse is reinforced by the simple drum patterns and the steady crotchets of the rhythm guitar and walking bass. The punctuating rhythm between phrases in the verses provides variety and throughout the song, shorter rhythms within each crotchet beat are swung, as had been the practice in most popular music for many years. The main feature of this swung rhythm, which is indicated by the instruction '12/8 Feel' in bar 1, is the pattern ♩ ♪ which is notated as ♩. ♩ in the score.

Against this firm backing Perkins makes much use of **syncopation** in the vocal part (for example, bars 15, 17, 21 and 23), becoming increasingly adventurous in the final chorus – compare bars 61–64 with bars 17–20, noticing how he fills beats that were previously silent. He also makes much use of syncopation in the patterns of parallel 4ths for lead guitar in both of the instrumental breaks.

Exercise 6

1. How many *different* chords are used in *Honey Don't*?

2. What type of instrument plays the bass part in this song? The performer uses a technique known as slap bass – what does this mean?

3. Describe what is meant by a 'walking bass' and explain how it relates to the harmony in NAM 52.

4. What influences of the blues can you find in this song?

5. What term describes the type of word setting in *Honey Don't*?

6. Which drum-kit instruments are represented by the three different levels of notes on the drum stave in the score of NAM 52?

7. What are the pitches of the blue notes in the first verse of the vocal part of this song?

8. How is 12-bar blues harmony treated in this song?

A Day in the Life (Lennon and McCartney)

The Beatles' rapid rise to fame began in 1962, the year of their first two hit singles, although John Lennon and Paul McCartney had been performing together since 1957. They were joined by George Harrison in 1958 and the group worked with two other musicians before Ringo Starr became their drummer in 1962.

The group's early years had been spent learning their craft by playing cover versions of American songs. As they began adding their own songs, written by Lennon and McCartney, they established the concept of a group working creatively together, rather than just being the backing for a solo singer.

The group image was reinforced by the Beatles adopting similar haircuts and wearing similar clothes, but it was the quality of their music that attracted international attention. American artists had dominated popular music for decades, but by the early 1960s the blues-based styles of early rock had given way to cute songs about teenage romance. The time was right for something new to fill the void, and that was provided by the energy and originality of British groups, and in particular the Beatles.

Context

NAM 54 (page 487)
This song is not included on the CDs that accompany the New Anthology.

The album

In late 1966 the Beatles decided to abandon concert performances because the incessant screaming of their adoring fans often made it impossible to hear the music, and they resolved instead to work as a studio band. The decision was prompted by the success of the album *Pet Sounds*, from the leading American group the Beach Boys, released in May 1966. Over a year in the making, it was the first successful concept album in which all of the songs are related and Paul McCartney later revealed that it was the inspiration for the Beatles' eighth album, *Sgt. Pepper's Lonely Hearts Club Band*, released in 1967.

The album uses the old theatrical device of a performance within a performance to create an impression that it is not the Beatles we hear but Sgt. Pepper's Lonely Hearts Club Band – an imaginery Edwardian concert band which presents a vaudeville of fantasies in styles old and new. The band's title is significant – they create an illusion for lonely people but they themselves are lonely and it is this theme of loneliness, and how it is covered up, which links their songs.

This simple but effective device allowed the Beatles to create a concept album embracing a far broader range of musical styles than that found in the Beach Boys' *Pet Sounds*, in which the songs are linked by their musical similarity. It provides the opportunity to juxtapose music hall (*When I'm Sixty-Four*) and community songs (*With a Little Help From My Friends*) with surreal fairground music (*Being for the Benefit of Mr Kite!*) and the psychedelic imagery of songs such as *Lucy in the Sky with Diamonds*.

A Day in the Life is the last song on the album. As in many of the Beatles' later songs the lyrics are subtle and the music is sophisticated. John Lennon composed the verses, Paul McCartney contributed the bridge, and the Beatles' producer (the classical oboist George Martin) directed the orchestra and effects.

The Beatles also sought to engage the listener by including with the album Sergeant Pepper cutouts, a collage of portraits to decipher and a printed version of the complete lyrics. This last feature was most unusual at the time and reflects the fact that, unlike the words of most earlier pop songs, the lyrics are often ambiguous and open to interpretation.

To create the illusion the album begins with tuning-up, audience noises and applause. To maintain the illusion, the separate tracks are closely spaced and sometimes overlap (a deliberate feature to make it difficult for radio DJs to break up the concept by playing individual tracks). The illusion is seemingly brought to an end by a reprise of its opening number, now at a more urgent tempo and with its title line curtailed to produce poignently insistent repeats of 'Sergeant Pepper's lonely, Sergeant Pepper's lonely, …'.

This reprise concludes the performance by Sgt. Pepper's Lonely Hearts Club Band, but it is not the end of the album. *A Day in the Life* appears at the end of the album, like an epilogue outside the context of the show. This at last is the Beatles performing. John Lennon's sardonic commentary on the news strikes an icy tone … ('a lucky man who made the grade … rather sad … just had to laugh … he blew his mind out in a car … didn't notice the lights had changed'). Paul McCartney's interpolated middle section creates ambiguity – was the first half of the song as illusory as Sergeant Pepper himself? At first it might seem so – an alarm clock is heard … 'Woke up, got out of bed'. But the ensuing account of humdrum existence quickly reverts to dreaming – he gets on a bus, goes to the upper deck, where smoking was allowed in those days, has smoke (of what?) and 'goes into a dream'. Lennon's final stanza loses all sense of coherence ('Now they know how many holes it takes to fill the Albert Hall; I'd love to turn you on') and so does the concluding music. Is this all still part of the illusion? After the final colossal chord a locked playout groove presents sounds from the post-production party and an inaudibly high tone put there at Lennon's request, 'to annoy your dog'. So is this, at last, the return to reality?

Despite worries about the scale of the project, the Beatles recorded 16 songs (including three not used in the final album) in 129 days. The final mono mix of all the material was completed on 21 April 1967, matters such as the stereo mix (stereo still being relatively new in pop music at this time) and the order of tracks being left largely to George Martin. The album was released on 1 June 1967 and received considerable critical acclaim, although a few found it contrived. At the time the pop single was still the main way of marketing pop music and part of the signficance of *Sgt. Pepper* was the role it played in establishing the importance of the album as a vehicle for more complex musical ideas in pop music. It was soon followed by concept albums from other groups, by double and even triple albums, rock operas and similar large-scale works.

Sgt. Pepper is also significant for its approach to recording, in which the studio is no longer used as a way to capture the sound of a live performance, but as a tool in its own right – one of the consequences being that such music becomes difficult, if not impossible, to recreate in live performance. Above all, its significance is in its demonstration that pop music can be very much more than a transient three-minute song. As a coherent, entertaining and sometimes moving statement of the aspirations and counter-culture of its age, *Sgt. Pepper* has remained one of the great works of popular music, returning to the top of the charts decades later with its release on CD in 1987 and again in 1995.

A Day in the Life begins as the final chord of the previous song fades away. It creeps in, almost unnoticed, with an acoustic guitar outlining the chord pattern (G–Bm–Em–Em⁷–C) that will be used in the following verses, joined after two bars by piano and bass. The drum entry in bar 5 is just a simple quaver rhythm on maracas. A key element is the dispassionate delivery of the lyrics. The singer's detachment is expressed through panning Lennon's voice hard to the right of the accompaniment in the stereo field and through motifs that sound more like repetitive thoughts than a melodic line – short, jumpy figures in free rhythm, frequently coming back to the same intervals.

Although the bass descends through a complete though slightly decorated scale of G major at the start of each verse, the tonality is ambiguous because the dominant chord (D major) is totally avoided and the use of the chord on the flattened leading-note (F major) towards the end of the verses adds a distinctly modal element.

Notice how the vocal line differs slightly in each verse, reflecting the essentially improvisatory nature of the singing. In verse 2 the tension begins to mount. The full drum kit enters immediately after

A remastered version of *Sgt. Pepper's Lonely Hearts Club Band* was released by EMI in 2009.

Commentary

Form			
1–4		Intro	4 bars
5–14	Verse 1		10 bars
15–23	Verse 2		9 bars
24–34	Verse 3		11 bars
35–46		Transition	12 bars
47–57		Bridge	11 bars
58–67		Transition	10 bars
68–78	Verse 4		11 bars
79–89		Coda	11 bars

The *Sgt. Pepper* songs are linked musically as well as by the theme of loneliness in their lyrics. One of these links is a bass line built on descending scale patterns, which occurs in four of the songs on the album.

Note that some editions of NAM have the first chord symbol in bar 24 and the second in bar 74 incorrectly printed – they should be G and F respectively, to match the other verses.

The mixolydian mode on E consists of the pitches E–F♯–G♯–A–B–C♯–D–E. In the verses, the F♮s in the accompaniment come from the mixolydian mode on G: G–A–B–C–D–E–F–G.

'He blew his mind out in a car' and the previous ten-bar verse is shortened to nine bars. In bar 22 a semitonal figure in semiquavers appears which will be of significance later – like so many of the melodic motifs in the song, it hovers around the note B – after which the vocal range is extended to reach a climactic top G. At the end of verse 3 the semitonal figure is **inverted** (the principal note is still B) and this is the idea taken up by the orchestra and transformed into an **atonal** spiral of sound for the transition.

The tempo is tightened for McCartney's bridge section, which is focused on the tonal area of E major although, as in Lennon's verses, there is a strong modal element, with prominent use of D♮ in the accompaniment, the characteristic flat seventh degree of the mixolydian mode on E (see *left*). The two sections are complementary in other respects. Like Lennon, McCartney uses repetitive intervals (mainly 3rds) rather than stepwise melody, and assymetric structures made up of 2½-bar phrase lengths. And while Lennon's motifs mainly centre on the 4th between B and upper E, McCartney's focus on the 5th between B and lower E (thus reversing the normal role of the two singers, in which Paul McCartney usually took the high notes).

In the second transition (bars 58–67) Lennon's **vocalisation** reflects the idea of a dream, and is underpinned by massive root-position triads in a rising **circle of 5ths**, twice outlining the pattern C–G–D–A–E with the full weight of orchestral brass.

The final verse is musically similar to verse 3 (although notice how 'the Albert Hall' is decorated with concerto-like piano chords). However, significantly it has left and right channels reversed – several commentators have remarked how this gives the effect that something has been fundamentally changed by the reminder of reality in the bridge. But the lyrics are now the most trivial of snippets from the newspaper, and they are dealt with in just the same deadpan tone as the report of the car accident in verse 1. The reappearance of the atonal orchestral spiral links the coda to the earlier transition, but this time it leads to a dramatic silence. This is followed by the brilliant light of a chord of E major, reverberating for 42 seconds and seeming to resolve the ambiguous tonality, modality and atonality of the previous sections.

After the final chord of our song has died away, the album finishes with a 'locked groove' (a device that causes a tiny part of the record to play incessantly) consisting of noise from the post-recording party, recorded twice, chopped into pieces, reassembled in a different order and then played backwards – a return to reality that is as strange and innovative as the songs that preceded it.

Much of the material in the song is deceptively simple. The bass in the verses is formed from simple descending scales; the vocal motifs are rhythmically free but short and of limited range – in verse 1 they generally begin and end on the same pitch although Lennon gradually broadens their range later. The accompaniment in the verses is restrained – the drum part is very sparse at the start but builds throughout the song, providing a firm contrast in the bridge. The 40-piece orchestra is used sparingly but with colossal effect. Its dissonant crescendo in the first transition removes the ense of key and the cymbal fill at its end (bar 44) removes the ense of pulse – only to be replaced by the clock-like ticking of the major piano chords in bar 45. In the second transition the rchestra's role is more subtle, simply underpinning the bass of he root-position harmony. The reappearance of the atonal spiral n bar 79 acts as a structural device, linking the coda with the irst transition. But this time it leads to a dramatic silence followed y the E major chord on three pianos, overdubbed four times and upported by George Martin playing a harmonium.

Exercise 7

. How does the introduction of *A Day in the Life* relate to the verses of the song?

. How does the bass-guitar part relate to the left-hand part of the piano in bars 5–8? Can you think of the term to describe this relationship?

. Almost all of the phrases in the verses begin after a quaver rest on the strong beat. What do you notice about the starts of most of the phrases in the bridge? How else does the bridge contrast with the verses?

. Write short notes to show the ways in which the music reflects the lyrics in NAM 54.

. In what ways is *Sgt. Pepper's Lonely Hearts Club Band* significant in the history of pop music?

Sample questions

or an idea of the type of questions that are set in Section A of the paper, see pages 73–75. Obviously, the two xtracts to be used in 2017 will come from the set works you have studied in this chapter, rather than the two rinted on those pages. Here are some sample questions for practice in answering Section B of the paper.

Part B: Investigating Musical Styles

nswer *either* Question 3(a) *or* Question 3(b). You must answer both parts of the question you choose. You hould spend no more than 45 minutes on this part of the paper. Remember that you are not allowed to onsult recordings, scores or notes while answering the questions.

(a) INSTRUMENTAL MUSIC

i) Describe the stylistic features of Corelli's Trio Sonata in D, Op. 3 No. 2 (fourth movement) which show that this music was composed in the Baroque period. **(10)**

ii) Compare and contrast the melodic writing and instrumental textures in *Harold in Italy* (third movement) by Berlioz and the Septet in E♭ (first movement) by Beethoven. **(18)**

)R

(b) VOCAL MUSIC

i) Describe the stylistic features of *Honey Don't* by Carl Perkins which show that this is an example of early rock and roll. **(10)**

ii) Compare and contrast the structure and textures of *Sing We at Pleasure* by Weelkes and *My Mother Bids Me Bind My Hair* by Haydn. **(18)**

(TOTAL: 28)

hinegold Education publish a book of practice tests covering sections A and C of this paper, *Edexcel AS Music Listening Tests*. More practice questions for section B are in the *Edexcel AS Music Revision Guide*.

Set works for 2018

Instrumental music

Piano Sonata in B♭, movement 1 (Mozart)

NAM 22 (page 253)   CD2 Track 12
Alfred Brendel (piano)

This was a set work in 2015, so you will find a discussion of it on pages 79–81 of this guide. Remember to complete the exercise on page 81 before continuing.

Prélude à L'Après-midi d'un faune (Debussy)

Context and style

NAM 5 (page 86)   CD1 Track 5
Concertgebouw Orchestra
Conducted by Bernard Haitink

The faun in Debussy's 'Prelude to the Afternoon of a Faun' is an ancient pagan nature-god, guardian of herds and patron of country pursuits. The inspiration for the piece was a poem by his friend Stéphane Mallarmé, the great French poet. The faun awakes in the shimmering heat of a summer afternoon and languidly plays his panpipes while watching two nymphs. His passion aroused, he seizes the water nymphs, but they are frightened by his burning kisses and the vision vanishes. As night falls he stretches himself voluptuously on the sand to sleep.

Debussy described the work as a prelude because he intended to follow it with two further movements. These were never written and so NAM 5 is the complete piece. It is sometimes described as a tone poem – a type of orchestral work that uses music to tell a story or convey an image – although Debussy made it clear that his music was intended only as 'a very free illustration of the poem'. It is designed for the concert hall, and was first performed on 22 December 1894 in Paris, although it is also heard in theatres where it is performed as a ballet score.

Structure and style

Bars	Form	Bars	Subsections
1–54	A	1–30	A¹
		31–36	Transition
		37–54	A²
55–78	B		
79–93	A		Recap of A¹ only
94–110	Coda		

The *Prélude à L'Après-midi d'un faune* has a **ternary** structure followed by a **coda** (see *left*). The languid faun's theme (bars 1–4) is heard in sharp keys centred on E major in the two flanking sections (bars 1–54 and 79–110). The central section is based on a more impassioned theme in flat keys (centred on D♭ major) which is heard three times (woodwind in bars 55–62, upper strings in bars 63–74 and solo violin in bars 75–78). Listen to the music and make sure that you can recognise these main ideas. Try to decide what you feel are the most important features of the music and then see if you agree with our list *below*:

➤ Complex rhythms that disguise a regular pulse

➤ Melodic variation (rather than the development of motifs)

➤ Rich colourful harmony that often seems to obscure the keys of the music rather than define them

➤ Subtle orchestral textures.

All of these features contribute to a style of music in which the atmosphere created by colour, tone and texture seems to be more important than clearly-defined phrases and structures. This later

Romantic style is known as Impressionism. The term is borrowed from French painting of the period, in which there is a similar interest in conveying the impression of light and movement, rather than giving an exact representation of shapes.

Debussy's rhythms are as fluid as an Impressionist painter's brush strokes and he uses chords for the colours they create, rather than in the functional way we saw in Mozart's Classical sonata. The result is often a succession of gentle discords that obscures any clear sense of tonality, looking forward to 20th-century music more than back to the tonal styles of the past.

Debussy's melodic style is very different to the balanced phrasing of Mozart's themes. When we examine the way Debussy treats his opening flute melody we find that he:

Melody

- Repeats it unchanged with an accompaniment of fluttering **tremolo** strings (bars 11–14)

- Lengthens the first note and decorates the melody of bar 3 with demisemiquaver triplets (bars 21–22)

- Ends the phrase with a fast version of the first bar (bars 26–27)

- Slows the whole melody down (bars 79–82 and 86–89).

Debussy's main interest is not in manipulating and developing melodies, but in presenting the same theme in various rhythmic and melodic variants, and in different textures and harmonisations.

One of the most characteristic features of Debussy's style is the use of the **whole-tone scale**. Look at the clarinet solo in bar 32 (it is repeated by the flute in the next bar). Each pitch is one whole tone away from its neighbour – there are no semitones in this scale to give it tonal direction, and so it is another means of both adding colour and avoiding clear tonal direction.

Debussy's orchestral palette requires ten woodwind, four horns, two harps and enough strings to manage the divided and solo parts in bars 95–100. The only percussion are antique cymbals – small disks of brass or bronze, tuned to specific pitches. Note that:

Orchestration

- The cor anglais and the four horns sound a perfect 5th lower than printed

- Clarinets in A sound a minor 3rd lower than printed (the players change to clarinets in B♭ at bar 44, and these sound a tone lower than printed)

- The viola part is printed in the alto C clef, in which the middle line of the stave represents the pitch of midde C

- Double basses sound an octave lower than printed.

Harps have seven strings per octave, each of which can be raised by a semitone or a tone by means of pedals. The pitches required at the start are specified in bar 1 of the harp part. Make sure you understand the many French terms used in the score (less obvious ones are explained on page 537 of NAM) and the notation for bowed and fingered tremolo (explained on page 16 of this book).

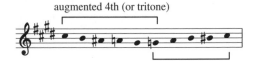

augmented 4th (or tritone)

The importance of instrumental colour is apparent in the very first bar, in which the augmented 4th outlined by the opening motif (shown *left*) is presented in the distinctive bottom octave of the flute's register. The lower notes of the flute are very quiet and so Debussy leaves the melody unobscured by any accompaniment. The tone colour then changes to that of soft horns, with a delicate harp **glissando** and muted (*sourdine*) string accompaniment.

The last five bars contain many examples of instrumental subtlety. Muted strings are divided into 12 parts to play the tonic chord in bar 106, but the two top notes are played by unmuted solo violins. Muted horns subtly colour the middle range and against this chord two harps play the four-quaver groups. In bar 107 muted horns and muted violins play the chromatic fragment from the opening motif of the work in unrelated triads. In bar 108 the flute adds a 6th to the tonic chord (echoed by a harp harmonic), while the violins play an appoggiatura (A♯) that lasts six beats before it resolves. The chord at bar 109¹ is the same as the first chord of the work (in bar 4), but this time it resolves to a tonic chord of E major. Antique cymbals sound the root and 5th of the key chord and almost inaudible pizzicato cellos and basses bring the work to an end.

Harmony

There are few root-position and first-inversion triads of the sort Mozart used throughout his sonata. Debussy's chords are often chromatic and he uses dissonance freely, although for colour and atmosphere rather than for emotional tension. He was also fond of strings of parallel dissonances, as can be seen in the string accompaniment to bar 24, shown *left*. The pattern F♯⁷–Bm⁷–Am⁷ is heard twice in the last six quavers, the cellos moving in parallel 7ths throughout these chords.

105   106

E major: V¹³   V⁹   V⁹   I

A further taste of Debussy's harmonic style can be seen in the final perfect cadence of the work (shown *left*). There is little tonal tension – the cadence seems to be enveloped in a haze of sound. This is partly attributable to the fact that the leading note (D♯) puts in a late and very quiet appearance in the dominant chord, and partly by the diatonic discords (7ths, 9ths, 11ths and 13ths above the dominant) that add sensuous colour rather than tonal direction. Debussy goes out of his way to ensure that a regular pulse will not be apparent by introducing lazy duplets and groups of four, completely disguising the compound-time beat as the music drifts timelessly to a close.

Exercise 1

1. What is a glissando (harp, bar 4) and what does the term *cuivré* mean (first horn, bar 92)?

2. Explain as precisely as possible how the second violins should play bar 11. Take into account the instruction in bar 5 as well as the information in bar 11 itself.

3. The circles over the last four harp notes of the piece indicate **harmonics**. What does this mean?

4. Write a short paragraph on Debussy's use of rhythm in this work.

5. What identifies the style of NAM 5 as Impressionist?

Sonata for Horn, Trumpet and Trombone (Poulenc)

This was a set work in 2015, so you will find a discussion of it on pages 81–83 of this guide. Remember to complete the exercise on page 83 before continuing.

| NAM 19 (page 242) | CD2 Track 8 |
| Nash Ensemble | |

New York Counterpoint, movement 2 (Reich)

Steve Reich first came to attention in the late 1960s and early 1970s as one of several composers who rejected the complexity and dissonance of much mid 20th-century art music in favour of a less intellectual style in which simple musical patterns are subjected to systematic processes of gradual transformation. At first described as process music or systems music, this is the style that we now call **Minimalism**.

Although Reich's music has become more complex and multi-layered over the years, the repetition of short patterns continues to play an important part in his work. He has also retained a lively interest in music technology, writing many works that combine pre-recorded and live performance, or that use synthesisers.

New York Counterpoint was commissioned by the Fromm Music Foundation (one of America's most important patrons of new music) for the clarinettist Richard Stolzman. Written in 1985, it is part of Reich's series of 'counterpoint' works that each explore the idea of a soloist playing live against a backing tape they recorded earlier. He had used the idea in various earlier pieces, but this particular series started with *Vermont Counterpoint* (for flute) in 1982 and has continued with *Electric Counterpoint* (for electric guitar) written for Pat Metheny in 1987, and *Cello Counterpoint* (2003).

The first performance of *New York Counterpoint* was given by Richard Stolzman on 20 January 1986 at the Avery Fisher Hall in New York. The title of the work refers to the bustling city life reflected in the music and to the contrapuntal textures that are generated by the staggered entries of the clarinet parts.

New York Counterpoint consists of three movements, in the order fast–slow–fast. NAM 12 is the central movement, although its use of mainly semiquaver patterns gives the rhythm a much greater sense of urgency than in most slow movements.

Reich uses the key signature of B major, but since the clarinet is a transposing instrument the music will sound a tone lower when played on the standard clarinet in B♭ (and the bass clarinet parts will sound a 9th lower – that is, an octave plus a tone). Since all the parts transpose in a similar way, it is simpler if from here on we refer only to what you see in the score, rather than to the actual sounds you hear on the recording.

Although the music is entirely **diatonic**, it doesn't use functional harmony and cadences to define key, as Mozart did in his Classical sonata-form movement. And although it uses the key signature of B major, the principal focus of the movement often centres upon the pitch E. We could therefore say that it uses the **lydian mode** on E, shown *right*. This differs from a scale of E major in having a raised fourth degree (A♯), marked * in the example.

Style and context

| NAM 12 (page 176) | CD1 Track 16 |
| Roger Heaton | |

Commentary

The bar numbers given here match those in the score. Notice that in performance, five of the two-bar units in the first section are repeated.

The modal quality of the work is enhanced by the fact that the melodic parts are restricted to the notes of a **hexatonic** (six-note) scale – the pitch D♯ occurs only in the pulsating **homorhythmic** textures that periodically combine with the counterpoint. The first of these starts in bar 27, but even here the tonic triad of B major reiterated in parts 7–9 is clouded by the repeated C♯ in part 10.

In older styles, composers used contrasts in key and thematic material to structure their music, as we saw in NAM 22. There are no such contrasts here – in fact, the opening two-bar motif is heard in one form or another throughout the whole movement. Instead, Reich structures his music through the careful control of texture.

Although the movement is not punctuated by cadences, it falls into two distinct sections. The first (bars 1–24) is characterised by a steady build-up of contrapuntal complexity with parts initially entering in pairs like this:

➢ Two parts in the first two bars

➢ Four parts in bars 3–8

➢ More parts are added at bar 9, but initially these double existing strands for four bars, so a real six-part texture doesn't emerge until bar 13

➢ A seventh part is added from bar 21.

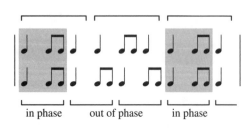

In the second section (bars 25–65), the three-part canonic ostinato continues while the live clarinettist plays a 'resultant melody' – a melody that results from doubing and combining fragments of other parts being played at the same time (see *left*). This section is also distinguished by the addition of three dissonant four-part chords, each played as repeated semiquavers. These fade in and out on clarinets 7–10. The first two last for six bars and the third for eight, after which the entire pattern repeats.

The homorhythmic texture thus introduced makes a vivid contrast with the counterpoint that continues around it, but finally the chords disappear, leaving six more bars of fading counterpoint, followed by a three-note fragment of the opening motif in the final bar.

Many Minimalist composers use a technique known as phasing, in which repeating patterns of different lengths gradually move from being in phase when they coincide to being out of phase when they do not. A very simple example is shown *left*.

in phase   out of phase   in phase

In this work, phasing can most clearly be seen in the opening bars. For clarity the example *below* shows only the upper of each pair of parts and omits the repeat signs. When the live clarinet enters in bar 3 it plays the same motif as clarinet 7, but half a beat later. When heard against the original motif (which continues in clarinet 7) it is a half-beat out of phase, and this creates a **canon**:

Only four notes are imitated at this point – the greyed-out notes are replaced by rests. But look at bar 5 and you will see that the canon continues out of phase despite the missing notes. Reich fills in one more note (A♯) in bar 6 – and after this the live clarinet gets to play the entire canonic entry, still half a beat out of phase.

Now look at the live clarinet entry in bar 13 of the score. Do you see that it has now moved one whole beat out of phase? The importance of the phasing process is that it causes expected rhythmic accents to be thrown 'out of sync', giving rise to complex new patterns as metrically different versions of the same idea are heard simultaneously.

The repetitions of the two-bar patterns create melodic **ostinati** which centre on an hypnotic alternation of the chords of E major and F♯ major, but the phasing causes the chords to overlap and change at different times in different parts. The harmonic basis of the work can more easily be seen if we show the accompaniment to the live clarinet like this (for clarity the parts for clarinets 1–3 are transposed down an octave):

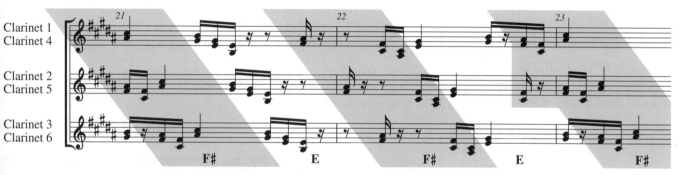

The constant overlap of these two chords generates numerous diatonic dissonances as the texture thickens, but the repetition blends them into a gentle wash of harmonic colour, and the use of a hexatonic scale for the contrapuntal parts avoids the particularly dissonant clash that would occur if D♯ was included in the melodic lines.

However, with the arrival of the first homorhythmic interjection comes the first use of D♯ and therefore much more gritty harmony. The three different chords heard in this section are B major over C♯ in the bass (bars 27–32), a chord based on 4ths (E, A♯, D♯, G♯) in bars 33–38, and F♯ major over G♯ in the bass (bars 39–46). These three chords are then repeated. They do not have a harmonic function – there is no progression towards a tonic. Their purpose is to provide contrast with the two chords of the counterpoint by adding to the dissonance level, as well as by offering a contrasting texture and different rhythm.

A notable aspect of the work is its use of a single instrumental colour (clarinet tone in the score, but Reich has also approved a saxophone arrangement of the work) and the use of technology (multi-track recording) to enable all 11 parts to be delivered by a single performer. The clarinet parts cover a modest range of just over two octaves (extended to two and a half octaves for the bass clarinet). Nevertheless, this is enough to exploit the distinctively different timbres of the clarinet in low, middle and upper registers, and Reich's control over textural change ensure plenty of variety.

Although the entire movement is written in triple metre, the pulse is not easy to detect at the start because of the fragmentary nature of the opening motif. Indeed, although it is **syncopated**, without a clear pulse this is not immediately apparent. It is only as more parts join in that the regular pulse begins to emerge. From bar 21 there are semiquavers throughout every beat until the final bar, and the triple metre becomes totally clear.

Exercise 2

1. How do the clarinet parts in the first two bars relate to each other?

2. How do the parts played by clarinet 5 and the live clarinettist in bars 3–6 relate to the music heard in bars 1–2?

3. In which bar does the live clarinettist start playing material unrelated to the pre-recorded tracks?

4. Define what is meant by phasing, giving an example from bar 21 onwards in NAM 12.

5. Twentieth-century music is often divided into tonal and atonal styles. Is NAM 12 tonal or atonal?

6. Most of the melodic material in NAM 12 derives from the motif heard in its first two bars. How does Reich create variety in this movement?

7. To what extent do you feel that playing to a backing tape in *New York Counterpoint* compromises the spontaneity of live performance?

Vocal music

The six vocal works set for 2018 have all been discussed in earlier chapters of this book:

NAM 33: **Flow my tears** (Dowland)
See pages 112–114.

NAM 35: **Ohimè, se tanto amate** (Monteverdi)
See pages 87–89.

NAM 38: **Der Doppelgänger** (Schubert)
See pages 65–66.

NAM 32: **The Lamb** (Tavener)
See pages 91–93.

NAM 51: **I'm Leavin' You** (Howlin' Wolf)
See pages 68–70.

NAM 56: **Tupelo Honey** (Van Morrison)
See pages 96–98.

Make sure that you complete the exercises at the end of each of these six sections. Question 5 in the exercise on page 98 should be changed to read:

Compare the use of harmony in *Tupelo Honey* and *I'm Leavin' You*, referring to differences in the ways that chords are decorated in both songs.

For an idea of the type of questions that are set in Section A of the paper, see pages 73–75. Obviously, the two extracts to be used in 2018 will come from the set works you have studied in this chapter, rather than the two printed on those pages. Here are some sample questions for practice in answering Section B of the paper.

Part B: Investigating Musical Styles

Answer *either* Question 3(a) *or* Question 3(b). You must answer both parts of the question you choose. You should spend no more than 45 minutes on this part of the paper. Remember that you are not allowed to consult recordings, scores or notes while answering the questions.

3(a)   INSTRUMENTAL MUSIC

(i)   Describe the stylistic features of Debussy's *Prélude à L'Après-midi d'un faune* which show that this music is an example of Impressionism.   **(10)**

(ii)   Compare and contrast the structure and rhythms of Poulenc's Sonata for Horn, Trumpet and Trombone (first movement) and *New York Counterpoint* (second movement) by Reich.   **(18)**

OR

3(b)   VOCAL MUSIC

(i)   Describe the stylistic features of *I'm Leavin' You* by Howlin' Wolf which show that this song is an example of rhythm and blues.   **(10)**

(ii)   Compare and contrast the vocal writing and word setting in Dowland's *Flow my Tears* and Schubert's *Der Doppelgänger*.   **(18)**

                                                                                                (TOTAL: 28)

Rhinegold Education publish a book of practice tests covering sections A and C of this paper, *Edexcel AS Music Listening Tests*. More practice questions for section B are in the *Edexcel AS Music Revision Guide*.

Glossary

Note that some of the terms in this glossary may apply to set works that you are not studying.

Accented passing note. A dissonant note sounded on the beat and filling the gap between two harmony notes. In NAM 22 the notes F and A in the right hand of bar 53 beat 4 are accented passing notes, clashing with the underlying C^7 chord. *See also* **Appoggiatura** and **Passing note**.

Acciaccatura. An ornament printed as a small note with a slash through its stem and flag (♪) that is either played as short as possible, or is played with the main melodic note and immediately released. It often forms a discord with a harmony note, as is the case with the acciaccaturas in the second half of bar 15 in NAM 37.

Alberti bass. An accompaniment pattern in which the notes of a chord are repeatedly sounded in the order low, high, middle and high again. It is named after an obscure Italian composer who was addicted to the device. See NAM 22, bars 71–80 (left hand).

Anacrusis. One or more weak-beat notes before the first strong beat of a phrase, as in bar 5 of NAM 52 and bar 8 of NAM 53. Often called a 'pick-up' in jazz and pop music.

Anticipation. A note played immediately before the chord to which it belongs. The anticipated note is often the tonic in a perfect cadence, as in NAM 1, where the semiquaver G at the end of bar 426 anticipates the tonic in the final chord of the movement.

Antiphony. The alternation of different groups of instruments and/or singers. There is a short antiphonal exchange between wind and strings in bars 47–49 of NAM 17; a longer example is the antiphony created by the two groups of instruments at the start of NAM 14.

Appoggiatura. A dissonant non-chord note, often approached by a leap, that resolves by moving to a chord note. It is like a **suspension** but without the preparation. Appoggiaturas are sometimes written as small notes, like ornaments, as in bar 12 of NAM 37, where the C♯ in the vocal part clashes with B in the accompaniment before resolving on the same note.

Arco. An instruction for string players to resume bowing after using some other technique, such as **pizzicato**, as seen in NAM 3, bar 53.

Articulation. The degree of separation between notes. In NAM 23, slurs in the first piece indicate that it should be played smoothly (legato). Most notes in the second piece are marked with staccato dots, indicating a detached style of performance. At the start of the third piece, the combination of staccato dots and slurs indicates mezzo-staccato – the notes should be only slightly detached.

Atonal. Western music without a note that acts as a home note to which all other notes are related. This means, in particular, that atonal music avoids major and minor keys, and modes. NAM 8 is atonal.

Augmentation. A proportionate increase in the note-lengths of a melody. The last bar of NAM 32 is an augmented version of the previous bar. The opposite of augmentation is **diminution**.

Augmented-6th chord. A chromatic chord based on the sixth degree of the scale (the flattened sixth degree if the key is major) and the note an augmented 6th above it. The chord also contains a major 3rd above the root and may include a perfect 5th or augmented 4th above the root. An augmented-6th chord can be seen on the last beat of bar 80 in NAM 22 (left hand), where the key is G minor and the augmented 6th is formed by the notes E♭ and C♯. The chord resolves when the two notes forming the augmented 6th move outward by a semitone to the dominant, as occurs on the first beat of bar 81 in the same piece.

Auxiliary note. A non-chord note that occurs between, and is a step away from, two harmony notes of the same pitch. In bar 6 of NAM 22 the second semiquaver (C) is an upper auxiliary and the fourth semiquaver (A) is a lower auxiliary. The harmony note is B♭.

Avant-garde. A term referring to composers or works seen as breaking new ground, such as NAM 11.

Backbeat. A term used in pop music to describe accenting normally weak beats (beats 2 and 4 in $\frac{4}{4}$ time). In bars 3–4 of NAM 51 the backbeats in the drum part are marked with accents.

Balanced phrasing. *See* **Periodic phrasing**.

Baroque. A term referring to music written in styles typical of the period 1600–1750, such as NAM 1, 15 and 21.

Bend. *See* **Pitch bend**.

Binary form. A two-part musical structure, usually with each section repeated, as in the first piece in NAM 23. In longer binary-form movements the first section often ends in a related key and the second section modulates back (perhaps by way of other related keys) to the tonic. This can be seen in the two dances of NAM 21, and in NAM 15, where the first sections end in the dominant key (A major) and the second sections end in the tonic (D major). Binary form is often represented as ‖:A:‖:B:‖ but there is not normally any contrast in mood or theme between its two sections as there is in the ABA structure of **ternary form**. *See also* **Rounded binary form**.

Bitonality. The use of two different keys at the same time, as in bars 4–6 of NAM 31, where the choir parts outline E♭ major but the accompaniment outlines C major.

Blue note. A term used in jazz and blues-based music for a note (usually the third, fifth or seventh degree of the major scale) that is made more expressive by slightly lowering its pitch. In the vocal part of NAM 52 the note G♮ is the blue 3rd of E major and the note D♮ is the blue 7th.

Break. A term used in pop and jazz for an instrumental solo within a song, as occurs in bars 33–44 of NAM 57.

Cadence. The last notes of a phrase, suggesting a point of repose. When harmonised the chosen chords can define the degree of completion more exactly. *See* **Perfect cadence**, **Imperfect cadence**, **Interrupted cadence**, **Plagal cadence** and **Phrygian cadence**.

Cadential $\frac{6}{4}$. A triad in second inversion is called a $\frac{6}{4}$ chord because its upper notes form intervals of a 6th and a 4th above its bass note. A cadential $\frac{6}{4}$ is chord Ic used before a perfect cadence (Ic–V$^{(7)}$–I) or as the first chord of an imperfect cadence (Ic–V). It is one of the most characteristic sounds of the Classical style and can be found in NAM 22, where a perfect cadence in F major is formed by the progression Ic–V^7–I in bars 57–59.

Canon. Music in which a melody in one part fits with the same melody in another part even though the latter starts a few beats later. The device occurs in the type of song known as a round. In NAM 34, the entire first soprano part in bars 43^3–50 is sung in canon by the second soprano three beats later. *See also* **Counterpoint**.

Chamber music. Ensemble music intended for only one performer per part, such as NAM 16. The term originally referred to music that was suitable to be played in a room (or chamber) of a private house.

Chromatic. A word meaning 'coloured', used to describe notes outside the current key or mode. They are added for colour and do not cause a change of key. Accidentals are not necessarily chromatic. Bars 1–8 of NAM 15 are in D major and the G♯ in bar 4 is chromatic because it does not belong to that key – G♮ returns in the very next bar. However, the G♯ in bar 9 has a different effect. It is part of a **modulation** to A major which, unlike the previous example, is confirmed by a cadence in this new key in the next bar. The music from here until bar 19 is in A major and the G♯s used in this section are not chromatic – they are **diatonic** notes in the new key of A major. *See also* **Tonality**.

Circle of 5ths. A series of chords whose roots are each a 5th lower than the previous chord. In practice the series would soon drop below the lowest note available on most instruments, so the bass usually alternates between falling a 5th and rising a 4th, producing the same series of pitches. NAM 39 starts with a circle of 5ths in bars 1–9.

Classical. A term often used for any sort of art music, but more specifically referring to music written in styles typical of the period 1750–1825, such as NAM 16, 17 and 22.

Coda. The final section of a movement. In tonal music the coda will often consist of material to confirm the tonic key. For example, the coda of NAM 2 (bars 122–133) contains three perfect cadences in the tonic key of D major. *See also* **Outro**.

Codetta. A little **coda**. The final section of a part of a movement.

Conjunct. Movement to an adjacent note (a tone or a semitone away) in a melody, also known as stepwise motion. In the first 12 bars of NAM 13 the top part is entirely conjunct. The opposite of conjunct is **disjunct**.

Consonance. Harmonious. Opposite of **dissonance**.

Continuo. Abbreviation of *basso continuo*. A continuous bass part of the Baroque period played on one or more bass instruments and which also provided the foundation for improvising harmonies on chordal instruments such as the harpsichord, organ and lute. This was done in accordance with the conventions of the time, guided by any **figured bass** given in the part (*see* NAM 15). The term is also used to to mean the instrumental group that plays the continuo part.

Contrapuntal. A texture that uses **counterpoint**.

Contrary motion. A term used to describe simultaneous melodic lines that move in opposite directions. In the first piece in NAM 23, the melody and bass move in contrary motion throughout the first six bars – when the melody rises, the bass falls, and vice versa. *See also* **Oblique motion**, **Parallel motion** and **Similar motion**.

Countermelody. A melody of secondary importance heard at the same time as (and therefore in **counterpoint** with) a more important melody. In NAM 17 the horn melody in bars 250–253 is combined with a cello countermelody.

Counterpoint. The simultaneous combination of two or more melodies with independent rhythms. There may be some **imitation** between the parts but counterpoint can also be non-imitative. Whole movements may be contrapuntal, such as the gigue in NAM 21, or the music may alternate between contrapuntal and other textures, such as NAM 18, where a section of **fugal** counterpoint begins at bar 67. The term is now often used interchangeably with **polyphony**.

Cross-rhythm. A passage in which the rhythmic patterns of one or more parts runs counter to the normal accentuation or grouping of notes in the prevailing metre. The effect of 'two-against-three' in bar 3 of NAM 39 is an example of a cross-rhythm.

Development. The central section of **sonata form**. The term is also used more generally to describe the manipulation and transformation of motifs and themes in any sort of music.

Dialogue. A texture in which motifs are passed between different parts. In NAM 35, the falling 3rd in bar 1 is exchanged in dialogue between pairs of parts throughout the first four bars. This is not imitation, because there is no overlap between these motifs.

Diatonic. Pitches of the prevailing key and music which contains only those pitches. The first two complete bars of NAM 37 are purely diatonic. Bars 3 and 6 are not diatonic as they contain **chromatic** notes which colour the harmony although they do not establish a new key. The D♯s in bars 15–21 are diatonic because the music is in E major in this section, and D♯ is part of this key.

Diminished-7th chord. A four-note chord made up of superimposed minor 3rds (or their **enharmonic** equivalents), creating an interval of a diminished 7th between its outer notes. In the first piece in NAM 23, the notes C♯–E–G–B♭ in the second half of bar 1 form a diminished-7th chord.

Diminution. A proportionate reduction in note-lengths. In the melody of NAM 22 the first two notes of bar 3 occur twice in diminution in bar 5. The opposite of diminution is **augmentation**.

Discord. *See* **Dissonance**.

Disjunct. Melodic movement by leaps rather than steps between adjacent notes, as in NAM 8. The opposite of disjunct is **conjunct**.

Dissonance. Two or more sounds that clash, producing a discord. The perception of what sounds discordant has varied over time. Before the 20th century it was normal for the tension produced by on-beat discords to be 'resolved' by means of the dissonant notes moving to a concord. In the final bar of NAM 22 the left hand outlines notes of the tonic chord of B♭ major, but the E♭ and C in the right hand clash with this. This dissonace is resolved when these two right-hand notes drop to notes of the tonic chord in the second half of the bar. Since about 1900 dissonance has often been used as an effect in its own right.

Dominant preparation. A passage focused on and around the dominant chord to create an expectation that the tonic key will return, often at the end of the development section in **sonata form** (as in bars 87–93 of NAM 22).

Double-stopping. The performance of a two-note chord on a string instrument, as occurs in the first-violin part of NAM 16 at bar 41.

Échappé. A non-chord note that moves by step from a harmony note and then leaps in the opposite direction to another harmony note: *see* page 37.

Enharmonic. The same pitch notated in two different ways. The final note of NAM 9 could have been written as A♭ but it is enharmonically notated as G♯ because it functions as a link to the next movement which is in a sharp key.

Episode. *See* **Rondo form**.

Exposition. *See* **Sonata form**.

False relation. The simultaneous or adjacent occurrence *in different parts* (e.g. treble and bass) of a note in its normal form and in a chromatically altered form. In NAM 35 a false relation occurs in bar 56 between the F♯ and the F♮. In NAM 41 an example of a simultaneous false relation between E♮ and E♯ occurs on the third beat of bar 14.

Figure. A clearly-defined melodic fragment such as the six notes heard in the ripieno violin 1 part in bars 14–15 of NAM 1. This is repeated in sequence in the next six bars. When a figure such as this is repeated exactly, varied, or used in sequence the result is called figuration. *See also* **Motif**.

Figured bass. Numbers and other symbols below a basso **continuo** part to indicate the harmonies to be improvised by chordal instruments, as in NAM 15.

Fill. A term used in pop music to indicate that a passage which is embellished or filled out in performance is not notated in full in the score, as occurs in bar 44 of NAM 54 or in the section starting at bar 17 in NAM 51. The term is also used for a brief improvised flourish (often on drums) to fill the gap between one section of a pop song and the next.

Fugal. In the style of a **fugue**, as in the opening of NAM 15.

Fugue. A type of composition based on a melody that initially enters in succession in each of several parts. This is called the subject (or the answer if it is transposed). While each subsequent part introduces the subject, the previous part continues with a new idea called the countersubject that fits in counterpoint with the subject. After each part has introduced the subject or answer these ideas are manipulated in a variety of ways, often including **stretto**.

Functional harmony. Progressions of chords, particularly $V^{(7)}$–I, that define the key(s) of a piece of music. In NAM 1, the progression I–V–I is heard four times in the first 12 bars, firmly establishing G major as the tonic key.

Genre (pronounced jon-ruh). A category or type of composition, such as the piano sonata, the string quartet or the madrigal.

Ground bass. A melody in a bass part that is repeated many times and which forms the basis for a continuous set of variations. The second part of NAM 36 (the $\frac{3}{2}$ time section) uses a ground bass.

Harmonic. On string instruments (including the harp and guitar) a very high and pure sound produced by placing the finger on a string very lightly before plucking or bowing. Harmonics are indicated by small circles above the harp notes in bars 108–109 of NAM 5.

Harmonic rhythm. A term used to describe the rate at which chords change. In bar 1 of NAM 16 there are two chords (I and V^7), but in bars 9–12 the harmonic rhythm is much slower – chord V lasts for two bars and then chord I lasts for two bars.

Hemiola. A rhythmic device in which two groups of three beats ('strong–weak–weak, strong–weak–weak') are articulated as three groups of two beats ('strong–weak, strong–weak, strong–weak'). See the example printed on page 77.

Heterophony. A texture in which simple and elaborated versions of a melody are heard together, as in bars 26–39 of NAM 2, where the oboe melody is accompanied by a decorated version of the same tune in the first-violin part.

Hexatonic. Music based on a scale of six pitches. The vocal melody of the chorus in NAM 57 (bars 25–32) is hexatonic – it contains six of the seven pitches in C major, but avoids the leading note (B). The accompaniment to this tune, though, is not hexatonic. *See also* **Pentatonic**.

Homophonic. A texture in which one part (usually the uppermost) has the melodic interest to which the other parts provide an accompaniment (as opposed to a polyphonic or contrapuntal texture, in which all the parts are melodically interesting). The last five bars of NAM 30 are homophonic; they consist entirely of block chords and so could also be described as a chordal or **homorhythmic** texture. The opening of NAM 39 illustrates a different type of homophony, referred to as 'melody-dominated homophony', or 'melody and accompaniment'.

Homorhythmic. A type of homophonic texture in which all of the parts move in the same rhythm, such as in the first four bars of NAM 38 or in bars 79–81 of NAM 9.

Hook. In pop music, a short melodic idea designed to be memorable and repeated a number of times in the song. If the motif is sung to the title words of the song, as in NAM 55, it is known as a 'title hook'.

Imitation. If a motif in one part is immediately taken up by another part while the first part continues with other music, the motif is said to be treated in imitation. The imitation is usually not exact – some intervals may be modified, but the basic melodic shape and rhythm of the opening should be audible. The imitative entry often starts at a different pitch from the original. NAM 15 begins with imitation in all three parts. If the parts continue in exact imitation for a number of bars, they will form a **canon**.

Imitative point. A motif that is used as the subject for **imitation**.

Imperfect cadence. Two chords at the end of a phrase, the second of which is the dominant, as in NAM 37, bars 3^6–4.

Impressionism. A musical style particularly associated with late 19th- and early 20th-century French music. Just as Impressionist paintings often blur objects and explore the effects of light, so Impressionist music frequently blurs tonality, using chords primarily for the atmosphere they create rather than as **functional harmony**, and exploring unusual and delicate tone colours. NAM 5 is typical of the Impressionist style.

Interrupted cadence. Two chords at the end of a phrase, the first of which is the dominant and the second being any chord other than the tonic (most often chord VI, as in bar 26 of the third movement of NAM 23, where the cadence is V^7–VI in the key of E minor).

Inversion (1). An interval is inverted when its lower note is transposed up an octave while the other note remains the same (or vice-versa).

Inversion (2). A chord is inverted when a note other than the root of the chord is sounding in the bass. In NAM 2 the first chord in bars 9–12 is the tonic chord of D minor in root position, but the second chord in each of these bars is the dominant chord in first inversion (A major, with its third, C#, in the bass).

Inversion (3). A melody is inverted when every interval is kept the same but now moves in the opposite direction (e.g. a rising 3rd becomes a falling 3rd). The alto part in bars 5–6 of NAM 32 is an exact inversion of the soprano part above it.

Lick. In pop music, a short pattern of notes improvised by a guitarist to decorate a vocal melody, as in the lead-guitar part of bars 6–14 in NAM 51.

Lied (plural *Lieder*). The German for song, used more specifically to refer to 19th-century settings of German poetry for solo voice and piano, such as NAM 38. Its French counterpart is the **mélodie**.

Melisma. Several notes sung to one syllable, as in bar 22 of NAM 39.

Mélodie. The French for melody, used more specifically used to refer to 19th-century settings of French poetry for solo voice and piano, such as NAM 39. Its German counterpart is the *Lied*.

Metre. The organisation of a regular pulse into patterns of strong and weak beats. For example, alternate strong and weak beats are known as duple metre, while the recurring pattern 'strong–weak–weak' is known as triple metre.

Minimalism. A musical style of the late 20th century characterised by static or slowly changing harmonies and the interaction of short patterns that repeat and change over time, as in NAM 12.

Modes. These are usually taken to mean seven-note scales other than the modern major and minor scales, although some people refer to even these as the major mode and minor mode respectively. The aeolian mode consists of the notes A–B–C–D–E–F–G–A. Although it begins and ends on the note A (like A minor) it differs from A minor in that is has G♮ as its seventh note, not G#. All of the notes in the last four bars of NAM 32 belong to the aeolian mode transposed down a 4th to start on E (E–F#–G–A–B–C–D–E).

Modulation. The process by which music changes from one key to another. NAM 1 begins in the key of G major. The introduction of C#s from bar 15 onwards indicates the start of a modulation to the dominant key of D major. The new key is confirmed by a succession of I–V–I progressions in D major, starting in bar 23.

Monophonic. A texture that consists of a single unaccompanied melody, as in the first phrase of NAM 32.

Monothematic. A movement constructed from material that derives from a single theme, such as NAM 16.

Monotone. A single pitch repeated a number of times. The vocal part in bars 60–65^1 of NAM 52 is sung to a monotone on E.

Mordent. An ornament consisting of a rapid move from a main pitch to an adjacent note and back again (*see* pages 37–38).

Motif. A short but memorable melodic fragment which is subject to manipulation through techniques such as sequence, inversion, extension and so forth. For example the motivic material heard in the first wo bars of NAM 16 forms the basis of almost all he thematic material in the entire movement. *See also* **Figure**.

Neapolitan 6th. The first inversion of the triad on he flattened second degree of a scale. In the key of [minor this is a chord of F major in first inversion, ıs used on the first beat of bar 155 in NAM 1.

Neoclassical. An early 20th-century style that combined forms and techniques from the 18th century with a more modern approach to elements such as rhythm, harmony and instrumentation. NAM 7 and NAM 19 both show the influence of Neoclassicism.

Oblique motion. A term used to describe the relationship between a melodic part that remains on a single pitch while another moves away from it (as at the start of the third piece in NAM 23, where the melody remains on B while the bass moves down chromatically) or towards it (as at the start of NAM 30, where the bass remains on C and the soprano moves down towards it). *See also* **Contrary motion**, **Parallel motion** and **Similar motion**.

Ostinato. A melodic, rhythmic or chordal pattern repeated throughout a substantial passage of music. For example, the four-note pattern starting in bar 163 of NAM 31 is played 31 times in succession by pianos, harp and timpani. In popular music and jazz a melodic ostinato is known as a riff. A **ground bass** is a type of ostinato.

Outro. In pop music, the closing section of a song – the opposite of an intro (introduction). An outro is essentially a **coda**, although an outro is more likely to have a fade-out ending rather than finishing with a clear cadence. NAM 53 ends with a fade-out outro, while NAM 57 ends with a coda that comes to rest on the tonic chord, but the two terms are often used interchangeably.

Parallel major and **parallel minor**. Keys that share the same tonic, such as D major and D minor, are known as parallel keys. The two keys are sometimes described as the tonic major and tonic minor. The main key of NAM 2 is D minor, but at bar 100 it moves to the parallel major key (D major) for the final section.

Parallel motion. A type of **similar motion** in which the parts move in the same direction *and* maintain the same or similar vertical intervals between notes, as in the opening of NAM 24 and in the parts for women's voices in bars 26–29 of NAM 41. *See also* **Contrary motion**, **Oblique motion** and **Similar motion**.

Passing note. A non-chord note that most commonly fills the gap between two harmony notes a 3rd apart. In the third bar of NAM 1 the second quaver in both recorder parts is a passing note between harmony notes belonging to the chord of G major. *See also* **Accented passing note**.

Pedal (or 'pedal point'). A sustained or repeated note against which changing harmonies are heard. A pedal on the dominant (NAM 16, bars 16–28) tends to create excitement and the feeling that the tension must be resolved by moving to the tonic. A pedal on the tonic anchors the music to its key note (NAM 16, bars 107–111^1). A pedal on both tonic and dominant (a double pedal) is used at the start of NAM 3. If a pedal occurs in an upper part, rather than the bass, it is called an inverted pedal.

Pentatonic. Music based on a scale of five pitches. You can find one such scale by playing the five black notes on a music keyboard. In NAM 57 the vocal melody in bars 5–12 is pentatonic since it uses only the pitches C, D, E, G and A. However, the accompaniment is not pentatonic since it includes the other two pitches of C major (F and B). *See also* **Hexatonic**.

Perfect cadence. The progression V–I at the end of a phrase, as in the last two chords of NAM 15.

Periodic phrasing. Balanced phrases of regular lengths (usually two, four or eight bars) – a style particularly associated with music of the Classical period. The introduction to NAM 37 consists of a four-bar statement ending on the dominant, balanced by a four-bar answer ending on the tonic.

Phrygian cadence. A type of **imperfect cadence** used in minor keys. It consists of the chords IVb–V, as in bars 15^4–16 of NAM 33.

Pick-up. *See* **Anacrusis**.

Pitch bend. A term used in pop and jazz for an expressive short slide in pitch to or from a note, particularly a **blue note**. In NAM 51 pitch bends are indicated by curved lines in the score, for example in bars 9–10 of the lead-guitar part.

Pizzicato. An instruction to a player of a bowed string instrument to pluck the strings instead of bowing them, as seen in the violin and cello parts at bar 32 in NAM 3. *See also* **Arco**.

Plagal cadence. The progression IV–I at the end of a phrase. For example the last two chords of NAM 38 are IVc–I in B minor, with a major 3rd in the final tonic chord that creates a **tierce de Picardie**.

Polarised texture. A term referring to Baroque pieces in which there is a wide gap between the bass part and the melody line(s), as in NAM 15. In performance, this gap is filled by improvised chords played on a **continuo** instrument such as an organ, harpsichord or lute.

Polyphony. The simultaneous use of two or more melodies. The opening of NAM 26 is polyphonic. Nowadays, the term is often used interchangeably with **counterpoint**, although it is more common to use polyphony when referring to Renaissance music.

Quartal harmony. Chords built from superimposed 4ths, rather than on 3rds as they are in triads. Quartal harmony is used in bars 23–28 of NAM 24.

Recapitulation. *See* **Sonata form**.

Refrain. A passage of music that returns at intervals throughout a work, especially in **rondo** form, although the term is also used to refer to the chorus of a song in verse-and-chorus form.

Register. A specific part of the range of a voice or instrument. For example, the first-violin part in NAM 18 starts in a low register, but climbs to a high register in bars 135–137.

Renaissance. A term referring to music written in styles typical of the period 1400–1600, such as NAM 26 (c.1528) and NAM 34 (published 1598).

Rhythm and blues. A style of popular music that developed initially among African-Americans in the late 1940s. It combined the driving rhythms of jazz with the slow blues and, as it came to be used as dance music, louder instruments were introduced, including electric guitars, saxophones and drum kits. Rhythm and blues was an important element in the development of rock and roll in the 1950s and its influence on rock music continued for some years to come. NAM 51 is a rhythm-and-blues song, and can be compared with NAM 52, which is an example of early rock and roll from the same period.

Riff. *See* **Ostinato**.

Ritornello form. A structure used for large-scale movements in the late-Baroque period, such as NAM 1. An opening instrumental section (called the ritornello) introduces the main musical ideas. This is followed by a contrasting texture, featuring one or more soloists, and often based on similar material. Sections of the opening ritornello, often in different keys, then alternate with the solo textures until, at the end, the complete ritornello (or a substantial part of it) returns in the tonic key. The fragmentary nature of most of the ritornello sections gives the form its name – ritornello means a 'little return'.

Romantic. A term referring to music written in styles typical of the period 1825–1900, such as NAM 3, 18, 23, 30, 38 and 39.

Rondo form. A musical structure in which a **refrain** in the tonic key alternates with contrasting episodes, creating a pattern such as ABACA or ABACABA. NAM 16 is a rondo.

Rounded binary form. A common type of **binary form** in which material from the opening returns towards the end of the second section, transposed to the tonic key if necessary. The structure could be represented as $\|{:}A{:}\|{:}BA^1{:}\|$ and is used in the first movement of NAM 21 and the first two pieces in NAM 23. Rounded binary form differs from **ternary form** (ABA) in having a B section that does not provide a clear contrast and that leads without a break into the abbreviated repeat of the opening material.

Rubato literally means 'robbed' and refers to shortening some beats and lengthening others in order to give an expressive, free feel to the pulse. The use of rubato is particularly associated with Romantic piano music, such as NAM 23.

Sequence. The *immediate* repetition at a different pitch of a phrase or motif in a continuous melodic line. A series of such repetitions is frequently used in the spinning-out of Baroque melodic lines, as in bars 69–75 of NAM 1 (where recorders perform an ascending sequence based on the initial three-note figure).

Similar motion. A term used to describe simultaneous melodic lines that move in the same direction. In bars 67–70 of NAM 3 the two clarinet parts move in the same direction. *See also* **Contrary motion**, **Oblique motion** and **Parallel motion**.

Slide. A melodic ornament consisting of two or more short notes, normally printed in small type, that rise rapidly to the main note, as shown in bar 15 of NAM 37.

Sonata form. The most common structure for the first movement (and often other movements) of sonatas, symphonies, concertos and chamber works in the Classical period and later. The essence of sonata form is the use of two contrasting tonal centres (tonic and either dominant or another closely related key such as the relative major) in a first section called the exposition; the use of a wider range of keys to create tension and excitement in a central section called the **development**; and a recapitulation in which music from the exposition is repeated in the tonic key. *See* NAM 22 and *see also* **subject**.

Sprechgesang. German for speech-song. A type of vocal production halfway between singing and speaking, used in NAM 40.

Stepwise movement. *See* **Conjunct**.

Stop time. A style of accompaniment in pop music and jazz in which most of the band stops playing continuously and instead contributes punctuating chords or isolated motifs in support of a soloist. The effect is marked as 'stop chorus' in NAM 51 (bar 15), but a similar technique can be heard in bars 6–13 of NAM 52, where the singer is accompanied only by drums, with the rest of the band playing short chords between the vocal phrases.

Straight quavers (or straight eights). In jazz and pop music, quavers that are played evenly rather than being played as **swing quavers**.

Stretto. The telescoping of imitative parts so that entries come closer to each other than they originally did. At the start of NAM 15, the first-violin melody is imitated by the second violin two bars later, and the bass joins in after a gap of a further two-and-a-half bars. When the inverted form of this melody appears in bar 20, it is treated in stretto, each of the lower parts entering after a gap of only one bar.

Strophic. A song that uses the same music for every verse (such as NAM 37), as opposed to one which is **through-composed** (such as NAM 38).

Subject (1). One of the sections in the exposition of a movement in **sonata form**. The first ten bars of NAM 22 contain the first subject of this sonata-form movement.

Subject (2). The melody upon which a passage of imitation is based, such as the opening of the cello part in NAM 9.

Substitution chord. A chord that functions in a similar way to the simpler chord that it replaces. For example, in NAM 57 Fm^7 is substituted for the simpler chord of F in the second half of bars 13, 15 and similar places.

Suspension. A device in which a note is first sounded in a consonant context (the preparation) and is then repeated (or held) over a change of chord so that it becomes a dissonance (the suspension itself). Finally, there is a resolution when the suspended note moves by step (usually downwards) to a consonant note. These three stages can be seen in the violin 2 part of NAM 15: the note A is prepared in bar 17 (it is part of both chords in that bar), it then sounds against B in violin 1 at the start of bar 18 (this is the actual suspension) and it resolves by falling to G♯ (thus forming part of the prevailing chord of E major) in the second half of that bar.

Swing quavers. Also known as swung quavers. In jazz and pop music the division of the beat into a pair of notes in which the first is longer than the second. Swing quavers may be notated as ♪♪ or as ♪.♪ but are performed closer to ♩ ♪ in both cases. They are indicated by instructions above the time signature at the start of NAM 51 and NAM 52, but in NAM 41 the ♪.♪ rhythms are swung without any specific instruction – their use is simply part of the style of the song. If even quavers are required in places where they might otherwise be swung, they are described as **straight quavers**.

Syllabic. A style of vocal writing in which, generally speaking, each syllable is set to just one note, as in NAM 34.

Syncopation. Off-beat accents or accents on weak beats. In the first bar of NAM 33 the note on the word 'fall' is syncopated by a leap to a high note on the weak fourth beat and the suppression of the next strong beat in the melody by the use of a tie.

Ternary form. A three-part musical structure in which a middle section is flanked by two identical or very similar passages. The form can be represented by the letters ABA, or ABA^1 if there are differences in the A section when it returns. NAM 18, NAM 19 and NAM 30 all make use of ternary structures. *See also* **Rounded binary form**.

Tessitura. The part of the pitch range in which a passage of music mainly lies. For example, the lead vocal in NAM 55 is in a high tessitura, especially obvious in bars 25 and 43.

Texture. The relationship between the various simultaneous lines in a piece of music (melody, harmony and bass). *See* pages 45–46 for more detail.

Through-composed. A song that uses mainly different music for each verse (such as NAM 38) rather than one which is **strophic** (such as NAM 37).

Tierce de Picardie. A major 3rd in the final tonic chord of a passage in a minor key. For example NAM 33 is in A minor, but the C♯ in bar 24 is a tierce de Picardie that makes the last chord A major.

Timbre (pronounced tam-bruh). Tone colour. The clarinet has a different timbre to the trumpet, but the clarinet also has different timbres in various parts of its range. The timbre of an instrument can also be affected by the way it is played, for example by using a mute or plucking a string instead of using the bow.

Tonality. The use of major and minor keys in music and the ways in which these keys are related. Not all music is tonal – some is modal (based on one or more **modes**) and some (like NAM 59) makes use of non-western scales. Western pieces that use neither keys nor modes, such as NAM 8, are described as **atonal** (without tonality).

Tonic major and **tonic minor**. *See* **Parallel major** and **Parallel minor**.

Transcription. The notation of music that was previously not written down or that existed in some other type of notation. The scores of popular music, jazz and world music in NAM are all transcriptions from recordings. The term is also used in the sense of 'arrangement' to describe music that has been adapted for different performing resources. In NAM 20, bars 1–16, 33–48 and 82–98 are free transcriptions of the three eight-bar phrases in NAM 33.

Triad. A three-note chord formed from two superimposed intervals of a 3rd.

Trill. An ornament consisting of the rapid alternation of two notes a step apart. The symbol for a trill is *tr* and can be seen in bar 37 of NAM 22.

Tritone. An interval of three tones, such as B to the F above, as occurs between the outer parts on the last beat of bar 16 in NAM 34. Other examples occur at the ends of bars 10 and 13 in this piece.

Turn. A four-note ornament, indicated by the symbol ∾. It starts a step above the written note, drops to the written note, falls to the note below and finally returns to the written note. The vertical stroke through the turn symbol in bar 62 of NAM 22 indicates an inverted turn, in which the order of notes described above is reversed.

Turnaround. In popular music, a short passage at the end of a section designed to lead the music back to the tonic key for a repeat of an earlier section. For that reason, it usually ends on chord V^7 of the home key, as in bars 33–34 of NAM 53.

Tutti. 'All' – the full ensemble, or a passage of music intended for the full ensemble. In bar 89 of NAM the word 'tutti' signifies the entry of the full orchestra following the violin solo in the previous six bars.

Unison. A term used to describe two or more people performing the same note or melody at the same pitch. In NAM 2 the bassoon plays in unison with the cellos for the first eight bars. In a wind part, the instruction 'a 2' (seen in bar 1 of the oboe part in the same score) means that both instrumentalists should play the same notes in unison. The term is also used to describe women and men (or boys and men) singing the same melody, as in bars 11, 13 and 14 of NAM 32, although this is more accurately described as singing in octaves.

Virtuoso. A performer of great technical skill. The term is also used to describe music which requires a high level of technical skill.

Vocalising. Singing to vowel sounds rather than real words as in the parts for women's voices, starting at bar 26 in NAM 41.

Walking bass. A bass part that maintains the same note-lengths throughout a substantial passage, as in much of NAM 52, starting at bar 14.

Whole-tone scale. A scale in which there is a whole tone between all adjacent notes. It occurs in the clarinet and flute solos in bars 32–33 of NAM 5.

Word-painting. The musical illustration of the meaning or emotion associated with particular words or phrases, such as the use of the highest note in the song for the word 'Happie' in NAM 33.

For further help on musical terminology, consult the *Rhinegold Dictionary of Music in Sound* by David Bowman, which provides detailed explanations of a wide range of musical concepts and illustrates them using a large number of specially recorded examples on its set of accompanying compact discs. The *Rhinegold Dictionary of Music in Sound* is published by Rhinegold Education, ISBN 978-0-946890-87-3.

Index of works